CW00858921

Mount up with wings like eagles

MOUNT UP
WITH WINGS LIKE EAGLES

Justification, Regeneration, Sanctification, and Glorification

BY ERIC A. FOLDS, PhD

XULON PRESS

Xulon Press
2301 Lucien Way #415
Maitland, FL 32751
407.339.4217
www.xulonpress.com

This book investigates the reality of the supernatural and how God sees us like he does the eagle. We review what we have come to know as Pneumatology. We examine the great eagle and the supernatural work of God in pneumatology. We look at the great doctrine of justification by faith alone and the paradox between this truth and a final judgement of works. We look at the history of the Holiness Movement and review Holiness and Sanctification as it was taught by early Reformers. This book shows us another view of justification by faith alone and sanctification that may have been lost since the early apostolic church age. The conclusion can help anyone overcome guilt, depression, and anxiety.

The book also probes into the results of over 150,000 man- hours spent by scientists, historians, and scholars on the scientific explanation for the image of a crucified man inside of the Shroud of Turin. This work also examines the historical evidence for Jesus Christ and the history of his empty tomb. Did Jesus Christ really rise from the dead? If so, what does that mean for you and the universe? The book reveals how that God loves us and shows the extent that he has went to save us. This book reveals the gospel message and the truth about his grace.

The simplicity of the gospel message in presented in biblical events and stories. We take an in-depth look into Theology in the nature, extent and necessity of the Atonement. The book compares the doctrinal views of the Limited Atonement, Universalism, and Unlimited Atonement and other historical views which are compared and explained. We probe into historical theology while comparing Calvinism to Augustinianism, and Arminius doctrine. We examine Antinomianism. The book reveals the truth about The Election, Predestination, Perseverance of Saints, and the theology of the Atonement.

Author's Note: The book is for scholarship, educational, nonprofit, and informational purposes. Students of the College and Seminary or congregants will utilize the book for educational purposes. The author is not engaged in rendering any professional services to the reader. If the reader requires personal assistance and advice, a competent professional should be consulted. The author's intent is to spread the Gospel of Jesus Christ to every possible city, town, village, and country, and to support tax exempt, religious or charitable organizations. The content of the book is the sole opinion of the author based on The Word of God, the leading of the Holy Spirit, facts of history, and the words of Jesus Christ Himself. All of the information contained in the book have been shared in the ministry. The data has been maintained in notes from sermons prepared and for research and educational purposes for students of a Seminary and parishioners of tax exempt, nonprofit charitable organizations. All proceeds are designated for donation to a nonprofit organization. This book could be used as an aid in evangelism or for a Christian College or Seminary.

Due to the changing nature of the Internet, if there are any web addresses, links, or URLs included in this manuscript, these may have been altered and may no longer be accessible. The views and opinions shared in this book belong solely to the author and do not necessarily reflect those of the publisher. The publisher therefore disclaims responsibility for the views or opinions expressed within the work.

Unless otherwise indicated, Scripture quotations taken from the King James Version (KJV) – *public domain.*

The information should enable the reader to compare theological systems from centuries ago to their present form and learn what is revealed in the scriptures by Jesus Christ.

Paperback ISBN-13: 978-1-66286-113-0
Ebook ISBN-13: 978-1-66286-114-7

TABLE OF CONTENTS

PREFACE

The main thesis is justification by faith alone, but also the paradox of justification in a final judgment of works. We discuss Pneumatology and the supernatural workings. Manifestation of the power and glory of God is revealed. Miracles and wonders are discussed. The paradox of justification by faith alone and a final judgement of works is explained and solved.

The magnificent doctrine of glorification and ascension is elaborated on with transformation. The History of the Holiness Movement is also explained and how justification corresponds to the theological doctrine of hamartiology, sanctification, glorification, positional holiness, and practical holiness. The book is put together with the intent to encourage the reader about his and her identity. The conclusion can help anyone overcome guilt, depression, and anxiety.

We provide truth and insight into hamartiology and justification by faith alone as the prerequisite to glorification. We also find how the Spirit of God still works supernaturally with regeneration and distributing spiritual gifts to believers. This is about manifestation, power, and God's anointing. Some personal stories are shared.

The eagle is an extraordinary bird. The bird soars like no other. God has compared his people to the eagle! How does this bird teach us about ourselves? Is it possible that we can find some truth about our spiritual journey on earth from this wonder in creation? Do we see any parallel between the journey of an eagle and our movement forward toward our destiny? Why can't we find another bird with such an extraordinary vision and what makes the eagle one of a kind? Why does God compare the Christian to the eagle?

This book is about your flight in this life. It can help explain why you can rise to another level through your storms. It is about perseverance and determination. How does one mount up with wings like an eagle? It's about being extraordinary in a strength that comes only from God. It's about becoming what we were intended to be. It is about identity. This book is about knowing who you are and why you are. The eagle flies above and beyond the storm. The book is shrouded in some mystery. God became man!

This book is about an extraordinary ascension into a greatness that was not possible without supernatural help and a work that was already accomplished for us by God. The eagle flew and he landed at his destination. He was equipped for the journey. His wings were made for him! He soared on a strong wind thermal.

How do we reconcile the great doctrines in eschatology with theological anthropology, justification, hamartiology, soteriology and sanctification? How do we know for sure that we are saved and that we will enter the gates of Heaven and see Jesus' face in peace?

What does the doctrine of justification by faith alone have to do with holiness and final salvation in the end? How do we reconcile what is taught by people who believe that spiritual gifts have ceased with phenomena reportedly experienced by Charismatics or Pentecostals around the world? What happened in the Holiness Movement? Does God finish salvation with us in this this life or does he do this with our glorification in the next life?

1

Mount up with wings as eagles

God uses the eagle to symbolize greatness and for extraordinary abilities that transcend the normal and that are beyond our abilities. The prophet Isaiah encourages the people before and during their captivity and exile in Babylon by saying, "He giveth power to the faint; and to them that have no might he increases strength. Even the youth shall faint and be weary, and the young men shall utterly fall: But they that wait upon the Lord shall renew their strength; they shall mount up with wings as eagles; they shall run and not be weary; and they shall walk, and not faint" (Isaiah 40:29-31, King James Version). Something extraordinary was about to happen! God has used the eagle to speak figuratively of us rising above our circumstances!

A move of God is about to sweep through our lives!

Wait on the Lord

Who are we waiting for? In chapter forty of the book of Isaiah, the prophet describes God and reveals a few things about himself. He measures the waters of earth in the palm of his hand, marked off the heavens, and collects every particle of dust on the earth in a basket (Isaiah 40:12). He knows the exact weight of all the mountains, islands, and hills (Isaiah 40:12, 15). He sits on a throne above planet earth watching us and dwells in a tent made from the canopy of heavens (Isaiah 40:22).

He causes earthly rulers to wither with his breath (Isaiah 40:24). Brings out the stars each night by calling them each by name (Isaiah 40:26).

God is God and we are not. We wait on him because he can do what we cannot. He can do with us what we were told to do, but what we cannot do with ourselves on our own. We are helpless and hopeless without him! That is what the Hebrews learned when they were in captivity in Egypt and that is a lesson again when Judah was in Babylon! Wait on the Lord! We wait on the Lord to answer our prayers. We wait on the Lord to deliver us! We wait on the Lord to renew our strength. We wait on God to heal, set free, revive, manifest. We wait on God to do what only God can do!

The eagle rises to great heights but has no jet engine behind him. His body is designed to maximize the power of the air, as he soars on unseen currents with great agility and east. The prophet Isaiah is inspired to get us to see ourselves as creatures, designed to rely on the unseen, something greater than ourselves. The eagle is not weak because he is dependent on the power of the air, but he is built for the air to be his greatest strength!

The Psalmist says these words, "I remain confident of this: I will see the goodness of the Lord in the land of the living. Wait for the Lord; be strong and take heart and wait for the Lord" (Psalm 27:13-14). Remember that God's timing is perfect. Micah said this, "But as for me, I will wait for the God of my salvation; my God will hear me" (Micah 7:7). Jeremiah said these words in his lamentations, "The Lord is good to those who wait for him, to the soul who seeks him" (Lamentations 3:25).

Waiting for the power and for glorification at the eschaton

The Old Testament word "wait" means the same thing as the New Testament "tarry" that's brought up in the book of Acts. The disciples were told by Jesus Christ, "Tarry ye in the city of Jerusalem until you be endued with power from on high" (Luke 24:49). This was the resurrected savior proclaiming, before his ascension to heaven, that they would have power sent to them and within them! Real power was coming from Heaven and down into them! They needed to wait for this endowment of power in Jerusalem before traveling anywhere to preach the gospel. This is also a promise to every other believer. This is the spirit of truth to teach them and guide or comfort them (John 14:15-31).

They needed to be where he told them to be in order to receive this power and needed to make sure that they did not run ahead of him. They were helpless and without strength to overcome spiritual issues and battles to come without this power! They needed this power to proclaim the gospel message. The book of Acts is a continuation of the ministry of Jesus Christ on the earth as the Holy Ghost through people (Acts 1:1). Jesus had said that the Holy Ghost was coming to comfort them, but then said that it was he who would come to them to comfort (John 14:18). What could this mean to anyone struggling with fear, anxiety, depression, trauma, addiction, and other issues? The power that brought the Son of God back to life can live inside of you! Look at the potential! Think of the possibilities of what wonderful things could happen! We can overcome with God in us!

Luke later explained, "You shall receive power after the Holy Ghost has come upon you" (Acts 1:8). The Holy Ghost is the power that raised Jesus Christ from the dead that is now living in the born-again believer (Romans 6:10-11). Please take a moment and think about what this would mean to the men that were going out into the world to proclaim the gospel and for every other believer too.

We also find over in the nineteenth chapter of the Acts of the Apostles that the believers in Ephesus had not received this Holy Ghost and had not ever heard about it. How shall they call on whom they have not believed and how shall they believe in whom they have not heard and how shall they hear without a preacher. How can they preach unless they are sent by God to preach it (Romans 10:14-15)? A believer won't experience what the preacher hasn't told them about. Mount up with wings as the eagle!

Glorification

Paul says these profound and timeless words to the Church in Rome, "For whom he foreknew, he also did predestinate to be conformed to the image of his Son, that he might be the firstborn among many brethren. Moreover, whom he predestinated, them he also called; whom he called, these he also justified; and whom he justified, these he also glorified" (Romans 8:29-30). Glorification is God's final act of saving man.

The Apostle Paul revealed that we are waiting for the salvation of our bodies by saying, "For we know that the whole creation groans and travails in pain together until now. And not only they, but ourselves also, which have the first fruits of the Spirit, even we ourselves groan within ourselves, waiting for the adoption, to wit, the redemption of our body. For we are saved by hope, but hope that is seen is not hope: for what a man sees, why does he yet hope for? But if we hope for that we see not, then do we with patience wait for it" (Romans 8:24-26). Did you see that? We are still waiting for our bodies to be redeemed. Your flesh is not saved yet. Flesh has not been delivered. We are saved because we wait in hope for things that hasn't happened yet! But salvation is real because he said we already have the victory, and he has come to live inside of us as the Holy Ghost!

Did you get saved? Okay! Did you know that there are aspects of salvation that is yet to come, and that everything is not happening during your lifetime? What is glorification? Paul is referring to God's final act to remove sin out of the life of saints in the eternal state. Glorification is an aspect of Christian soteriology and Christian eschatology. This is God taking lust, sin, death, and all other faults out of your existence entirely! Remember this, "If we say that we have no sin, we deceive ourselves, and the truth is not in us, but if we confess our sins, he is faithful and just to forgive us and to cleanse us from all unrighteousness" (I John 1:8-9). Hamartiology is the aspect of Christian theology that identifies sin, its effect on themselves and their posterity, and how it still affects everyone today.

Glorification refers to the nature of believers being changed after death, rapture or at his second coming with the ultimate sanctification and perfection of the believer. The believer receives deliverance and liberty from the bondage and decay of the body into the glory and liberty of the children of God (Romans 8:21). The believer will, at glorification, be made glorious, holy, and blameless (Ephesians 4:27). He is changed in a moment or in the twinkling of an eye (I Corinthians 15:51). The glorification of the Christian is that we shall share in Christ's glory when we are in our resurrected bodies in the new heaven and the new earth, experiencing deeper fellowship with God and not being at risk of falling away into sin.

The glory of God is the state of incomparable greatness in which God dwells and through which he is compared to his creatures. This is when we live with God and share in his glory forever. We will be raised to a new life in a new body with Christ in the new heavens and the new earth. We won't have his glory but share in his glory as creatures who will now be dwelling in an eternal light.

The glory of God is incomparably greater than anything that can be seen on the earth. No human effort can elevate a man or woman this far above the human condition. Sin marred the creation and affected everyone to come on earth, but also made us as a marred image of the glory of God's image and less like him than before the fall, Glorification involves completely overcoming the damage caused by sin and being transformed from the material to the resurrection world!

Mount up with wings as eagles

The process of sanctification is at work in us now. The scriptures say, "And we all, with unveiled face, beholding the glory of the Lord, are being transformed into the same image from one degree of glory to another. For this comes from the Lord who is the Spirit" (2 Corinthians 3:18). We are moving from one degree of glory to the next now. This is not something that happens because of our prayer and fasting or vain efforts to be like God. Paul reveals that the Spirit of God makes all of this happen in all who are in Christ Jesus. Some theologians call transformation over time "progressive sanctification," meaning that we will become more and more like him as we are changed by the Spirit over time. However, we only reach final glory in the next life or when Jesus returns!

The Hebrew writers says, "Follow peace with all men and holiness, without which no man shall see the Lord" (Hebrews 12:14). The word "follow" from the New Testament Greek means to pursue. We are pursuing what we have yet to attained in its totality. However, we go from glory to glory and one level of overcoming to the next.

We are in pursuit of what God is doing to sanctify us now. We can see what we have overcome, and we know that God is producing his fruit in our lives. We can also sense that everything is not finish yet. He finishes all at glorification! Wait on the Lord! We will develop and grow spiritually over time. Wait on the Lord! We shall be changed! Never give up and quit during your period of transition from one degree of glory to another.

The glorified body will be immortal (Romans 2:7). The body at glorification is imperishable, powerful, and spiritual (II Corinthians 15:43-44). God's honor, praise, and holiness shall be realized in us and through us at glorification in a way that it is not now. We will have the divine nature. We will no longer be burdened with a sin nature and will changed to immortals with a more direct access to God. Until he returns or we depart from our bodies, we are burdened with original sin. Hamartiology Theologians call this original sin. Some call it the doctrine of total human depravity. There remains an affect that the fall continues to have upon all.

Paul described the reality of this sinful nature when he elaborated on how he sometimes did what he hated and did not know how to perform that which was good, but despite the reality that his inward man delighted after the law of the Lord (Romans 7:14-25). Paul put it like this, "For we know that the law is spiritual: but I am carnal, sold under sin" (Romans 7:14).

Paul says" Now it is no more I that do it, but sin that dwells in me. For I know that in me (that is, in my flesh) dwells no good thing: for desire to do right is with me, but how to perform that which is good I find not" (Romans 7:18). Paul explained why people needed glorification when he wrote these words, "For the good that I would I do not: but the evil which I don't want to do, is what I do" (Romans 7:19). He then says, "Now if I do that that I don't want to, is no more I that do it, but sin that dwells in me. I find then a law, that when I would do good, evil is present with me. For I delight in the law of God after the inward man: But I see another law in my members, warring against the law of my mind, and bringing me into captivity to the law of sin which is in my members. O wretched man I am! Who shall deliver me from the body of this death" (Romans 7:20-24)?

Our spiritual vision is still distorted and tainted due to the original fall of man, Paul says, "For now we see things imperfectly, like puzzling reflections in a mirror, but then we will see everything with perfect clarity. All that I know now is partial and incomplete, but then I will know everything completely, just as God now knows me completely" (I Corinthians 13:12-13, New Living Translation). The best theologians are still not aware of the depths of God's Word and what is revealed that is right in front of his eyes.

When does all this redemption of the body happen? We know that this hasn't happed yet or people in church would not stumble or fall. At the last trumpet, when Jesus comes, the saints undergo an instant transformation. Wait on the Lord! We shall be changed, in a moment, in the twinkling of an eye (I Corinthians 15:53). Glorification is God's final act of salvation and when he gives us a perfect nature and eradicates everything sinful out of us in the eschaton.

Going from one degree of glory to another

But right now, and at this time we are currently beholding the glory of the Lord and are being transformed into his image "from one degree of glory to another" (2 Corinthians 3:18). This text that I just cited again does not refer to our final glorification, but to the work of the Holy Ghost in our lives that is transfiguring us right now! God is sanctifying us in the Spirit and in truth (Jude 24-5, John 17:17). We move from one level to the next. This is a doing of God. People will overcome sin in this life! They will be set free! Jesus saves! We will see fruit in their lives, but we will know that there is more fruit they'll need to bear.

Paul says this deep spiritual truth, "Therefore if any man be in Christ, he is a new creature: old things are passed away: behold, all things are become new" (2 Corinthians 5:17). How could all things have become new while everyone is still waiting for the redemption of the body? How is the man a new creature in Christ? His spirit is born again, but his flesh is not!

The newness of life that believers walk in is a reality that is not here in the present material world, but a reality that comes from beyond the final judgment., from the life of the age to come. The works of a believer cannot be reduced to a mere condition of obtaining entrance into the age to come. They are the works and reality of the age to come that has broken forth into this present time in Jesus Christ.

Christ is our righteousness that is alive and at work in us and working out how he wants us to be. Everything is not complete. Wait on the Lord. He is still working on us! I just want to caution you not to believe that there is not more salvation that Christ will do in and through us! He finished salvation at the cross, but he is not finished working on us yet! More is coming! There may also be things that born-again believers are waiting for God to do in terms of redemption in this life and in the one to come! Wait for the Lord!

Wait on the Lord for your new body

The new body will not be subject to the current laws of sin and death that Paul described that was warring with him in his regenerated state in Romans 7:14-25. We don't know if the new body will be like the one that Jesus had after his resurrection and able to eat food and be touched, but also able to appear and vanish without a notice. It could be that the spiritual body will have passed through a stage that was typical of what happened at the ascension of Christ.

This would mean that everything about the body would have been raised to a higher spiritual plateau, comparable to that of angels. The glorified state in heaven will not be a return to the Garden of Eden. The tree of life will be there, but not the tree of the knowledge of good and evil. The Devil won't be there either. The believers are assured in the Book of Revelation that the very circumstances that led to the original fall are not in heaven. The World as it once was, will now be gone! The lust of the flesh is gone! The lure of the forbidden is gone! Satan is also nowhere to be found!

Wait on the Lord! Glorification is the future and final work of God upon Christians where he transforms our mortal physical bodies to the eternal physical bodies in which we will dwell forever. It is guaranteed to the believers in Christ Jesus, "And those whom he predestinated, he also called, he also justified; and these whom he justified, he also glorified" (Romans 8:30). All surroundings also change. Glorification is the theological term used to describe the final removal of sin from the lives of Christians at the end of time. This begins with justification (being made right with God based on what Christ did), sanctification (the life-long process of being made holy in a practical sense), and glorification (the final work of God removing sin and mortality from the believer at the rapture or when he receives his new body).

We will experience perfect joy in God's presence as stated, "Now unto him who is able to keep you from falling and to present you fault-less before the presence of his glory with exceeding joy, to the only God, our Savior, Jesus Christ our Lord, be glory, majesty, dominion, and authority, before all of time and now and forever. Amen." (Jude 24-25). Men will not be faultless until final glorification, but they will make progress in sanctification. We keep in mind in our lifetime that only Jesus Christ can present us faultless before God. God has not decided to do every aspect of sanctification in this life. We are imperfectly sanctified now but shall be perfectly sanctified then. He has saved some things for later. Wait on the Lord!

Paul mentions that Christ has given us a citizenship in heaven and that he will transform our earthly body to be like his glorious body, by the power that enables him even to subject all things to himself (Philippians 3:20-21). Our body will become fully glorified in eternity. The post-resurrection body of Jesus was able to recognize his followers. He was able to eat, but it was not necessary for his survival. He could appear in one room despite the door being locked. Now at this time the scriptures say, "No longer will there be anything accursed, but the throne of God and the Lamb will be on it, and his servants shall worship him" (Revelation 22:3).

Although it has not yet been revealed what we shall be, we know that, when he returns in great glory, we shall be like him, for we shall see him as he is (I John 3:2). We will be perfecting conformed to the image of Christ and have a divine nature that is free from the consequences of sin originating out of the fall. Everyone who hopes for this and hopes in him purifies himself (I John 3:3). There is something special about waiting for God to do something awesome and hoping for what he already said that he will do! God makes this happen!

The word "wait" means many things in the Word of God. The Hebrew word means to wait actively with anticipation, hopefully watching for God to act. This is trusting God to do something that we are expecting him to do.

The prophet Isaiah says, "They that wait upon the Lord shall renew their strength, they shall mount up with wings as eagles, they shall run and not be weary, they shall walk and not faint" (Isaiah 40:31). We are growing and developing toward perfection now, but there will come a time when each believer shall have it in its entirety!

Extraordinary Vision

The eagles have vision that is 6-8 times better than humans. We can illustrate this by explaining that if an eagle was sitting on one end of a football field, it could read the pages from a book or newspaper at the other end of the football field. Eagles have vision like a binocular. The eagle can use both eyes simultaneously to magnify things to view an object. The human can see things that are very far away, but everything is blurry, and he is unable to see very small things or miniature details far off like an eagle.

The prophet Isaiah was called the eagle-eye prophet in our Bibles because he could see the future as it would transpire and hundreds of years beforehand. He could see, hear, and listen afar off. He knew the future "supernaturally" to include specific details about the purpose of the death of Jesus Christ on the cross and many circumstances that would surround his death. Isaiah had the vision of the eagle when it came to future events. The Bible prophecies that came to pass with accuracy and precision are proof of the authenticity of the Word of God!

The eagle, as a bird, can see a fish underwater from over a mile away and see other objects up to three miles away. The eyes work independently from one another. They can focus on a fish with one eye and look for a path or obstacles with the other eye. It is a gift to have extraordinary vision and to be able to see a targeted goal afar off.

Have you ever met anyone before that could somehow see things that you could not see or know things that it seemed impossible to know? Have you ever met someone that knew what would be happening next? The prophet Amos says, "Indeed, The Sovereign Lord does nothing until he reveals his "secret" plan to his servants the prophets" (Amos 3:9, New Living Translation).

Personal Testimony of the Supernatural

Several years ago, I was about to leave home. I told my wife that I was going to run a few errands. I was driving down the road and I heard God tell me in my Spirit to go home and say to your wife, "I am the Man of God and I have come to give you a Word from the Lord". I knew I was being told this in my Spirit. I then returned home.

When I returned home, my wife asked as to why I returned. I then told her that I was driving down the road and God told me in my Spirit to return home and say, "I am the Man of God and I have come to give you a Word from the Lord". She then listened for moment to what God told me to share. Tears started rolling down her eyes. She then asked me to watch a segment of a live sermon that was broadcast from Columbus, Ohio that she was watching online while I was gone.

My wife then rewound the live television broadcast to show me what the Pastor said while I was gone. The Pastor said when I was gone, "If you want to hear the Man of God to give you a Word from the Lord then pray on your knees right now and he will send a Man of God to you to give you a Word from the Lord". My wife said that she then got on her knees to pray to God and asked for a Man of God to give her a Word from the Lord. She said that after this it was in about seven minutes that I returned to the house and said, "I am the Man of God and I come to give you a Word from the Lord".

I am not a billionaire or famous, but the Lord Jesus Christ talks to me by the Holy Ghost!

The Holy Ghost speaks to his people

God provides supernatural guidance and speaks to people about where, when, and to whom ministry should go. This was surely the case when Phillip spoke to the Ethiopian eunuch as it is written, "And the Spirit said the Phillip, "Go over and join this chariot" (Acts 8:29). The Spirit's role in providing guidance for evangelical outreach and missionary work is seen in the book of Acts regarding the ministry of Paul and says, "While they were worshipping the Lord and fasting, the Holy Ghost said, "Set apart for me Barnabas and Saul for the work to which I have called them" (Acts 13:2). We then find these words written, "So they, being sent forth by the Holy Ghost, departed unto Seleucia, and from thence they sailed to Cyprus" (Acts 13:4). The Holy Ghost communicates directly to our spirit and guides us down the pathway that God desires for us to take! Mount up with wings as eagles!

We also find that Paul was guided by the Holy Ghost and forbidden to minister to some people with these words written, "And they went through the region of Phygia and Galatia, having been forbidden by the Holy Ghost to speak the word in Asia. And when they had come up to Mysia, they attempted to go into Bithynia, but the Spirit of Jesus did not allow them" (Acts 16:6-7). Mount up with wings as eagles will most definitely mean being led by the Holy Ghost with what we do next and where to go from here.

Extraordinary gifts

As I think about the vision of the eagle, I think about how people can have some extraordinary talents or gifts. The prophet, Isaiah, Daniel, Enoch, the Apostle John, and many others often narrated events with precision that would happen decades and sometimes thousands of years in the future. The events happened exactly how they were narrated. Everything that was prophesied about the purpose of the life, death, and resurrection of Jesus Christ by the prophet Isaiah, happened exactly as foreseen beforehand.

Sometimes men or women in life have yet to discover their gift. There is an Old Proverb that says, "A man's gift makes room for him, and brings him before great men" (Proverbs 18:16). We may think of spectacular things happening with people or even someone growing into awesomeness but remember that it's often due to an extraordinary gift. Like the vision of an eagle, people can have gifts that transcend the ordinary.

God makes them great because of his strength and his work in their lives. I will never forget these profound words spoken by God to Jeremiah, "Before I formed you in the belly, I knew you, and before you came out of the womb, I sanctified you, and ordained you as a prophet to the nations" (Jeremiah 1:5). Did Jeremiah have a choice? He surely did! But remember that God's eternal decree and daily providence work together to bring his purpose for our lives forward. God is Sovereign.

Daniel could see like the eagle and supernaturally interpret dreams

When we look into the Old Testament, we find that the prophet Daniel had the ability to know what a King had dreamed, but also to tell him what his dream meant and what God was going to do in the future for ages to come with kingdoms on earth. The magicians, astrologers, and soothsayers that King Nebuchadnezzar sought out for the interpretation of his dream, did not know and couldn't figure it out. God can do things with men by his Spirit that other people in the world cannot do in their worldly wisdom, knowledge, and education.

Daniel explained to the King what the dream meant and how that the King would lose his kingdom and have it restored 7 years later. Daniel explained to the King that all of this would happen to him because he did not give the glory to God for giving the kingdoms to him. Also, he wrote much about four future world empires and kingdoms that would rise up on the earth in the future.

Daniel's interpretation of the dream included defining the stone that would fall on all Kings of the earth to move all of the world empires away from the earth. This stone spoke of is Christ in prophecy and God's kingdom being set up on earth to remove the others (Daniel 2:1-44). How were these things possible? Mounting up with wings as the eagle is about God showing up through us and in our lives to manifest what we cannot manifest on our own. This is possible with faith! We hope for this. We wait for this with expectancy and joy!

Elijah and Elisha's gift to soar above

Many of you may remember how that the prophet Elijah had a supernatural anointing (Spirit of God) that rested on him in his lifetime to do miracles. Elijah performed many miracles. One of the most memorable is when a foreign leader sent men to capture him with a captain and 50 men. The prophet Elijah said to them, "If I am a man of God, let fire come down from heaven and destroy you and your fifty men! Then fire fell from heaven and killed them all" (2 Kings 1:10).

This happened two more times that Elijah called fire from heaven that burned up a caption and his fifty men! God moved the heavens to fight for him and sent his fire out of heaven against his enemies at his word! This was a manifestation of the power of God showing up against the enemies of a servant of God! I would not encourage anyone to pray for fire to destroy enemies, but I do warn God's enemies that God can send his judgment down!

Another notable miracle was him challenging King Ahab and Jezebel at Mt. Carmel to ask their false God, Baal, to send fire to a bull on an altar to consume it if their false God was real. Nothing happened. Elijah then called on God in heaven and we find that God then sent fire out of heaven to not only set ablaze the sacrifice, but the wood, the altar, and the dust around it. The people then fell to their knees and proclaimed that the Lord is God (I Kings 18:1-39).

A secret to mounting up with wings as eagles

God is still looking for people to put their sacrifice on an altar and to cry out for deliverance so that he can answer! God sent the needed rain after sending fire to the altar to burn up the sacrifice. The rain ended a drought and brought fruitfulness to their land! God does what we can't do. Elijah had mounted up with wings as the eagle! God moved and that is what we hope for!

He called on God of heaven to do something and God showed up in his life in a supernatural way. Fire fell from the sky to consume the sacrifice and the needed rain came after the fire was gone! Mount up with wings as the eagle is to have God swoop through our lives and bring about a breakthrough that we cannot. This is something that we can pray for!

The scriptures teach us about why God heals our land by saying, "If my people, which are called by my name, shall humble themselves, and pray, and seek my face, and turn from their wicked ways; then will I hear from heaven, and will forgive their sin, and will heal their land" (2 Chronicles 7:14). God heals that land because the people humble themselves to petition him in prayer. They cry out to God. The people also sought the Lord and turned from their wicked ways! King David said these words, "The righteous cry, and the Lord hears, and delivers them out of all their troubles" (Psalms 34:17).

Traveling in a supernatural vehicle

One extraordinary and supernatural event that happened in the life of Elisha was his departure from the earth. There appeared a whirlwind and horses of fire with a chariot of fire. Elisha boarded a vehicle that pulled up in front of him and he was taken to heaven in a chariot of fire. He gave his protégé, Elijah, a double portion of the spirit that was upon himself before boarding the fire chariot from heaven (2 Kings 2:1-18).

Elijah asked for this double portion of the Spirit of God. His mentor, Elisha, mentioned that if he saw him when he boarded the chariot that it would be so! All these extraordinary events were things that God wanted us to know about so that we can see what is possible. There are doors that can be opened supernaturally and things that are not possible with ordinary people that do become possible when God is with a Son or Daughter of God!

A new dimension

All of Elijah's extraordinary acts and miracles were examples of men soaring above and beyond the ordinary dimension of the natural or the flesh and into another realm of supernatural power. His departure on a fire chariot from heaven symbolizes how that God's people are supernaturally transported to heaven after they depart the earth. We must keep in mind that when we walk with God that he can transport us to another place by supernatural means. This can happen while we are still alive!

John wrote these words, "I was in the Spirit on the Lord's Day and heard behind me a great voice and a trumpet" (John 1:6). John was there. He wrote down what he saw! This was a vision. But he still wrote what he saw and was there in the Spirit. Can you imagine what it would have been like to write down events that were to happen thousands of years into the future?

The Apostle Paul also had an experience that transcends space and time. How did he see it and how did he know it? God showed him! Paul spoke of himself in the third person and said, "I know a man in Christ fourteen years ago was caught up to the third heaven. Whether in the body or out of the body I do not know-God knows! And I know that this man-whether in the body or apart from the body I do not know, but God knows-was caught up to paradise" (2 Corinthians 12:1-4). God can show us amazing things and give us experiences that are so phenomenal that words cannot express or utter.

Entering God's Throne of Grace

The kingdom of God is not like the earth. God elevates us above and beyond the realm of the earth. We are transported spiritually and enter God's throne of grace when we pray and then we can obtain mercy and help from God when we ask (Hebrews 4:16). This is only possible when we are born again and experience the birth of the spirit that Jesus spoke about.

We mount up with wings as the eagle by the power of the Spirit of God. We pray and ask God for this gift and God's intervention! The chariot of fire that came to take Elijah to heaven was a supernatural event that God manufactured! Elijah was not seeking out this experience. God does what men cannot do in their own strength! Men will also experience the supernatural at times they were not seeking out the experience.

We soar above to new heights and greater depths in God by the wings of the eagle. Jesus said these words, "That which is flesh is flesh; and that which is born of the spirit is spirit. Marvel not that I said unto you, Ye must be born again" (John 3:6-7). When a man or woman is born again it means they have experienced a supernatural event inside of their spiritual man! That event is a miracle! It's an act of God! Only God can birth someone again in the spirit and put them into his kingdom by that birth. This is also how we know that people cannot bring about their own spiritual growth and development. God is God. He has set the church in place in put spiritual gifts in the church gatherings for this (Ephesians 4:11).

Elijah's protégé

There was a prophet of God that lived named Elisha. Elisha was the predecessor of the prophet Elijah. Elisha had a double portion of the Spirit of God that was on his mentor Elijah. The prophet Elisha soared as the eagle. He was a miracle worker. This was an extraordinary gift that came from God. The miracles that he worked were examples of how the Spirit of God can do extraordinary feats in the life of a believer. There is an extraordinary power on the earth that is here to help us take our flight!

We find that Elisha parted the Jordan River. He raised a woman's son from the dead. He caused bread to supernaturally multiply. He caused an ax head to float on the water after it fell underneath the water and sunk. Elisha smote the Syrian Army with blindness and later caused their sight to return. A man was even brought back to life after Elisha died, but when the bones of another dead man accidentally touched the bones of the corpse of Elisha. Elisha had performed many more miracles in his lifetime.

God's gifts are what causes people to become great. Elisha had God's spirit on him! He was anointed! Jesus also promised to the church they he was sending them a supernatural gift, "You shall receive power after that Holy Ghost has come upon you" (Acts 1:8). What was this power for? What is this power? Have you ever wondered about what the Holy Ghost was?

After the descent of the Holy Ghost on the Day of Pentecost, we will find later that Peter healed a paralyzed man that was bedridden by simply telling him that Jesus heals him and to rise and make up his bed. Peter also raised Tabitha from the dead after she got sick and died. People were mourning her death when Peter came on the scene (Acts 9:32-43).

Paul raised a man from the dead. The Word of God also says, "And God wrought special miracles by the hands of Paul: so that from his body were brought unto the sick handkerchiefs or aprons, and the diseases departed from them, and the evil spirits went out of them" (Acts 19:11-12). Mount up with wings as the eagle may mean one thing to one individual and another special manifestation of God's grace or power to someone else. God will do extraordinary things with and through his people.

Gifts that come only from God

James put it like this, "Whatever is good and perfect is a gift coming down to us from God our Father, who created all the lights in the heaven. He never changes or casts a shifting shadow" (James 1:17, New Living Translation). God has many different types of gifts that he has given his people to work wonders on the earth. The gifts given to men in the field of medicine, quantum physics, science, astrophysics, music, arts, and many other disciplines are simply not possible without their being supernatural phenomena interacting with and through man. There are also gifts that are spiritual gifts which come from God's anointing being on us.

The Gift of the supernatural strength and Power

I just want to mention that this story of mounting up with wings like the eagle is speaking symbolically of the believer doing something extraordinary that is far beyond his natural ability. Can you remember the story of Samson? Samson fought the Philistines and said one day, "With the jawbone of a donkey, I've piled them in heaps, with the jawbone of a donkey have I've killed a thousand men" (Judges 15:16). Samson's extraordinary strength came from God and that allowed him to defeat 1000 Philistine men in a single fight by himself!

Maybe you can remember to story of Samson killing a lion with his bare hands when he was a child. Samson had his final act of judgment against the Philistines after losing his strength. He pushed those pillars in the temple to bring down the temple and slayed all of them. This was an extraordinary gift that came from God! There was strength and power on him because the Spirit of God rested on him to do certain acts.

God's anointing

This historical lesson about Samson shows us that we need a gift that comes only from God to give us strength to overcome our enemies and to win our battles! The Word of God says, "And it shall come to pass in that day, that his burden shall be taken away from off thy shoulder, and his yoke from off thy neck, and the yoke shall be destroyed because of the anointing" (Isaiah 10:27). The anointing is the burden-removing, yoke-destroying power of God.

A yoke was used around the neck of two animals to join them together in slavery. The anointing is God being on flesh doing what flesh cannot do. The anointing is what delivers God's people and sets the captive free. The anointing is God's super added to the natural. In Acts 10:38 we see the impact of the anointing on the life and ministry of Jesus. The scriptures say, "And you know that God anointed Jesus of Nazareth with the Holy Ghost and with power. Then Jesus went around doing good and healing all who were oppressed by the devil, for God was with him" (Acts 10:38, New Living Translation).

The anointing that rested on Jesus produced the results and touched the lives of people around him. Mounting up with wings as the eagle is about God himself working the supernatural through us beginning with being born again. The context in the book of Isaiah in the tenth chapter is about the anointing removing a burden by the historical liberation of an entire nation from slavery, but them being taken out of captivity to the Assyrians empire. This was a doing that the people could not do in their own strength. This is and was "as always" the anointing of God moving supernaturally to set the captives free.

Feathers and their purpose

The eagle is nothing less than an airplane, but not one the was built by man. One thing that we discover when we study the animal kingdom is that feathers are unique to birds. We notice that other animals do not have feathers. That is because they were not engineered to fly.

We know that the soft feathers keep the bird warm and provide insulation to help regulate the body temperature. The eagle was prepared in advance to do what it does in the weather and through the storm. The down feathers actually trap the air in small spaces, but that stops the body from losing heat. The feathers help to regulate the temperature of the body of the bird.

The contour feathers are overlapping and contain structures that make the bird very streamlined and aerodynamic for flight. Every bird cannot fly. The penguin is a great example of a bird that isn't engineered for flight. Flight feathers are very specialized contour feathers that are attached to the wings. This gives a very large and flat surface like the wings of an airplane. This large and flat surface that stretches outward and an angle are necessary for flight. The eagle was built to fly.

The Flight of an eagle

When we notice the flight of an eagle it is very fascinating to see. We may not realize the amount of creativity and knowledge of aerodynamics that is needed for a creature to be designed to fly. This could not have been accidental or a chance event. Birds fly when air flows over the top of a wing.

The front of the wing must be thick, and the back has to be very narrow to allow the wings to cut through the air. The design of the wing is what allows the force of the air to go over the top of the wing to lift the body of the bird. The bird can only fly when the pressure of the air under the wings is larger than the weight of the bird. When the air moves fast over the top of the wing, the ability of the eagle to lift upward is greater. Keep in mind that the flying isn't possible without the wind to give the eagle its lift.

Built for your flight

When you study the structure and makeup of the bones of an eagle, you'll find that they have very hollow bones. The hollow bones make them very light compared to the size of their bodies. They have over 7,000 feathers. The eagle has very broad wings and they are needed to lift his prey upward. The feathers on the tail are designed to allow the eagle to steer during his flight. The bald eagle spends more time soaring during a flight than flapping their wings. This is because the wind is heavily relied upon during their flight, but not their own strength and endurance. Have you ever considered that you were engineered for a specific purpose?

Moving with the strength of the wind

The warm air is lighter than cold air. The cold air that surrounds the wind thermal is sucked inward as the heated air rises. The study of wind reveals that the warm air rises like a balloon. Have you ever seen anyone rises upward in a giant balloon that men built? The warm air rises and floats on the cool air below. Once the eagle is in the wind thermal, the eagles soar and use very little energy to stay in flight. They soar on the wind and in the strength of the wind.

The eagle spreads his wings straight out to soar on wind currents. He doesn't rely on his own strength to take him throughout his journey. He uses the wind currents. The eagle learns to fly without flapping the huge wings that they do have. Eagles would get very tired and burnout if they relied on their own strength to take them everywhere by flapping their wings.

Eagles wait for a big gust of wind that rises. The eagle may wait for days until they catch a strong wind thermal. They will then use a combination of flapping their winds and soaring on the wind currents to move them toward wherever they want to go. The wind does the work. The eagle will do something, but most of the work is done by the wind. The people of God wait on the Spirit of God to move and for him to manifest himself to them. The Word of God says, "For all who are led by the Spirit of God are the sons of God" (Romans 8:14).

Mount up with wings as eagles

What does it mean to mount up with wings as eagles? The picture of an eagle takes us all the way back to the days of the Exodus of Israel from the land of Egyptian. The Israelites were God's chosen people, but they were in bondage as slaves to the Egyptians! Sure, they wanted to be delivered. They wanted to come out, but they did not have the ability or strength to bring themselves out! God says to the Israelites after bringing them out, "You yourselves have seen what I did to the Egyptians, and how I bore you on eagles' wings and brought you to myself" (Exodus 19:4, New Living Translation).

With strength and power like the eagle, God swooped in and carried his people away and out of Egypt. God used Moses to perform many miracles and eventually drowned Pharoah's army in the Red Sea when they attempted to capture or pull them back into captivity. God had in history orchestrated that the deliverance of Israel out of bondage to the Egyptians and Pharoah would be symbolic of redemption of our deliverance out of sin and from bondage to Satan.

God compares himself to the eagle! However, he tells us to mount up with wings as the eagle. That means that we must go in his strength. God becomes our deliverance and our salvation! He becomes the strength, deliverance, salvation, and redeemer of his people. The people are in bondage and not able to bring themselves out of the situation that they are trapped in.

·Many years later, Judah is now in trouble again. They are on the brink of exile. They are about to be taken captive by the Babylonians. They hear the prophetic messages from Isaiah and know that they will be losing everything. God then inspires the prophet to speak to them to comfort them. He wants them to know that they will come out of bondage by their captor, and it will be in a strength that they do not possess on their own.

The Assyrians had already taken the North from Israel. Babylon was about to take the South. Israel needed the eagle. They needed their Savior to act. They needed the eagle. They needed another Exodus. This was the promise of a brand-new Exodus where God swooped in and rescued his people again from bondage.

The new Exodus included the promise of a coming Savior. The people would return to their homeland in Jerusalem but also have eternal deliverance once they put their trust in the Savior! The scope of the new Exodus would be global. The new Exodus would bring them from Babylonian captivity, but it would encompass much more for all who put their trust in the coming Savior!

The Wind symbolizes the Spirit

All throughout the scriptures we find the wind used as a metaphor to symbolize the supernatural and the spirit. We see Zechariah saying the following, "Not by might, nor by power, but by my spirit, says the Lord" (Zechariah 4:6). Zechariah wanted the people to know that the Spirit of God is what be their strength and give them the victory in the battle! They would not be able to conquer or subdue the enemy on their own. This is why that we have to continue to speak about Jesus' promise of the Holy Ghost in the life of a believer.

Judah had to mount us with wings like the eagle. This meant trusting the Lord and having faith in him. This meant believing that the deliverer would do what he said he would and to keep believing while they were waiting. They were not to give up. They were not to quit. They were to focus their vision on their goals. They were to live in hope. They did not know how the promise would come to pass, but they had to continue to believe that God would do it! Keep hoping. Never stop believing that God will bring you out in his appointed time!

They were not to doubt, but to believe the good news! They were not to live in fear or anxiety, but to trust God's Sovereignty. Judah was not able to overpower the Babylonian or the Persian Army in their own strength. God had to move and set them free from their captivity. Likewise, men do not have the ability to overcome addictions or bondages to the flesh or Satan, but Jesus Christ can set them free. Jesus said that he came to set the captives free in Luke 4:18. The anointing destroys the yoke!

They were not to investigate the past and burden themselves with guilt and depression. They were coming out! They would mount up with wings like the eagle! God was going to do what he said that he would do! As the eagle soars in the strength of the wind, God's people would be rescued and delivered by the strength of the spirit of God. The Lord becomes our strength! The scriptures say, "God is our refuge and strength, a very present help in the time of trouble" (Psalms 46:1).

God is our deliverer

When we think of God as a deliverer it may bring back many memorable events in the scripture. Do you remember how that God shut up the mouth of lions for Daniel when Daniel was in the lion's den? We may recall how that God prevented the three Hebrew boys from being burned in the flames after they refused to bow down to worship the statute. The people saw an angel that appeared like the Son of God that was in the furnace. The King threw them in the fire, but they did not burn and none of their garments were even allowed to have the scent of the smoke or flames on them. God delivered them from their situation.

We can tell people to quit things and to come out, but they need a deliverer and cannot come out on their own. It's a supernatural move of the Spirit. I have concluded that people can be saved but need deliverance from certain bondages in their walk with God. I call it saved, but not delivered! People must repent. They must be willing in their minds to come out and then God will bring them out!

God anointed a Pagan King
to deliver Israel from bondage

God anointed a Persian King named Cyrus and commissioned him to destroy the bars of Babylon's prison and to set Israel free and to set free the captives from other nations. The Persians conquered the Babylonians in 538 BC. The captivity of Judah had been a 70-year judgement to Judah for her sin. Cyrus was the King of Persia. King Cyrus then made a decree as soon as becoming King, to announce that Judah could return to Jerusalem to rebuild their temple.

Cyrus explained that the God of Jerusalem was God of all, but that God had given him all nations and directed him to make this announcement! When Judah was set free it was a doing of the Lord and nothing that they could have done in their own strength. Once God does something it will have an immediately impact. However, after Cyrus announced that they were free, they still had to take a 700-mile journey back to Jerusalem.

Once God has opened the door and cleared the way for us to take our journey back to our rightful place, we will know that it is time for us to move! This is a "type" of Christian journey. We are on our way to heaven, but we must take our journey. God has cleared the way for us to come and now he wants us to pursue heaven. We soar above the earthly realm by the power of the Holy Ghost. We soar to heaven too in a strength that comes from God!

The only way that they could run and not be weary or walk and not faint would be that they had supernatural help. The wings of the eagle that brought the people out of Egypt had now acted in their favor to set them free from Babylonian captivity. They only way that they could not faint on their journey or during all the tribulation and trials of life would be for the Lord himself to live through them and give them supernatural strength. They also had to hold on to hope and live in expectation of God's promise through Isaiah being fulfilled in its due time.

We mount up with wings as the eagle when we believe Jesus and trust him for our deliverance and our salvation. We walk in his spirit. We'll overcome our captivity, but not in our own strength. The wind carries the eagle above the storm. When God compares us to the eagle, he wants us to have the insight that his spirit gives us supernatural help. Hear is what Luke says about the descent of the Holy Ghost on the day of Pentecost, "But you shall receive power after that the Holy Ghost has come upon you" (Acts 1:8). The power that Luke is talking about is arising out of a promise that Jesus Christ made to his disciples prior to his ascension.

27

God called us Gods

Word of God says these illuminating words, "And the Lord said to Moses, See, I have made you a god to Pharaoh: and Aaron your brother shall be your prophet" (Exodus 7:1). God said this because Moses mounted up with wings as the eagle. He operated with the power of God and what he said and done originated with God! It was God working through a man and doing what a man could not do in his own power and strength! Jesus quoted Psalm 82:6 in the gospel in John 10:34. Jesus said, "Is it not written in your law, I said, you are gods? If he called them gods to whom the Word of God came-and the scripture cannot be broken-do you say that the one that God sent into the world and anointed, "You are blaspheming," because I said, "I am the Son of God?" (John 10:33-36).

When Jesus cited Psalm 82:6, he was referring to the power delegated to the Judges in the Old Testament to make decisions and rule or act on behalf of God. This is delegated power and authority to act for God. However, this doesn't mean that men are the eternal and Most High God of creation. Nevertheless, when we look at what it means to mount up with wings like an eagle, keep in mind that God moves and acts in and through us by his Spirit to do things for him and that God manifests himself through us! The eagle depends on the wind of the unseen world. Healing the sick and raising the dead or working a miracle during the early days of the church were acts done by God and through people! Mount up with wings as the eagle!

The strength of the Spirit
in Regeneration and overcoming

Jesus made one of the most astonishing revelations about entering the heaven above when he said, "Except a man be born again, he cannot see the kingdom of God" John 3:3). Nicodemus was perplexed. He asked Jesus as to how a man could go back into his mother's womb to be born again. Christ was not talking about the fleshly man going back into his mother's womb to be born again.

He was talking about a spiritual rebirth. Jesus then said, "Verily, verily, I say unto you, except a man is born of water and of spirit, he cannot enter into the kingdom of God. That which is flesh is flesh, and that which is spirit is spirit. Marvel not that I said unto you, you must be born again. The wind blows where it listeth, and you hear the sound thereof, but can't tell whence it cometh, and whither it goeth; so is every one that is born of the Spirit" (John 3:5-8).

Do you see how Jesus compared the wind to the spirit? The wind and the spirit of God of both invisible and mysterious. But just as the wind carries the eagle, the spirit will literally lift a man out of his sinful condition. He overcomes because he is born again. He can avoid the pit because he is born again. He will be tempted. He may even fall. However, he cannot stay as he was in his past life. He is born again.

Being born again is not something that any individual can do on his own. This is the spirit of God birthing a man's spirit into his kingdom by breathing into him a new, regenerated, spiritual life that he has never had before. The spiritual man that was spiritually dead in sin is revived and given life in Christ who died for his sins and rose from the dead.

Paul explained this regenerated new life and the spiritual cleansing to Titus by saying, "Not by works of righteousness which we have done, but according to his mercy he saved us, by the washing of regeneration, and renewing of the Holy Ghost" (Titus 3:5). The Holy Ghost is God's spirit that Jesus promised to every believer. The Holy Ghost is the wind of the spirit that causes the eagle to soar above the storm! We mount up with the wings of the eagle when we rise above things on the earth. Our mind and our spirit is elevated above. The Word of God says, "Set your affection on things above, not on things on the earth" (Colossians 3:2).

The Power that lives within

As we have seen above, the Holy Ghost is God's power. Here is what the Roman author says about the Holy Ghost, "But if the Spirit of him that raised up Jesus from the dead dwell in you, he that raised up Christ from the dead shall also quicken your mortal bodies by his Spirit that dwelleth in you" (Romans 8:11). Did you see that? The power that raised up Jesus' body from death is alive and dwelling inside of the believer that has experienced being born again! Pray and ask God to fill you with the Holy Ghost and power! God will birth you into his kingdom! We mount up with wings as the eagle by soaring in a supernatural power. This is Christ himself living in us. The Holy Ghost is real!

The Holy Ghost is our Comforter

Jesus said these words about the Holy Ghost, "And I will pray the Father, and he shall give you another Comforter, that he may abide with you forever; Even the Spirit of truth; whom the world cannot receive, because it seeth him not, neither know him: but you know him: for he dwells with you and shall be in you. I will not leave you comfortless: I will come to you" (John 14:16-18. Christ makes it clear that the world cannot receive this Comforter. He also identifies that he is the comforter that is coming to live inside of them! The gift of the Holy Ghost is only for the ones who have put their trust in Christ as being the Son of God who died for their sins and rose again.

Peace to a troubled mind

I have sat down and talked to many men throughout the years that either attempted suicide more than once or that were contemplating ending it all. Depression and guilt are real spiritual issues. The stories of abuse and trauma or abandonment and betrayal from either a parent, loved one, lover, or spouse often caused many to suffer from what clinicians would diagnose as post-traumatic stress disorder. Jesus then identifies what the comforter will do by saying, "But the Comforter, which is the Holy Ghost, whom the Father will send in my name, he shall teach you all things, and bring all things to your remembrance, whatsoever I have said unto you. Peace I leave with you, my peace I give unto you: not as the world giveth, give I unto you. Let not your heart be troubled, neither let it be afraid" (John 14:26-27). The Spirit gives peace to a troubled mind. He gives comfort and leaves us no reason to be afraid of anything within our hearts.

Rest in your soul

Mounting up with wings as the eagle is all about getting the victory and the power and strength that comes from the Lord himself. This victory includes overcoming things like anxiety, fear, depression, anger, rejection, guilt, and grief. All these things could overtake anyone, but that is when we leap into our comfort with the Holy Ghost and power. We can mount up with wings as eagles to rise above or overcome them. He does the work through us by the Holy Ghost. Jesus said these words to troubled souls, "Take my yoke upon you. Let me teach you, because I am humble and gentle at heart, and you will find rest for your souls" (Matthew 11:29, New Living Translation).

The rest is in what Jesus taught and what we believe about him and his teachings. This comes from us trusting him to save us, provide for us what we need as our shepherd, deliver us from enemies, rescue us from sin. We are born again once we repent of sin and believe the gospel! We have a supernatural comfort in our souls once we are filled with the Holy Ghost!

Manifestation of power

The Holy Ghost also manifests itself through us by what the spirit does through us! Mark says this about the believer, "And these signs shall follow them that believe; In my name shall they cast out devil; they shall speak with new tongues; They shall take up serpents; and if they drink any deadly thing, it shall not hurt them; they shall lay hands on the sick and they shall recover" (Mark 16:17-18). These words were spoken by Jesus and I'm not adding anything to the Word of God or taking anything away. Jesus said that all of these signs would only follow those who believed!

The Day of Pentecost

The descent of the Holy Ghost on the day of Pentecost was about the manifestation of God's presence and power. Peter said that the event that transpired on the Day of Pentecost by the power of God was a fulfillment of prophecy that was spoken of by the prophet Joel that says, "And it shall come to pass that in the last days, saith God, I will pour out my spirit upon all flesh: and your sons and daughters shall prophesy, and your young men shall see visions, and your old men shall dream dreams" (Acts 2:16-17). You all may want to ask God if we are still in the last days or not and what does it mean that sons and daughters would prophesy! The scriptures and circumstances indicate that we are still in the last days!

John the Baptist also spoke of the baptism of the Holy Ghost by saying, "I indeed baptize you with water unto repentance: but he that comes after me is mightier than I, whose shoes I am not worthy to bear: he shall baptize you with the Holy Ghost, and with fire: Whose fan is in his hand, and he will thoroughly purge his floor, and gather wheat into the garner; but he will burn up the chaff with unquenchable fire" (Matthew 3:11-12).

John the Baptist is talking about how that Jesus will baptize his followers with the Holy Ghost. Christ is the one who baptizes with the Holy Ghost. We have seen that the Holy Ghost is the spiritual life that enables the believers to overcome. He will also gather the believers with him in the end of the age and separate them from the unbelievers who did not trust him for forgiveness and eternal life!

The Holy Ghost falls on Ephesus believers

Being born again is being regenerate or brought to spiritual life by the power of the Holy Ghost! It is not possible for anyone to live a life of victory over sin and Satan without Christ giving them spiritual life and baptizing them with the Holy Ghost. The Holy Ghost and the power of the anointing is what destroys the yoke of captivity. Believers are justified by faith alone as we shall discover in upcoming chapters, but the power of the Holy Ghost is a special gift that can come at the time of justification or after one believes!

Notice what happens when Paul traveled to see believers who had not been baptized with the Holy Ghost. The scripture says, "While Apollos was in Corinth, Paul traveled through the interior regions until he reached Ephesus, on the coast, where he found several believers. "Did you receive the Holy Ghost when you believed?" he asks them. "No" they replied, "we haven't even heard that there is a Holy Ghost." "Then what baptism did you experience?" he asked. And they replied, "The baptism of John." Paul said, "John's baptism called for repentance from sin. But John himself told the people to believe on the one who would come later, meaning Jesus." As soon as they heard this, they were baptized in the name of the Lord Jesus. Then when Paul laid his hands on them, the Holy Ghost came on them, and they spoke with tongues and prophesied. There were about twelve men in all" (Acts 19:1-7, New Living Translation).

This narrative reveals that it is possible to have believed the gospel and not to have heard about the Holy Ghost. It is also possible to have believed and not to have been baptized with the power of the Holy Ghost. The Holy Ghost manifested itself at the time of the baptism. God will manifest the Holy Ghost to his servants, and we will know that we have received it!

The truth about Spiritual Gifts

Throughout the years I have heard many debates and arguments about manifestations and whether they are for still for today. I have noticed that many Reformed Theologians teach that the spiritual gifts still operate in the church to include tongues and prophesy. But some Reformed Theologians believe that these gifts have ceased. This book is not about settling those debates or siding with any view but teaching the scriptures as they are written.

The men in Ephesus had not heard about the Holy Ghost and had not been filled with the Holy Ghost since they believed. When Paul told them about the Holy Ghost and prayed for them, they received the Holy Ghost.

The Holy Ghost only came on the believers in Ephesus after they had heard about him from the Apostle Paul. Paul said these words to the Romans, "For whoever shall call on the name of the Lord shall be saved. How then shall they call on him in whom they have not believed? And how shall they believe in him of whom they have not heard? And how shall they hear without a preacher?" (Romans 10:14). I am here to encourage men to believe God for everything that is possible!

The men spoke in tongues and prophesied once they received the Holy Ghost in this historical narrative. Men will need to pray and ask God for the Holy Ghost and make sure that you have received this precious gift of promise from the Father! The Holy Ghost is what empowers us to live a life of victory in the spirit. Men are born-again and regenerated by the Holy Ghost to walk in a newness of life as a new creature.

Agree with the Word of God

I can agree with everyone that two things are true when it comes to spiritual gifts. The Word of God says, "But one and the same Spirit works all these things, distributing to each one individually as he wills" (I Corinthians 12:11, New King James Version). All believers should agree that it is up to God's will as to who will receive which spiritual gift and why. That is simply what the Word of God says.

Second, The Word of God says, "Love never ends. As for prophecies, they will pass away; as for tongues, they will cease; as for knowledge, It will pass away. For we know in part, and we prophesy I part, but when the perfect comes, the partial will pass away" (I Corinthians 13:8). There is no doubt that the Word of God teaches that a time will come that prophecies, tongues, knowledge, and other gifts would cease.

As we saw above, a manifestation had not happened in Ephesus because they had not heard about the Holy Ghost. I have no doubt that some of these gifts may have ceased in many movements of God that preach the gospel. Why have the gifts ceased in some places and yet multiplied millions of people say that they are operating within their churches or religious organizations?

Have gifts ceased everywhere and do we know everything

The gifts are simply not operating in many churches. We also know that they did not operate with many believers throughout the Protestant Reformation. But can we say that they have already ceased everywhere?

I say that the text in I Corinthians 13:9 explains why some believers may not see things the same on these issues. He says in I Corinthians 13:9 that we know in part and prophesy in part!

Any knowledge given to the church by God through someone with the gift of knowledge is just a tiny picture of all there is to know of God and how God operates or what he is doing. Men have seen and spoken only a small window of the enormous picture of all there is to know about what God is doing in his church now and who he is!

Paul says in I Corinthians 13:9 that the perfect will come and that is when some of the gifts would cease. The Lord knows that the perfect is not already here. Glorification is the time when perfection comes. Paul says that when the perfect comes that there will be no need for some of the gifts.

God will still decide who receives gifts in his spiritual body now and why. All of the spiritual gifts are not for all believers to experience. All may not have the same gifts. We see that Pastors and teachers are mentioned in Ephesians 4:11 and every Pastor would agree that this is a spiritual gift! The ability to speak for God from the Word of God and to have wisdom and insight into spiritual issues is a gift from God!

God distributes gifts based on the measure of faith that he gives to each believer and based on what he has called or commissioned that individual to do. Our understanding of what is knowable is incredibly small based on what we read in I Corinthians 13:9. We know in part! The Word of God says, "Now he did not many mighty works there because of their unbelief" (Matthew 13:58, New King James Version).

What about the Gifts to Pastor and the Evangelist?

We know that no believers in church do believe that the gift to be a Pastor and to be an Evangelist has ceased in the church. This means that we can still rely on Ephesians 4:11 as being true. The Word of God says, "And he gave some apostles, and some prophets, and some, evangelists, and some pastors, and teachers" (Ephesians 4:11). Spiritual gifts are still operating through people in the church! Mount up with wings as the eagle! Hear God's voice and walk in his anointing to do his will and to obey his call and commission!

My own personal and unique experience

On March 23, 1988, I left a church revival, and nothing had happened supernatural when I was in there for me. However, when I started my car up and left the meeting, something supernatural happened that I will never forget. Suddenly, I started speaking in a language that I had never learned before and I couldn't understand it. However, I knew that it was supernatural and that it was God! This was not tongues that needed an interpretation because nobody was there to hear me, but me!

I knew this was God talking through me and the manifestation of the Holy Ghost, but I felt like my entire mind, spirit, and soul was being recreated and made all over again. Words on this page can not fully explain this. I spoke in unknown tongues from 9 pm all the way up until 4 am in the morning. This was 7 straight hours of speaking in either the tongues of men or the language of an angel as I drove around the city! What on earth was happening to me?

I knew at this time that I had undoubtedly been filled with the Holy Ghost because I had the same experience that men had on the Day of Pentecost and many times thereafter in the book of Acts. I have never presumed that everyone would have the same experience, but I am glad that I did. Everything inside of me seemed new and totally refreshed and made all over again. I knew that something had changed me forever. I could never be the same! However, I had accepted that Lord into my heart as my personal savior when I was only 6 years old. I rededicated myself to God and Christ when I was 14 years old. This was a different experience.

I found a verse of scripture about what had happened to me in the first letter to the Corinthian Church that says, "For if you have the ability to speak in tongues, you will be talking only to God, since people won't be able to understand you. You will be speaking by the power of the Spirit, but it will all be mysterious" (I Corinthians 14:2). Another version says it like this, "For he that speaks in an unknown tongue speaks not unto men, but unto God: for no man understands him; howbeit in the spirit he speaks mysteries (I Corinthians 14:2, New King James Version). Did you see that? We are not speaking to men, but to God when we speak in an unknown tongue! No interpreter is needed to speak to God in an unknown tongue!

Paul says a lot in the entire chapter, but I want to focus only on how this one verse applied to me and another. I did not know what I was saying and there was not an interpreter. According to this verse, I was speaking mysteries to God himself! Paul also said these words to the Corinthians, "He that speaks in an unknown tongue edifies himself;

but he that prophecies edifies the church" (I Corinthians 14:4). People build themselves up spiritually when they move in the spirit to speak in an unknown tongue. How does this happen and why?

Why speak in an unknown tongue?

I found out as to why God allows this gift to manifest itself to the church and to believers who do believe it is for them. The Apostle Paul says, "For if I pray in an unknown tongue, my spirit prays, but my understanding is unfruitful" (I Corinthians 14:14). We now find that the Holy Ghost is praying to God for us and through us in an unknown language. We won't understand what is being said because it is all a mystery. God knows!

There is nothing that anyone should be confused about because the person who is praying in an unknown tongue is speaking directly to God in a language that was not intended for anyone to understand! God has himself many mysteries! When you speak to God in an unknown tongue it means that you are praying in the spirit and the Holy Ghost is interceding for you in prayer based on what your needs are and in accordance with God's will!

The Holy Ghost as the Intercessor

This book is still about mounting up with wings like the eagle. One thing that the supernatural gift of the Holy Ghost does is a work to intercede for us in prayer. Paul said it like this to the Romans, "Likewise the Spirit also helps our weaknesses. For we do not know what we should pray for as we ought, but the Spirit himself makes intercession for us with groanings which cannot be uttered. And he that searches the hearts knows what the mind of the Spirit is, because he makes intercession for the saints according to the will of God" (Romans 8:26-27). We saw over in the Corinthian letter that the Holy Ghost is praying when we speak in an unknown tongue. We see in these verses to the Romans that the Spirit is interceding for us because we don't know what to pray for as we ought to.

These two verses are teaching us that we don't really know what God wants us to pray for. We are weak. We are frail. We have infirmities! Now comes the Holy Ghost to intercedes for us in prayer and sometimes words are not uttered at all when this happens! This is supernatural help with your salvation, healing, deliverance, peace, and much more. The Holy Ghost is a supernatural gift that helps the believer in his experience of salvation! We mount up with wings as an eagle with God's supernatural help!

Spiritual gifts and manifestation

Spiritual gifts are something that believers receive when they have been given the gift of salvation. The Holy Ghost imparts these gifts to the believers and so it is important to know what your gift is! Gifts are not things that we possess or own, but God showing up in our lives in various ways. This is called manifestation. The Word of God says, "There are different kinds of gifts, but the same Spirit distributes them. There are different kinds of service, but the same Lord. There are different kinds of working, but in all of them and in everyone it is the same God at work. Now to each one the manifestation of the Spirit is given for the common good" (I Corinthians 12:4-7).

Ministerial gifts

The flight for some will indeed be mounting up with wings as the eagle to do a work in the ministry that God has called and commissioned them to do. These gifts are the ways in which that God works through what believers do to serve others. The Word of God says, "There are differences of administration, but the same Lord" (I Corinthians 12:5). The Bible also tells us the a list of different gifts and their purpose when Paul narrates, "And he gave some apostles, some prophets, some evangelists, and some pastors and teachers, for the equipping of the saints for the work of ministry; for the edifying of the body of Christ, till we all come to the unity of the faith and the knowledge of the Son of God, to a perfect man, to the measure of the stature of the fulness of Christ (Ephesians 4:11-13). The Holy Ghost works these gifts through people. People are what they are because God made them to be what they are!

Helping

Many people refer to the ministerial gifts as the 5-fold ministry gifts. However, the Word of God also speaks of a gift for helping. We find these words written, "And God has placed in the church first of all apostles, second prophets, third teachers, then miracles, then gifts of healing, of helping, of guidance, and of different kinds of tongues" (I Corinthians 12:28). When I look back at my lifetime and how I have done things to help others, I have come to realize that this has been a spiritual gift operating all along.

Manifestation gifts

The manifestation gifts are for everyone to enjoy. This is a supernatural demonstration of the Holy Ghost's power to help other people in the ministry as well as to minister to ourselves. A message of wisdom is something that can help yourself and someone else at the same time.

Many people have not seen the Holy Ghost manifest himself to them in certain ways, but they can when they believe God and trust him for the manifestation. Manifestation is a gift.

Gifts are given when an individual trusts God and believes that God has the gift for him or her, but only God decides who receives manifestation. I still believe that God can manifest the Holy Ghost to everyone in the same way that it was manifested to me, but God alone must decide about manifestation.

The Holy Ghost enables us to soar above the natural

Here is what the Word of God says, "Now concerning spiritual gifts, brethren, I would not have you ignorant. You know how you were Gentiles, carried away unto these dumb idols, even as you were led. Wherefore I give you to understand, that no man speaking by the Spirit of God calls Jesus accursed, and that no man can say that Jesus is the Lord, but by the Holy Ghost. Now there are diversities of gifts, but the same Spirit. And there are diversities of gifts, but the same Spirit. And there are differences of administrations, but the same Lord. And there are diversities of operations, but it is the same God which works all in all. But the manifestation of the Spirit is given to every man to profit withal. For the one is given by the spirit the word of wisdom; to another the word of knowledge by the same Spirit; to another faith by the same spirit, to another the gifts of healing by the same spirit; to another the working of miracles; to another prophecy; to another discerning of spirits; to another divers kinds of tongues; to another the interpretation of tongues: But all these works that one and selfsame Spirit, diving to every man severally as he will" (I Corinthians 12:1-11).

Manifestation with a man that was supernaturally healed

I have shared this story on numerous speaking engagements. My wife told me about a friend of hers that had a significant person in their life that was in the hospital and in a coma. They told the family that the man could be taken off of the life support machine to die and that it was medically impossible for him to live any longer. I was asked my opinion. I told them to let the man stay on life support and that I would be praying for him in Jesus' name to come out of his coma.

I went to the hospital. I laid hands on him to pray in Jesus' name. He raised out of his coma and lived fifteen more years after being discharged from the hospital. This was a miracle and a gift of healing that worked. God allows this manifestation to happen so that the story could be shared with others as a testimony of what God can do! God has left many more signs and wonders for us that Jesus is real, Heaven is real, Hell is real, the Holy Ghost is real, the resurrection of Jesus from the dead was real, and salvation by the power of God is real!

A man who was raised from the dead by the Holy Ghost power

I was eating dinner with an Evangelist that attended our church and we went to a gathering of men who had various needs. We noticed when we arrived that a man had died. Firefighters and paramedics had tried to revive him. Staff told us that they had done everything that they could do. I asked the firefighters as to how long the man had been dead. The told me that the man had been gone for over 10 minutes and that they had done everything that they could do.

I looked at Mike and told him that if I only thought about him rising from the dead that he would have to come back to life. Mike then informed me that he was going to pray for him. I told Mike that I would lay hands on him. Mike started praying and then I bent over to touch his foot and he immediately came back to life. Firefighters were a bit surprised. I was not surprised. I had received periodic dreams time and time again of raising someone from the dead. I kept wondering when it was going to happen. I have shared this story before on social media and in church with Mike there. Mike has also spent time with me in the street ministry to share the gospel with others.

Mount up with wings as the eagle may mean raising someone from the dead or healing the sick depending on what your gift is. Some are miracle workers. Others have a gift of healing. People with a word of wisdom or a gift of knowledge or the gifts of helps may want to publish a book or broadcast to reach an international community of people that can benefit from the gift. We mount up with wings as the eagle because of the power of the Holy Ghost. God becomes our strength! Moses brought the children of Israel out of the land of Egypt by the power of God that was with him!

We can overcome addiction and sins by the power of God that is with us!

Motivational gifts

God will sometimes inspire our words or actions by the power of the Holy Ghost. Paul explained these type of motivational gifts by saying, "Having then gifts differing according to the grace that is given to us, whether prophecy, let us prophesy according to the proportion of faith; or ministry, let us wait on our ministering: or he that teaches, on teaching: or he that exhorts, on exhortation, he that gives, let him do it with simplicity, he that rules (leads) with diligence, he that shows mercy, with cheerfulness" (Romans 12:6-8).

Keep in mind that the motivation that people must do many things will often come from God. This includes hospitality, giving, saying things to encourage or to rebuke others, prophetic proclamations from the Word of God, teaching, mercy toward others. Mount up with wings as the eagle and move in the gifts that God has given. Never let anyone discourage you to quit or to stop walking in what you know God in doing or about to do through you!

Too Legit to Quit

Once you find out what your motivation is and what you have the strong desire to do, you'll likely have identified your gift. It's usually where your will is the strongest at and what you have the most ability and passion to do. The scriptures teach, "For it is God who works in us to will and do all according to his good pleasure" (Philippians 2:13). I have told people before that they were "Too Legit to Quit" and quoted M.C. Hammer and his song. However, it is true. People cannot quit many things because it is God who is working through them to motivate them to continue and to do what they are continuing to carry out!

Soaring above the world and things on the earth

I recently saw a video on social media about men in New York City that paraded through churches as "drag queens" (men who dress up like the women) and a video was made for youtubers of a drag queen delivering a sermon. The man who is born of God cannot be in a lifestyle of the deliberate and habitual practice sinning. He is identified as a child of God by what he does. The children of the devil are also manifested by what they do (I John 3:8-10).

It's not his strength that keeps him, but he mounts up with wings as the eagle. God gives him the grace to walk in victory above and beyond the trap of Satan. He overcomes the world, Satan, and the lusts of the flesh. Christ will get the glory in the end! A Christian may stumble and fall or even be overtaken in a fault and do some grievous sin (I John 1:8-9, Galatians 6:1).

Nevertheless, he will confess and get back up. He or she cannot stay in that state as a lifestyle habit because he is born of God! They shall mount up with wings as the eagle. They will soar above and beyond. If they do go into captivity as Judah did, they will come out and return to their homeland. They are set apart. Remember this, "Being confident of this very thing, he that has began a good work in you will perform it until the day of Jesus Christ" (Philippians 1:6).

The Spirit gives a new heart

The prophet Ezekiel said these words about the new covenant and what God was going to do for his people, "A new heart also will I give you, and a new spirit will I put within you: and I will take away the stony heart out of your flesh, and I will give you a heart of flesh. And I will put my spirit within you, and cause you to walk in my statutes, and ye shall fulfill my judgments, and do them" (Ezekiel 36:26-27). We can only soar above saying and doing many things if God changes our heart.

He remodels us on the inside and gives us a new spirit while he gives us a new heart. We can only mount up with wings like the eagle and soar above many things if God make us over again. This is a supernatural occurrence that happens at the birth of the spirit. People can ask God for the new birth to lift them out of the state or condition that their hearts may sink into again. The Holy Ghost does this work! This is called regeneration! It's making a man who is spiritually dead to come back to life again.

The valley of the Army of dry and dead bones that came back to life

One fascinating illustration of this occurrence is with Ezekiel's vision of the valley of dry bones! The Spirit of God took Ezekiel's spirit into a valley of dry bones. The bones were an exceedingly great army of people that were dead. All the flesh was no longer on their bones, and it appeared that they had no hope of restoration.

All appeared to be a dried up and worthless situation with no hope! God asked Ezekiel if the bones could live. God then told Ezekiel what he was about to do. God said that he would put flesh on them and cover them with skin, but also breath his life into them so that they could live. Here is an example of how men are revived from sin (Ezekiel 37:1-7).

God then told Ezekiel to prophesy to the bones. He spoke to the wind and after this happened, we find the army alive and standing up on their feet as a great army (Ezekiel 37:8-10). This story illustrates a few things. It shows the spiritual condition of Judah when they were in captivity to Babylon. There were hopeless and did not have the ability to come back to Jerusalem on their own. They were dead and had no hope of restoration.

This also shows us the spiritual condition of the lost or those that have fallen away. They cannot give themselves life. They can't come out! They can only revive, stand up, get the flesh on their bones again, grow skin, live spiritually, walk in victory, overcome, and come out of bondage to sin if they experience a revival! It is only God's doing!

God puts his spirit in them and gives them new life and a new heart. God will put their spiritual identity together and gives them spiritual life and power! This is what is means to mount up with wings like the eagle. It is a supernatural event where God gives men the Holy Ghost and power. He walks through them in a gift that only he can provide. The dead bones in the valley became an exceedingly great army!

Mounting up with the eagle's wings during restoration

Notice what God says after the people are restored and after God put the dry and dead bones with flesh and skin on them to breathe life into them, "And you shall know that I am the Lord, when I have opened your graves, O my people, and brought you up out of your graves, And shall put my spirit in you, and you shall live, and I shall place you in your own land: then shall you know that I the Lord have spoken it, and performed it, says the Lord" (Ezekiel 37:13-14). Restoration is something that God does. It would be nice if it were as simple as people doing what they heard a preacher say, but spiritual power and a supernatural creation with a restoration of the soul is needed. People need to be restored and only God can restore them!

Mount up with wings as the eagle

Jeremiah said these words about the heart, "The heart is deceitful and desperately wicked above all things, who can know it" (Jeremiah 17:9). David prayed, "Create in me a clean heart O God; and renew a right spirit within me" (Psalms 51:10). As we have seen, God creates a new heart in a man when he gives him a new spirit. Being saved is about having a new heart and a new spirit! Sometimes people must pray to God and ask him to restore them. David said that God restored his soul (Psalms 23:3). When people come to Christ for salvation it's about saving a soul from the hands of the enemy. Paul mentioned, "In meekness instructing those that oppose themselves so God can give them a repentance to acknowledge the truth; and that they may recover themselves out of the snare of the devil, who are taken captive by him at his will" (2 Timothy 2:25). Mounting up with wings like the eagle is about being free from the reach of the enemy or a predator!

Overcoming by the power of the Spirit

God has a purpose for saving us. He gives us the gift of eternal life. He loved us with an everlasting love. He called us to be his people. Peter says it like this in his epistle, "But you are a chosen generation, a royal priesthood, a holy nation, a peculiar people, that you may show the praises of him who has called you out of darkness into this marvelous light; Which in time past were not a people, but are not the people of God, which had not obtained, but now have obtained mercy. Dearly beloved, I beseech you as strangers and pilgrims, abstain from fleshly lusts, which war against the soul" (I Peter 2:9-11). Peter also says, "But as he which has called you is holy, so be ye holy in all manner of conversation. Because it is written, be ye holy; for I am holy" (I Peter 1:15-16).

The word holy means to set apart from the world and sin, but also to dedicate something or someone exclusively and wholly to God. The Holy Ghost gives men spiritual gifts and abilities to do what he or she cannot do in his or her own strength. The Hebrew author says, "Let us come boldly to the throne of grace, that we may obtain mercy, and find grace to help in time of need" (Hebrews 4:16). We come to God's throne in prayer, and he gives us the strength and help needed to overcome. We mount up with wings like the eagle after God empowers us to soar above the bondage that we were in!

The Holy Ghost also produces spiritual fruit in the life of the believer. This fruit is a work of the Spirit and cannot happen without God working through him or her producing the fruit. Paul says, "But the fruit of the spirit is love, joy, peace, longsuffering, gentleness, goodness, faith, meekness, temperance: against such there is not law" (Galatians 5:22-23). Spiritual fruit is the outward manifestation of the spirit's activity in the life of a born-again Christian. The fruit is what Christ produces through him or her as he or she yields to the work of the Spirit in his or her life.

Being raised up by his power

The fruit of the spirit is how he lives his life. This is his patience, love, contentment, joy about being a Christian and serving others, expression of kindness of love towards others, hospitality, unwavering faith and contentment in Christ and his work at the cross to save him, humility of mind and in relationships, and his self-control during temptations and trials.

This is his attitude, actions, motives, works, and his way of relating to God, God's Word, and people. Paul says to the Corinthian Church, "Therefore if any man be in Christ, he is a new creature: old things are passed away; behold all things are become new" (II Corinthians 5:17). As we think of God saying for us to mount up with wings as the eagle, keep this verse in mind, "And God has raised up the Lord, and will also raise up us by his power" (I Corinthians 6:14). We can do it as the Lord raises us up to walk by the power of the spirit!

How can anyone get things done that is impossible to be done in their own strength? I have met many people in many predicaments that were looking for a way out. They sincerely wanted to make a change. They wanted to overcome. They wanted to do better. But they needed to follow a simple strategy that could be learned from the eagle. They needed a source from the invisible world to help them reach their goals!

Our power and strength are weak and limited. People can only accomplish a few things in their own might. Here is what the Word of God says, "Hast thou not known? Hast thou not heard that the everlasting God, the Lord, the Creator of the ends of the earth faints not, neither is weary? There is no searching of his understanding. He gives power to the faint; and to them that have no might he increases strength. Even the youth shall faint and be weary, and the young men shall utterly fall: But they that wait on the Lord shall renew their strength; they shall mount up with wings as eagles; they shall run, and not be weary; and they shall walk, and not faint" (Isaiah 40:28-31).

God has used the eagle to symbolize our journey. The path of the eagle is a wonder to behold, but there is a lot of mystery. Once we read the book of Exodus, we'll find that God brought an entire nation out slavery and bondage in the land of Egypt by miracles, wonders, and signs with the staff of a shepherd named Moses. God then had Moses to narrate these words, "You have seen what I did to the Egyptians. You know how I carried you on eagle's wings and brought you to myself" (Exodus 19:4, New Living Translation). Did you see how God used the eagle to symbolize his strength in doing what the nation that they could not do in their own strength? However, in the book of Isaiah God says that we are to mount up with wings as the eagle!

The eagle has very powerful wings, but he learns how to catch the wind thermal so that he can fly in the strength of the wind. Men will recognize that their strength is limited. They will eventually find out that their might has a limit and that they are not strong enough to do many things. They get weary. They get tired. They faint. They know that they cannot make it through the storm in their own strength. They will feel like giving up on so many things. I want to encourage you to mount up with wings like the eagle. The eagle learns how to navigate through the wind thermals to soar almost effortlessly.

There is one important thing about this analogy that we should never forget. The eagle may leap off the tree or the edge of a cliff in order to be able to use the wind currents to soar in the strength of those thermals. The eagle has to take advantage of the opportunity that he gets when the currents come to him. He cannot stay sitting on the cliff and let the wind come and go or he will miss his opportunity to thrive. God will send opportunities your way. The spirit will also move and show us the way. We will be energized to speak a thing or to do something and we will know when the timing is right. We then must mount up with wings like the eagle. We move. We do. We soar. We survive. We know that if we don't do something now that this wind will come and go. We are led by the Holy Ghost!

The key to becoming what we are destined to be is moving when the current moves. They can fly to heights that no other bird flies and as high as some of our airplanes. But they cannot accomplish this extraordinary feat by flapping their wings due to their size and weight. The feat is done with the help of the wind thermals. We can find the eagle soaring at times on the wind, with their winds spread out and no flapping that is done on their part. This is symbolic of us working wonders by the power of the Spirit of God!

The eagle is also great at catching their fish. They have been given the gift to see them from far off and claws that capture them as they rise near to top of a stream or lake. Have you ever wondered how you could set such a goal and maintain the vision to carry it out? The eagle can see the prey from as far as a mile or more away and will glide downward toward the place where they are at. The eagle is mobile and realizes that he must go where he can hunt and capture the fish, quick and easy. We are all called to be the fishers of men. We are soul-winners!

You probably have saw the eagle flying alone in the skies. Sometimes what you have been called to do is unique to yourself. You cannot wait on the crowd to do what you are about to do. Your path and your destiny is for you. Being alone in what you are doing is not a bad thing. It may be a sign that you are soaring like the eagle. I sill remember the story of how David stepped out and killed Goliath. He was alone. He had his own destiny. He had to slay the giant. He had to answer his own call. He trusted the current. He trusted the wind. He trusted the spirit. He knew the Lord was with him.

Peter was also alone when he stepped out of the boat to walk on the water.

Eagles are courageous and bold. The eagle has been spotted going through the clouds of major storms. Most birds fly away from the storm and will hide until the storm is gone. The eagle has also been seen tearing off the head of a poisonous snakes with their beaks. When we mount up with wings as the eagle, we'll persevere despite our enemies. We are not afraid to confront the opposition. We may even move toward the adversary.

The eagle has been seen engaging in battle with venomous snakes and ripping their heads off by using their beak. Some have been seen flying with claws on the poisonous snake to take the battle to the air. We also know that the eagle takes advantage of those strong wind thermals to soar above the storms. This is a bird that knows how to utilize its God-given ability to fight a formidable adversary, but also to soar above the storm. Most birds hide in a place of safety until the storm has passed.

The interesting thing about God showing us a parallel between the eagle and the Christian is that the Christian is called to engage in spiritual warfare. He or she is also called to have faith in God to do things that it is not humanly possible to do without supernatural aid. Jesus said before his ascension, "These signs shall follow them that believe; in my name shall they cast out devils; they shall speak with new tongues; they shall take up serpents; and if they drink any deadly thing, it shall not hurt them; they shall lay hands on the sick, and they shall recover" Mark 16:17-18). Mounting up with wings like the eagle is able the believer doing in God's might that things he cannot do in his own. The believer must pray and rebuke devils and take dominion over spiritual enemies that come to destroy him or others. He takes the battle to the air when he ascends to God's throne-room in prayer!

When I think of the eagle soaring above the storm, my mind goes back to how Peter walked on the water. It took faith to believe that this could happen. Peter stepped out to walk on the water and he did walk on the sea for a while after Jesus gave him permission to come. However, he started sinking once he looked at the boisterous winds and the storm raging.

We must continue to believe God during circumstances that may look discouraging and too large for us. Pay attention to the God who is in control of the wind, but not to the storm itself. Our faith gives us the victory over fear, anxiety, depression, grief, trauma, and many of the most boisterous storms that rage in our lives. Mount up with wings as the eagle and soar above the storm. Don't let trials and tribulation keep you discouraged and perplexed. Wait on the Lord! Don't give up. Trust that the Lord will become your strength and move in awesome ways at his appointed time!

2

Christ accomplished our Sanctification and Holiness

One important thing to remember is that everyone who has believed the gospel and put their trust in him to save them has been set apart and sanctified through what he did at the cross. We have been cleansed of our sins because he carried them in his body to the cross, clothed in the righteousness of God, because Jesus took our sin away and became guilty for all our sins and gave us eternal life. The believer is sanctified by God, He is saved by grace through faith. Paul said it like this, "Much more then being justified by his blood, we shall be saved from wrath by him" (Romans 5:9).

The Hebrew writer says, "For it is God's will for us to made holy by the sacrifice of the body of Jesus Christ, once for all time" (Hebrews 10:10, New Living Translation). The one, perfect and eternal sacrifice is more awesome than the many, imperfect and temporary sacrifices of bulls and goats under the law. Man's ability to keep God's perfect law fell far short of the glorious standard of God that he demands of all who wish to please him or have a relationship with him. The Roman writer says, "All have sinned and come short of the glory of God" (Romans 3:23).

We cannot merit a standard with God of being sanctified or holy based on our own works of personal efforts to do the right thing. God's justice and his requirements of holiness was satisfied with Christ's work for us. Otherwise, we would remain dead in our trespasses and sins and always be separated from God without Christ's atonement for us. Our good works and acts of righteousness later in life, do not atone or make amends for violations of God's law earlier or at any time in life. However, "God so loved the world that he gave his only begotten Son that whosoever believes in him should not perish but have everlasting life" (John 3:16). The believer is set apart once and for all of time because of the offering of Christ that took their sin and guilt away!

We could never be sanctified and made holy by our good works or merit. Our efforts to keep the law and God's requirements have come short of the glorious standard. Paul says the Galatians, "Knowing that a man is not justified by the works of the law, but by the faith of Jesus Christ, even we have believed in Jesus Christ, that we might be justified by the faith of Christ, and not by the works of the law: for by the works of the law shall no flesh be justified" (Galatians 2:16). Paul adds to this and says a very profound statement, "I do not frustrate the grace of God: for if righteousness came by the law, then Christ is dead in vain" (Galatians 2:21).

This is the same principle that the Hebrew writer is trying to get the hearer of God's word to understand and sanctification and holiness. We are now set-apart, consecrated, and sanctified for God's good pleasure by Christ's offering made that one time at the cross! The blood of Jesus has paid the price for all of sin and for every person who trust in his atonement. He paid the full price for the righteousness of the law and the penalty for breaking the law. The Colossian writer said it like this, "He canceled the record of the charges against us and took it away by nailing it to the cross" (Colossians 2:14). The Hebrew writer also made this phenomenal revelation about what Christ accomplished for us, "For by one offering he has perfected forever them that are sanctified" (Hebrews 10:14).

I will be coming back to these verses a bit later. We know that Christ has already said that it is finished and done. We are holy and sanctified because he took our sin away at the cross and has pronounced to all that these things are already so. We cannot outdo or ever match the work that Christ has done to save us. Christ didn't die to make men savable, but he died to save them. He didn't die that their sin may be taken away by some effort of their own, but he put sin away at the cross. He came to put sin away by the sacrifice of himself. His death accomplished all the work of man's redemption and forever! We are holy. We are sanctified. He did it for us! True holiness is your faith in his work to save you!

Now I want to say a few things about the holiness and sanctification that we already have because of our faith in his atoning sacrifice that wiped out our sins. We too have been chosen to live a life on the earth that is set apart from the world and dedicated to God. One of the most cited verses about living holy in the Bible says, "Follow peace with all men, and holiness without which no man shall see the Lord" (Hebrews 12:14). The entire book of Hebrews is dedicated to narrating how that Christ himself is superior to the Old Testament priests, tabernacle, law, sacrifices, and everything contained in the Old Covenant. The first step of being holy is believing that Christ accomplished this for us when he took our sin away at the cross! We follow peace and pursue holiness by believing the gospel, living the gospel, and sharing the gospel!

Soaring like an eagle means doing something that is extraordinary. When God calls us to be his special people, he does something with us and through us that we cannot do in our own strength. The wind carries the eagle. The spirit carries us through our flight of sanctification and holiness. When we feel like that, we cannot make it or if we start struggling with guilt or even depression, mount up with wings like the eagle. Go through the storm in the strength of Christ and what he did for you.

3

The Holiness Movement
in history and God's Verdict

The holiness movement developed out of the Methodist church in the middle of the 19th century (the 1800s) in American church. It was an attempt to preserve the teachings of John Wesley. Holiness or sanctification that is taught now is different than what was taught during the Reformation. It's not that God's Word doesn't mention that the believer should be holy, but that the way that holiness was and has been interpreted in contrast to and in correlation with all other biblical revelation has evolved. The definition has changed. The concept or principle has also changed.

The Holiness Movement in history was an attempt to preserve the holiness teaching of John Wesley (1703-1791), the founder of Methodism.

However, there are scriptures about the subject too. Wesley had come up with the idea that grace had a second work after the new birth that blessed a believer with what is known as entire sanctification. Entire sanctification was thought of as a "second blessing" of grace to those that sought after it and that it included a complete eradication of sinfulness out of the fallen nature of man.

The Methodist Church eventually forsook Wesley's view of sanctification at the end of the 19th century, but the Holiness Movement continued to pioneer Wesley's view. The Holiness tradition led to what is now called the Keswick movement or Keswick Theology. The Keswick movement began at the end of the 19th century and became the most common way of understanding the Bible's teaching on holiness in fundamentalism and in many churches in evangelical tradition.

The Keswick movement is basically a continuation of Wesley's view of two entirely different works of grace-salvation and sanctification. Salvation is being forgiven. The Keswick movement, also called the Higher Life Movement, is a theological movement that originated in England in the early 19th century. It is heavily influenced by the teaching of John Wesley, John Fletcher, and Adam Clark.

The Keswick Convention began in 1875 in the United Kingdom as part of the higher life movement. The movement was founded by an Anglican, Canon T.D. Hartford-Baterby, and a Quaker, Robert Wilson. Keswick Theology taught that sanctification was up to believer and that he or she should seek the experience of sanctification and what was known and came to be known as a "second blessing" of grace.

Keswick Theology teaches that after salvation a believer must have a second experience or a second touch from God in order to experience entire sanctification. This later corresponded to the Pentecostal experience of the baptism of the Holy Ghost. Many Keswick teachers taught sinless perfection as a result of the second blessing or the Pentecostal experience of the baptism of the Holy Ghost.

The Wesley Connection

The doctrine of sanctification has been profoundly influenced by the founder of Methodism, John Wesley. John had an idea that wasn't taught during the Reformation that there was a separate and transforming work of grace that was after the new birth. The doctrine "Christian perfectionism," with some modifications, was fully embraced by his followers, especially in America. The Wesley view of sanctification was transmitted to us through successors and important movements, particularly Charles Finney and Asa Mahan, Phoebe Palmer, the Higher Life movement, Keswick Theology or the Higher Life Movement.

John Wesley (1703-1791), though ordained in the Anglican Church, developed a distinct doctrine of sanctification that he called "Christian perfection," "perfect love" (I John 4:8), "entire sanctification," "full salvation," and the second blessing." Wesley's view was set forth in his *A Plain Account of Christian Perfection*. He was influenced by the writings or earlier Catholic and Anglican mystical traditions.

Wesley believed that his view was completely biblical. He defined "Christian perfection" as "that habitual disposition of the soul which, in the sacred writings, is termed holiness; and which directly implies, the being cleansed from sin, from all filthiness of the flesh and spirit, and by consequence, the being endued with those virtues which were in Christ Jesus, the being so "renewed in the image of our mind," as to be perfect as our Father in heaven is perfect" (Works, 11:367). According to Wesley, Matthew 5:48 commands perfection ("Be ye therefore perfect, even as your Father which is in heaven is perfect," KJV), so it must be attainable in this life (Works, 11:390). Wesley also pointed to texts like I John 3:9, "Whosoever is born of God does not commit sin" (KJV). He believed that a sanctified Christian is so far perfect, as to not commit sin and that he and she was sinless.

Wesley taught that "entire sanctification" happens instantly by "a simple act of faith." (Works, 11:446). He taught that entire sanctification eliminated all sinful desires, destroyed moral depravity, removed all sinful desires of the heart, and delivered from all outward transgressions of the law. This doctrine taught that at entire sanctification the believer experienced complete purity of intentions, temperament, actions, and had perfect love for God and his neighbor. He believed at first that an individual could not lose entire sanctification, but later changed his mind and taught that if he did lose it that he could be instantaneously restored to perfection if he had fell from that state!

John Wesley did preach the gospel and he brought a revival to England. However, his teaching of entire sanctification obscured the biblical doctrine of sanctification. John Fletcher (1729-1785), strongly defended Wesley's doctrine of perfectionism. Fletcher became the chief organizer of Methodist theology. He often spoke of the entire sanctification as the baptism or "filling of the Holy Spirit." We know that God is baptizing men and women with the Holy Ghost. Does "entire sanctification" or perfection happen in his or her life at that time?

Coming to America

Wesleyan perfectionism was promoted heavily by the founder of the Methodist Church in America, Frank Asbury (1745-1816), but perfectionist doctrine also came to other groups outside of the Methodist Church. Charles Finney (1792-1875) also adopted the Wesleyan doctrine of entire sanctification. We credit Finney for being the father of modern revivalism. He was a lawyer, but after his conversion in 1821, he prepared for ministry under a Presbyterian Pastor in New York.

Charles Finney denied original sin and that men are sinners by nature (Lectures on Systematic Theology, 249). He believed that regeneration was a moral change in a person, a change of a person's will, and not a change of character, not the supernatural impartation of spiritual life to a spiritually dead person by the Holy Ghost (Lectures on Systematic Theology, 285). Finney also rejected the penal substitutionary death of Christ for sinners, arguing that it was only for moral influence (Lectures on Systematic Theology, 273). He argued that salvation was strictly up to our own initiative. Finney insisted "that the actual turning, or change, is the sinner's own act" (Finney, Sermons on Important Subjects, 20). Finney also denied the Reformation view of justification by faith, arguing that the righteousness of Christ is not imputed to the believer (Lectures on Systematic Theology, 385). Finney also viewed revival as something that man had to produce by tactics, he employed to generate excitement or interest in people. Finney was not a Methodist, but he taught entire sanctification and with the Oberlin

Seminary, he influenced holiness movements with American and British Methodism.

Phoebe Palmer (1807-1874) also influenced the entire sanctification movement in America. She was the most influential woman in the American Methodist during her time. The Methodist Church was the largest American denomination. Her book *The Way of Holiness* (1843) and her periodical *The Guide to Holiness (*first called *The Guide to Christian Perfection)* were influential in identifying these perfectionist teachings as the Holiness movement.

Ms. Palmer popularize Wesley's doctrine of entire sanctification. She followed Oberlin Theology and John Fletcher by identifying entire sanctification with the baptism of the Holy Ghost. She also developed a simpler and shorter method for receiving entire sanctification -her altar theology." Palmar taught that people can experience "entire sanctification" by coming to the altar. She taught that the altar is where you consecrate yourself entirely to God and where you had to believe that God consecrated and sanctified you. She also taught that Jesus words in Matthew 23:19 that the "altar sanctifies the gift," and correlated this verse to Exodus 29:37, 'whatever touches the altar shall be holy," This does not imply that God cannot do these things at the altar. But it does imply that God does not need the altar in the church to do it. God also has his own timing and process. God is Sovereign.

The altar theology of Palmar was adopted by holiness denominations such as Wesleyan Methodists, Free Methodists, Church of the Nazarene, Christian and Missionary Alliance, as well as the Salvation Army in addition to the Keswick movement in England (Dictionary of Christianity in America, 861). The Higher Life movement was also a part of the holiness movement, but outside of Methodist circles. The Higher Life movement focused on introducing perfectionist teaching to non-Methodists without using perfectionist language. The basic theology of the higher life-movement "was that while justification by faith brought cleansing from the guilt of sin, sanctification by faith brought cleansing from the power of sin and, consequently, a happy, or higher, Christian life" (Dictionary of Christianity in America, 526).

All of the teaching by John Wesley and his successors have led to many revivals and conversions. Could the teaching about sanctification and Christian perfectionism been taken a bit too far? Could it be more to the doctrine of sanctification? How does the Word of God present the doctrine of sanctification? Does sanctification mean that you attain perfection in holiness or entire sanctification within your lifetime? What will ultimately determine whether or not someone goes to heaven?

4

What is Holiness and Sanctification?

Many people still acknowledge that we must be justified by the righteousness that Christ has acquired but believe or at least act in practice as if we must be sanctified by a holiness, we bring about ourselves. If that were the case, we would not-contrary to the apostolic witness (Romans 6:14, Galatians 4:31)–live under grace and stand in freedom but continue always under the law. Evangelical sanctification, however, is just as distinct from legalistic sanctification as the righteousness that is of faith differs from that which is obtained by works of keeping the law.

We shall later define progressive sanctification a bit more and later. God does work through us as justified believers to make us more and more like Christ over time. Nevertheless, justification and sanctification are both done at the same time when a person believes the gospel. Sanctifying faith is the knowledge of the grace that God has revealed in Christ, a trust that he has forgiven all sins and made us holy and acceptable to God the moment that he made us right with God at justification.

Faith in Christ's work at the cross is not only what justifies us, but what sanctifies us at the same time. This faith must always accompany a Christian and play a permanent and irreplaceable role in sanctification. The Word of God reveals, "For by one offering he has perfected forever them that are sanctified" (Hebrews 10:14). God sees you as being sanctified and holy because you believe that Jesus Christ took your sin away in his body and that sin was nailed to the cross! The Hebrew writer said that we are perfected forever by his offering and that we are sanctified because of his work. Believe it!

Holiness is not a "second blessing" placed next to the blessing of justification. The Church must live in faith and in this fulness of sanctification. We have no need to work for a second blessing. God has promised that since Jesus has started a good work in us that he will continue to perform this until the day of Jesus Christ (Philippians 1:6). The Healthy Christian must continue to believe the gospel. The forgiveness of all of your sins is the source of your holiness and sanctification. We are sanctified and perfected forever because of what Jesus did.

Christians are sanctified by believing the gospel. They are sanctified by their justification. We shall discuss definitions of justification and different types of holiness, but never forget why God sees us as being sanctified at justification. Keswick Theology saw sanctification as something that believers should graduate into with Christian living. However, spiritual progress only takes place by God's grace. Men and women cannot sanctify themselves with self-effort and moral reformation. Regeneration is the act of God changing a man's heart at the new birth. This happens simultaneously with justification and sanctification. The Holy Spirit will then gradually change the believer into the likeness of Christ and produce his fruit in their lives.

As we continue through this book, keep in mind that justification by faith alone has everything to do with sanctification and holiness. It is important for the church in this century to understand this. Justification by faith is not only relevant for entrance of the people of God into heaven, but for final acquittal. But in between his justification and his final acquittal is a healthy growth in sanctification. This involves growing deeper into understanding and believing the gospel and in trusting Christ's work for us. When a person is justified and sanctified by faith alone, he is in union with Christ. Union with Christ produces the fruit of holiness in our practical lives. This is not a work of man, but a progressive work of the Holy Ghost.

We have probably heard this quoted to us, "Follow peace with all men, and holiness, without which no man shall see the Lord" (Hebrews 12:14). The word "follow" means to pursue. A medical student that is in pursuit of a career as a brain surgeon must graduate from medical school. He then must complete an internship as a brain surgeon. He only becomes what he is in pursuit of over time. The Christian is made holy and perfected forever at the new birth in his justifying moment. He pursues to overcome sin. John says, "He deceives himself if he says that he has no sin, but he will confess his sin and repent if he falls in his pursuit to overcome, and the blood cleanses him from all of his unrighteousness" (I John 1:8-9).

What is Holiness and progressive sanctification?

What I am about to share with you is very controversial, but it's theology and it's important. Theologians refer to the daily practice of living for God to become more holy as progressive sanctification. The idea is that if God did save us that he will continue to move us closer toward perfection. The word that is translated as holiness in the New Testament means to be "set apart." How can someone be holy if they have sinned?

The scriptures say, "All have sinned and come short of the glory of God" (Romans 3:23). The only solution to being a lawbreaker is to be set apart through the salvation offered through Jesus Christ. We see in John 3:16 that God so loved this world that he gave his Son so that whoever believes on him should not perish but have everlasting life. That's because when we believe on Jesus and trust him for our salvation, he cleanses us from sin and makes us holy (I John 1:7). John mentioned that the blood cleanses us from all sin in this verse. How and why does that happen?

Theologians refer to this concept of being cleaned from sin as positional sanctification. Paul said it like this to the Ephesians, "For by grace are you saved through faith. And this is not your own doing; it is the gift of God, not a result of works, so that none can boast" (Ephesians 2:8-9,

ESV). Grace is the unmerited favor of God that announces to you and all that you are holy because your sin has been taken away and nailed to the cross. Sin is gone because God said that it was gone! A believer is not a sinner because of his positional sanctification. We are saved by grace through faith as the gift of God. The gift of God is both eternal life, forgiveness, and God declaring that we are righteous and holy based on the performance of Jesus Christ having his blood shed to cleanse us from all guilt of all sin for all of time.

John says it like this, "If we say that we have no sin we deceive ourselves and the truth is not in us, but if we confess our sins, he's faithful and just to forgive us our sin and to cleanse us from all unrighteousness" (I John 1:8-9). How are we cleansed from all unrighteousness? Does God ever remove the passion to sin out of your fleshly nature in this lifetime? No! God erases your record and pronounces you to be not guilty! This is true! Now here this good news! Paul said to the Colossians, "Having cancelled out the certificate of legal demands (which were in force) against us and which were hostile to us. And this certificate he has set aside and completely removed by nailing it to the cross" (Colossians 2:14, Amplified Bible). God has nailed your entire record of sin and any ordinance to prove it to the cross and made you holy by Christ's performance at the cross!

In addition to being made holy in what theologians call positional holiness, we are called to live holy lives. First Peter 1:15 teaches, "As he who called you is holy, you also be holy in all your conduct." The previous verse adds, "As obedient children, do not be conformed to the passions of your former ignorance" (v.14). We are commanded to avoid the ways we practiced before becoming a Christian and live lives according to God's ways. We can only do this by the power of God's Spirit that enables us to follow the principles that we find in the Word of God. Throughout the years I have encouraged men and women to ask God to baptize them with the Holy Ghost. The Word of God says, "You shall receive power after that the Holy Ghost has come upon you" (Acts 1:8). This is important because men and women do not have the strength or capacity within themselves to cast out devils, heal the sick, overcome temptation, and be holy.

Theologians refer to this daily practice of living for God to become more holy as progressive sanctification. As we seek to follow God each day, we can increasingly become holy as we become more like Christ. However, progressive sanctification won't ever bring us to completion. We will never be perfect in our holiness or sanctification obtained in this life. The evidence shows that we still do sin at times. Paul wrote, "For I have the desire to do what is right, but not the ability to carry it out, For I do not do the good I want, but the evil I do not want is what I keep on doing" (Romans 7:18-19).

Paul described his experiences in Romans chapter 7 in verses14-25, however, the Christian need not assume that Paul never overcame whatever he struggled with or that he did not do have a practical righteousness in his life. Paul mentioned at the end of his life that he was pressing toward the mark and had not attained perfection over in his letter to the Philippians.

We still need to reconcile this reality and others with John's truth that was revealed in his epistle. John said, "If we say that we have no sin that we deceive ourselves and the truth is not in us" (I John 1:8). John also says, "The one who practices sin (separating himself from God, and offending him by acts of disobedience, indifference, or rebellion) is of the devil (and takes the inner character and moral values from him, not God); for the devil has sinned and violated God's law from the beginning.

The Son of God appeared for this purpose, to destroy the works of the devil. No one who is born of God (deliberately, knowingly, and habitually) practices sin, because God's seed (his principle of life, the essence of his righteous character) remains (permanently) in him (who is born-again-who is reborn from above-spiritually transformed, renewed, and set apart for his purpose); and he who is born again cannot habitually live a life characterized by sin, because he is born of God and longs to please him. By this the children of God and the children of the devil are clearly identified: anyone who does not prac-tice righteousness (who does not seek God's will in thought, action, and purpose) is not of God, nor is the one who does not (unselfishly) love his (believing) brother" (I John 3:8-10). What does this mean?

I love the purity of the verse the way that it reads. A Christian will always be able to go to this verse and point out that Christians don't do those things that a child of the devil does. I don't want to give an entire list of dos and don'ts here. But I can give you at least two examples. I think it is safe to say that a Christian isn't a bank robber or a serial killer. The man who is born-again is new in his spirit. He cannot do many things at all! However, John is referring to the inner spirit being that is born again. He is not talking about the flesh of man that is still unredeemed and waiting for glorification.

The flesh has sin, as John spoke of in I John chapter one and verse 8. He said that we deceive ourselves if we say that we have no sin based on that verse alone. Our sin can be anything from an indwelling passion or lust to covet or any other indwelling sin or work of the flesh in the carnal nature that Paul taught about and told us to mortify in Galatians and the 5th chapter. The indwelling desire to sin is sin based on the Ten Commandments.

His or her flesh has a nature of indwelling sin, but his spirit is born again and cannot sin. He is also not capable of sinning because his rela-tionship to the law has changed after believing the gospel as described in the above-stated verses. Paul taught, "Christ is the end of the law for righteousness, for every one that believes" (Romans 10:4) That means that we are no longer righteous by keeping the law, but we are not guilty, and we are justified as being sinless before God because of Christ crucified and risen again from the dead! His sacrifice for us took all our sin away once and for all of time (Compare Hebrews 10:14 with Hebrews 10:10).

It will only be in glorification that all sin will be removed from our lives and that we are made without spot, blemish, and wrinkle. Glorification is God's final act of salvation upon death or at the final trumpet of God. Paul described how that we shall be changed and how corruptible shall put on incorruption when our mortal bodies shall put on immortality in First Corinthians 15:51. This will happen at death or in the rapture. Lust is something that dwells in your body as a desire and a passion. The want to do something is sin. Paul mentioned these wants in Romans 7:7 when he said that he would not have known lust unless that law said not to covet.

Paul mentioned that the body is waiting for its own redemption in Romans 8:29-32. We find that this passage teaches that we will be brought into the glorious liberty of the children of God at that time. We receive a divine nature that is like Christ and our bodies that are sinful, decaying, and undone will then be perfected and free of sin and death. Paul described himself as doing the things that he hated sometimes in Romans 7:14-25 and as having not obtained perfection and still trying to meet the mark when he was near death in Philippians 3:13-14. Sin means to miss the mark. It doesn't matter if it is missing it by an inch or a mile.

What can we really do about guilt and shame? What happens when we look at ourselves and realize that we cannot stop what we are doing or change ourselves? What hope do we have? When I first came to God and gave my life to him, I was taught about how that God wanted us to be holy. Holy means set apart for God's use. Being holy also means sanctified and the words are interchangeable. How can someone be sinless? How can I set myself apart from the world to a degree that God would consider me holy? What would I do about guiltiness? How could I ever feel right or just before God?

The whole idea of becoming someone different that I was at the core of my nature surely wasn't within my power. What is considered holy seemed like a very high mountain to climb. I also had to be able to get past things that happened and accept myself for who I was and what I was. I was a sinner! I knew that God alone was entirely Holy, and I felt totally undone and incapable of turning into a flawless person without any faults or blemishes.

I kept hearing this verse cited in church after church, "Follow peace with all men, and holiness, without which no man shall see the Lord" (Hebrews 12:14). I have concluded that we have a positional holiness that is permanent based on the book of Hebrews. I have also concluded the Christ will make us his people that are "set apart" with how we live our lives on the earth. He will mature us in a practical holiness, but God won't finish all of his work with us until glorification. Nobody can entirely separate themselves from the fallen nature. However, they can overcome the works of it and it's deeds by the power of the Holy Ghost!

This meant that I had to be holy for me to see the Lord! But for some years after becoming a Christian, I still knew that I had not reached a practical holiness. Sin continued to live inside of me. I knew I was guilty because of what I thought about or because of what I felt like doing. There have also been those moments when I said or did something that I knew good and well that I ought not to have done.

5

Positional holiness

I found out that I was holy now that I gave my life to Jesus Christ. This has not changed, but I have missed the mark! The theme of the letter to the Hebrews is the aspect of holiness or sanctification which is considered to be positional. But this positional holiness is not a work that is produced through us as sinless perfection. However, it is the whole goal of being saved. It is how you know that you ae unconditionally loved. This positional holiness is why and how you know that God has accepted you and prepared you for the end of life. The positional holiness taught in the book of Hebrews is the glorious result of God declaring us holy because of the work of the Son of God who put sin away at the cross!

His sacrifice is why God sees us a holy and sanctified! The Hebrew writer says, "For by one offering, he has perfected forever them that are sanctified" (Hebrews 10:14). Sin has been taken away by Jesus Christ and nailed to the cross with him! John the Baptist had said these words about Jesus Christ, "Behold the Lamb of God that takes away the sin of the world" (John 1:29). After striving for a practical holiness and sinless perfection it is very refreshing to know that we are already holy! Christ has already won this for us!

The book of Hebrews contrasted the two covenants that God made with man and compared the Old Covenant with the New Covenant. The Old Covenant asked man to do something that God never got-that is perfect obedience; because man in his depraved natures which he inherited from the fall couldn't give it. The New Covenant guarantees all blessings and eternal life through the work of another; and from this knowledge comes a strong desire to be obedient on the part of whoever is the object of such love and grace.

The perfection that the Hebrew writer is talking about is not a moral perfection. This is a perfection of conscience and God's eternal proclamation of who we already are and what we have become when we put our trust in the work of Jesus Christ's death and blood that wiped all our sins away. We can approach God only because he sees you as being perfect and without sin to enter his presence. Christ came to do the will of God by pouring out his blood for our salvation to make us holy before God because of his work, "By the which will we are sanctified through the offering of the body of Jesus Christ once for all" (Hebrews 10:10).

The one sacrifice of Christ on the cross took all our sins away. No sacrifice would be needed to take sin away for the following year, but one offering wiped out the entire debt and record of sin once and for all! We are now holy in God's sight because of the sacrifice made by Jesus Christ if we believe it! Theologians call this positional sanctification. The position is permanent.

Our holiness and his offering stand or fall together. I believe the record. God declares that we are sanctified now. I can't teach anyone to grow into sanctification because you are already sanctified and holy. However, there is a progressive growth into more sanctification in our practical life. There is not greater work that we can do that can match or outdo what Christ has already done to save us! The positional sanctification is eternal and never ends.

The work of the Priest is done. He is eternal. His sacrifice covered all of time to include all your past, present, and future sin. The verse says, "For by one offering he hath perfected forever them that are sanctified" (Hebrews 10:14). How could anything be plainer and easier to understand than this! We are sanctified and holy because of what he did to take sin away by nailing to the cross! Whoever doubts this wonderful truth has not yet embraced the reality of what Christ has already achieved for your permanent position as being holy! He did not die to make men savable. He died to save men. He did not die so that men can put sin away by some effort of their own. He died to put it away and he did. The one atonement was all of the work of man's redemption and forever if he believes.

The one sacrifice of Jesus Christ took sin away. The writer to the Colossians said it like this, "He took the whole list of charges that were proven against us and nailed them to the cross" (Colossians 2:14). We are forever cleansed from guilt and condemnation by the blood of Jesus Christ. We are perfected forever and have a positional holiness that can't be undone if we truly have believed the gospel. There shall not be any double jeopardy in God's courtroom. God will not judge and condemn us for what he has judged and condemned Christ for already.

This is the power in believing the gospel! Heaven! The Hebrew writer said that we are perfected forever because the entire debt that we owed God was paid for by Jesus Christ. Christ lived the perfect life for us. He also paid our entire debt by suffering the penalty for our sin. God's grace is his free gift of declaring us righteous and holy because of what Christ performed. He was also pronounced guilty and condemned at the cross because of the lives that we are living. Paul said it like this, "He made him that knew no sin to be sin for us, that we may be made the righteousness of God in him" (2 Corinthians 5:21). The Reformers called this the great exchange! The sin that we struggle against and that we strive to overcome has been dealt a knockout punch. God has already taken it away!

Many have been perplexed by an expression used further in the same chapter. The Hebrew writer says, "For if we sin willfully after that we have received the knowledge of the truth, there remains no more sacrifice for sins, But a fearful looking for of judgment and fiery indignation which shall devour the adversaries. He that despised Moses' law died without mercy under two or three witnesses: Of how much sorer punishment, suppose ye, shall he be thought worthy who has trodden under foot the Son of God, and has counted the blood of the covenant, where he was sanctified, an unholy thing, and has done despite the spirit of grace?" (Hebrews 10:26-29).

First, we have already seen that we are sanctified by the one offering of Jesus Christ at the cross, his blood, and perfected forever. Forever means forever. Some who leave us or later claim that they no longer have faith in the Son of God or that they don't trust him or his blood anymore for their salvation would not actually be in the audience that the Hebrew writer is addressing. We know this from the last verse of this same chapter that says, "But we are not of those who draw back to perdition, but those who believe to the saving of the soul" (Hebrews 10:39, New King James Version).

The ones who fall away are those of whom John said, "They went out from us, but they were not of us; for if they had been of us, they would have continued with us: but they went out that they might be made manifest that they wee not all of us" (I John 2:19). Christ is the sanctifier and has been linked to his sheep with a bond that is indissoluble. He said, "They shall never perish, and none shall snatch them out of my hand or my Father's hand" (John 10:28-30). Never means never.

It is not our practical holiness or practical sanctification that gives us the title of "saints" and the right to our inheritance. His blood is what cleanses us from all unrighteousness. He is our righteousness and our sanctification before God as our eternal high priest. We have our positional holiness that is permanent. We have a full pardon for all our sins and for all of time. This is because of the one offering of Jesus' body that took our sin away. We are not one of those that reject the Son of God or draw back to perdition (Hebrews 10:39).

What did the Hebrew writer mean when he says, "For by one offering he has perfected forever them that are sanctified?" (Hebrews 10:14) He meant that the offering or body of Jesus took sin away. God had made laws about how sin is done away with. The law required a sacrifice and the blood of that sacrifice to be shed for sin to be removed. Christ came as that Lamb and shed his blood to take away the guilt of the sinner and to acquit the offender from the wrath due to him from God. This also gives him the right to inheritance and eternal life because God now sees the sinner as being sanctified and perfect since that one offering was for all of time. The redeemed are perfected forever. This is a full pardon for the past, present and the future.

Now God will also work through us to manifest righteous deeds and a holy lifestyle. The Hebrew writer says, "Follow peace with all men, and holiness without which no man shall see the Lord" (Hebrews 12:14). The word follow means to pursue. We must keep in mind that we can see him because of what he has done with our positional holiness. We are holy because we've been perfected forever. We ought to pursue faith to an in-depth understanding of this fact.

Pursuit of practical holiness is also progressive. A man can be in medical school and pursuing a career as a board-certified brain surgeon. He shall not confuse his pursuit of the goal as having attained the goal. He moves toward the goal each day. He studies. He does his homework. He learns. He does everything that he can to pass his exams. Pursuit is about sincerity. Do we really want to become what God intends for us to be?

Glorification is God's final act of salvation. This is when God redeems the body. He changes his saints in a moment or twinkling of the eye from mortal to immortality and from corruption to incorruptible. He gives them a divine nature and frees them from the presence of indwelling sin rooted within their natures. Paul described his struggle with this nature and went as far as to say that he sometimes did what he hated and that he was carnal but sold into sin as a captive (Romans 7:14-25).

6

The Wrath of God is Coming

Are we prepared for events that are about to unfold on the earth? These words are written about the Apocalypse, "And I beheld when he had opened the sixth seal, and, lo, there was a great earthquake; and the sun became black as sackcloth of hair, and the moon became as blood; And the stars of heaven fell unto the earth, even as a fig tree casteth her untimely figs, when she is shaken of a mighty wind. And the heaven departed as a scroll when it is rolled together; and every mountain and island were moved out of their places. And the kings of the earth, and the great men, and the rich men, and the chief captains, and the mighty men, and every bondman, and every free man, hid themselves in the dens and in the rocks of the mountains, And said to the mountains and rocks, Fall on us, and hide us from the face of him that sitteth on the throne, and from the wrath of the Lamb: For the great day is come, and who shall be able to stand?" (Revelation 6:12-17).

John is describing a period in the future when the wrath of God comes to the earth! How shall men escape the wrath of God? Who shall escape the wrath of God and why? My hope is that there will be something in this book that can explain how the epoch that we are in is designed to help us to escape the wrath of God to come! It's a horrific scene reading about the great leaders of the world and the mightiest men on earth that are running and crying out to mountains and rocks to fall on them and hide them from the one that is seen in the heaven that is sitting on a throne. The wrath of God is coming!

The Apostle Paul put it like this to the Church of Rome, "For the wrath of God is revealed from heaven against all ungodliness and unrighteousness of men, who hold the truth in unrighteousness; Because that which may be known to God is manifest in them'; for God hath shewed it to them" (Romans 1:18-19).

Loving people is about warning them of trouble that lies ahead and pointing them in the right direction to avoid doom. I want to share another horrific and dramatic scene from this prophetic book about events that are about to happen on the earth. John wrote this vision from God down and we have seen things unfolding in history that correlates to prophetic events that has already happened. We knew that Israel would become a state again and before that happened because of Bible prophecy. But many things are about to happen after the fifth angel sounds his trumpet. This shall take place once the fifth angel sounds his trumpet!

The Revelation says, "And the fifth angel sounded, and I saw a star fall from heaven unto the earth: and to him was given the key to the bottomless pit. And he opened the bottomless pit; and there arose smoke out of the pit, as the smoke of a great furnace; and the sun and the air were darkened by reason of the smoke of the pit. And there came out of the smoke locusts upon the earth; and unto then was given power, as the scorpions of the earth have power. And it had commanded them that they should not hurt the grass of the earth, neither any green thing, neither any tree; but only those men which have not the seal of God on their foreheads. And to them it was given that they should not kill them, but that they should be tormented five months: and their torment was as the torment of a scorpion, when he striketh a man. And in those days shall men seek death and shall not find it; and shall desire to die, and death shall flee from them" (Revelation 9:1-6). We now see creatures that were too cruel to be on the planet that God is now letting out after the 5th angel sounds his trumpet! They will seek men to torment them!

Look at the description of these creatures that are coming to bring the wrath of God to earth. John saw it! He writes, "And the shapes of the locusts wee like unto horses prepared for battle; and on their heads were as it were crowns like gold, and their faces were as the faces of men. And they had hair as the hair of women, and their teeth were as the teeth of lions. And they had breastplates, of iron; and the sound of their wings was as the sound of chariots of many horses running to battle. And they had tails like unto scorpions, and there were stings in their tails: and their power was to hurt men five months. And they had a king over them, which is the angel of the bottomless pit, whose name in the Hebrew tongue is Abaddon, but in the Greek tongues hath his name Apollyon" (Revelation 9:7-11).

Let us look at what happens when the sixth angel sounds his trumpet. John writes, "And the sixth angel sounded, and I heard a voice from the four horns of the golden altar which is before God. Saying to the sixth angel which had the trumpet, Loose the four angels which are bound in the great river Euphrates. And the four angels were loosed, which were prepared for an hour, and a day, and a month, and a year, for to slay the third part of men. And the number of the army of the horsemen wee two hundred thousand thousand: and I heard the number of them. And I saw the horses in the vision, and them that sat on them, having breastplates of fire, and of jacinth, and brimstone: and the heads of the horses were as the heads of lions: and out of their mouths issued fire and smoke and brimstone. By these three was the third part men killed, by the fire, and by the smoke, and by the brimstone, which issued out of their mouths. For their power is in their mouth, and in their tails: for their tails were like unto serpents, and had heads, and with them they do hurt" (Revelation 9:13-19).

God allows many men to live after this. But they did not repent of their deeds. They never felt any type of sorrow in their hearts about the wicked things that they did upon the earth. John writes this down, "And the rest of the men which were not killed by these plagues yet repented not of the works of their hands, that they should worship devils, and the idols of gold, and silver, and brass, and stone, and of wood: which neither can see, nor hear, nor walk: Neither repented they of their murders, nor their sorceries, nor of their fornication, nor of their thefts" (Revelation 9:19-21).

Repentance is a godly sorrow in the heart about doing wicked and evil things. Repentance is a change of mind about saying, thinking, or doing these activities. Men turn to God in repentance when they want God to forgive them and rescue them from the bondage or addiction of doing these wicked things. God didn't make man and put him on the earth to do the evil things that we have saw many men do. Jesus Christ said these words while on the earth, "I tell you that except you repent that you shall likewise perish" (Luke 13:3). When Jesus sent out his disciples to preach the gospel, he told them to preach repentance. Luke records this by saying, "And that repentance and remission of sins should be preached in his name among all nations, beginning at Jerusalem" (Luke 24:47).

We find that over in the book of Acts that men changed their ways after they repented of the sin in their lives. Luke narrates, "And many that believed came, and confessed, and shewed their deeds. Many of them also which used curious arts brought their books together and burned them before all men: and they counted the price of them and found it fifty thousand pieces of silver. So mightily grew the Word of God and prevailed" (Acts 19:18-20). When men confess Jesus and believe in him and his work to save them, they'll repent of their sin. Men repent when they believe the gospel. One of the biggest issues is rediscovering the true gospel and getting the good news out to all!

The time is running out for men to get saved from the wrath of God to come. Men will still need to stand before God if he doesn't return to earth and this will happen when they die. The Word of God teaches, "It is appointed to men once to die and after that the judgment" (Hebrews 9:27). Are you ready to stand before God on the day? Solomon described this final judgment by saying, "Let us hear the whole conclusion of the matter: Fear God and keep his commandments: this is the whole duty of man. For God shall bring every work into judgment, with every secret thing, whether it be good, or whether it be evil" (Ecclesiastes 12:14).

What would be your plea to God be as to why he should let you enter heaven with him?

John writes down the vision God gave him about a judgement that takes place before a great white throne in heaven and says, "And I saw a great white throne, and him that sat on it, from whose face the earth and the heaven fled away; and there was found no place for them. And I saw the dead, small and great, stand before God; and the books were opened, and another book was opened, which is the book of life: and the dead were judged out of those things which were written in the books, according to their works. And the sea gave up the dead which were in it; and death and hell delivered up the dead which were in them; and they were judged every man according to their works. And death and hell were cast out into the lake of fire. This is the second death. And whosoever was not found written in the book of life was cast into the lake of fire" (Revelation 20:11-15). Men stand before God and the records about his life on the earth are there. He is judged. Men are judged based on what they did in their lifetimes. He is thrown into a lake of fire if his name is not found written in the Lamb's book of life! Are you ready for that scene? Have you lived for God? Have you been forgiven by God? What must you do now?

We find another dramatic scene in this final book of the Bible. This scene describes a new earth and a new heaven. This scene also describes the types of people who cannot enter the new earth and the new heaven. John writes for God, "And I saw a new heaven and a new earth: for the first heaven and the first earth were passed away: and there was no more sea. And I John saw the holy city, new Jerusalem, coming down from God out of heaven, prepared as a bride that is adorned for her husband. And I heard a great voice out of heaven saying, Behold, the tabernacle of God is with men, and he will dwell with them, and they shall be his people, and God himself shall be with them, and be their God. And God shall wipe away all tears from their eyes; and there shall be no more death, neither sorrow, nor crying, neither shall there be any more pain for the former things are passed away. And he that sat upon the throne

81

said, Behold, I make all things new. And he said unto me, Write: for these words are true and faithful. And he said unto me, It is done. I am Alpha and Omega, the beginning and the end. I will give unto him that is athirst of the fountain of water of life freely.

He that overcometh shall inherit all things; and I will be his God, and he shall be my son. But the fearful, and the unbelieving, and the abominable, and murderers, and whoremongers, and sorcerers, and idolaters, and all liars, shall have their part in the lake which burns with fire and brimstone: which is the second death" (Revelation 21:1-8). How does anyone escape the horrors described in the lake of fire and brimstone? Did you see the different types of people that are going there?

After this description of the types of people that will not enter heaven, God gives us a description of heaven. He then says these words, "And there shall in no wise enter into it any thing that defileth, neither whatsoever worketh abomination, or maketh a lie: but they which are written in the Lamb's book of life" (Revelation 21:27).

Here is what Paul said to the Church of Rome, "All have sinned and come short of the glory of God" (Romans 3:23). There is not a man upon the earth that can merit going into heaven as it is described! The prophet Isaiah said it like this, "But we are all as an unclean thing and all of our righteousnesses are as filthy rags. And we all do fade as a leaf; and our iniquities, like the wind, have taken us away" (Isaiah 64:6). Something is terribly wrong that disqualifies us from entering paradise. What could that be? It's our sin!

Paul says it to the Church of Rome like this here, "As it is written, There is none righteous, no, not one" (Romans 3:10). Here are the words that we'll find in the last chapter of this book. John writes this down for God, "He that is unjust, let him be unjust still: and he which is filthy, let him be filthy still and he that is righteous, let him be righteous still: and he that is holy, let him be holy still. And, behold, I come quickly; and my reward is with me, to give to every man according as his work shall be. I am Alpha and Omega, the beginning and the end, the first and the last. Blessed are they that do his commandments, that they may have the right to the tree of life and may enter in through the gates into the city. For without are dogs, and sorcerers, and whoremongers, and murderers, and idolaters, and whosoever loveth and maketh a lie. I Jesus have sent mine angel to testify unto you these things in the churches. I am the root and offspring of David, and the bright and morning star" (Revelation 22:11-16).

Jesus says that the ones who shall have the right to the tree of life are they that do his commandments. What commandments did Christ give for us to follow? He gave out many commands and I don't want to minimize any. But keep in mind that Jesus taught people to repent and believe the gospel! He also commanded them to take the Lord's supper and to be baptized!

Repent means to change one's mind about his own beliefs. The Jews thought that they could earn salvation by keeping the law. Jesus wanted them to believe his message about the gift of eternal life that came to those that believed that he was the Son and God that died for their sins to take them away and that rose again for them on the third day! He instituted the Lord's supper and told them to eat the bread and drink the wine to remember that his body and his blood instituted the new covenant, but that new covenant was based on his works for our salvation and not our own! Christ built the bird for us to fly to heaven on! Believe it!

7

The Epoch of Grace

J ohn the Baptist describes Christ as being the Lamb of God that took the sins of the world away in John 1:29! Great news! Christ took your sin away and you should not have to worry about God's wrath if you believe and trust in God's Lamb. Paul put it like this to the Church of the Romans, "Sin shall not have dominion over you for ye are not under the law, but under grace" (Romans 6:14). The Lordship of sin over Christians had ended! Why? It's because we are no longer under the legal rule or principle of the Mosaic Law that counts us a transgressors or sinners and demands that we do this or that and be penalized if we don't. The law that proved that we are sinners and that condemns us to a curse and death. The law places us under God's wrath when we break it.

We are no longer under this law once we believe the gospel, but we are under God's grace or unmerited favor which grants us unconditional blessings. God gives us grace and declares us righteous and just simply because we believe the gospel and not because we are keeping or have kept the law. Sin no longer has dominion or Lordship over you because of the epoch dominated by grace.

Jesus fulfilled the epoch of the law by suffering the penalty for us breaking the law. He obeyed the law as a divine person in our stead and suffered the penalty as an eternal person, for us breaking the law in order that the benefit for us could last forever. He kept the law as our legal representative so that we could receive the reward of eternal life but based on the grace or unmerited favor of us being declared just because of his performance and what he did for us. Sin is an alien in the epoch of grace and is simply not with the believer anymore because he has no relationship with the law.

The Christian is no longer in the era dominated by the Mosaic law, but under the epoch of grace. Shall we continue in sin? No! We cannot. We have to change our view and see ourselves the way that God sees us. See ourselves as people that cannot sin because of our relationship with Christ and the fact that we have had to law fulfilled already by Christ so that we can be counted as not guilty. The Mosaic law pertains to the nation Israel, but not the church. But sin for everyone is breaking the law. The law will also be used to condemn the world that is not in a relationship with Christ.

Freedom from the law means deliverance. God delivers us from the attempt to measure up to its standards. He delivers us from the temptation of presuming that our works based on the keeping of the law can somehow justify us and make us right with God. The issue now is not how we behave, but what we believe. Do we believe that we are righteous in God's perspective because he took our sin away and placed it on the Lamb of God at the cross? Do we believe that we are right with God because of our own deeds, acts of righteousness, and works that justify us? Jesus said, "He that believes on him that sent me has eternal life and shall not be condemned but has passed from death unto life" (John 5:24).

The Christian is not under probation. When you are under probation, you'll be in trouble if you don't keep a rule and you will be locked up if you don't keep the terms and conditions of it. God does not accept us conditionally. God does what he does eternally. God does not leave our eternal destination to us to either earn or sabotage one way or the other based on our works. The believer is never under the law as a condition of acceptance with God. Grace doesn't originate within man and based on his merit of God's love or approval. Our acceptance with God depends on something the goodness and love that is in God. Our choice by God is not based on who and what we are or who and what we think we are that provokes God to give us his grace.

A few texts illustrate this concept to us in the Word of God. Paul says, "But to him that works not, but believes on him that justifies the ungodly, his faith is counted for righteousness" (Romans 4:5). Your belief counts as your righteousness now instead of your strict adherence to a set of laws or rules. Paul also says to that Church of Ephesus, "For by grace are you saved through faith: and that not of yourselves, it is the gift of God, not of works, lest any should boast" (Ephesians 2:8-9). Our righteousness is a declaration from God based on Christ's performance for us in his living and at the cross! It's a gift that is based on faith alone!

The epoch of sin is over for the believer. Paul said in his dissertation to the Romans, "The law was given that every mouth may be stopped and that the whole world can stand guilty before God" (Romans 3:19). The purpose of the Mosaic law was only to prove that man is unable to justify himself before God based on his works or what we call his performance. Every mouth can stop and the whole world is guilty of sin. Paul says these words to the Galatians, "Knowing that a man is not justified by the works of the law, but by the faith of Jesus Christ, even we have believed in Jesus Christ, that we might be justified by the faith of Christ, and not by the works of the law: for by the works of the law shall no flesh be justified" (Galatians 2:16). As we read on, we'll find Paul saying these words, "I do not frustrate the grace of God: for if righteousness came by the law, then Christ is dead in vain" (Galatians 3:21). God can't consider us right because we keep the Old Testament commandments. His righteousness has been revealed as being our faith in his work at the cross!

The Justification by faith alone paradox

A paradox exists when there are two truths that are both correct, but there is difficulty reconciling one truth with because they apparently contradict each other. Sometimes a reconciliation is not possible to solve a paradox and the solution is either in whole or in part a mystery. How could it be true that we are declared just and righteous before

God because of our faith alone in Christ and his declaration because of his matchless works at the cross, but also that we are not to be considered just or righteous on judgment day by faith alone without works to justify us? Which eschatological perspective should we have and why? Will we go to heaven because of Christ's works alone as a result of being saved by grace (unmerited favor) through faith as cited in Ephesians 2:8-9 or does God require us to do something on our part in this life to obtain our inheritance on that great day of judgment?

8

The paradox of justification by faith alone and judgment of works

P aul presented a dissertation that we are declared just from God by faith alone and without works, but also that works must justify us in the end. In two short chapters of the book of Romans, Paul says, "The hearers of the law are not justified, but the doers of the law" (Romans 2:13).

But we read, "Therefore we conclude that a man is justified by faith without the deeds of the law" (Romans 3:28). On the one hand, he is saying that it's not hearing the law that counts, but that you obey it and keep its rules by doing the works of the law to save you. On the other hand, he is saying that we are justified without keeping the deeds of the law and without doing the works, but because of our faith in Christ alone! Justification is when God says that we are not guilty and that we have right to eternal life based on a verdict he rendered which declared us right with God. We will have to ask ourselves if our acquittal takes place because Christ was judged and condemned for us already at the cross or if God will look at our works in whole or in part to justify us on that day.

Recent discussions by theologians and scholars about justification by faith and a final judgment of works show that Protestant theologians have proposed distinctions between different stages of justification-past, present, and future. The scholars who support the "new perspective on

Paul," believe that you "get into" salvation or the church by grace, but that you "stay in" and are ultimately justified by your works. However, it is crucial not to compromise the biblical teaching on justification by faith alone when we teach that the works which faith produces are somehow instrumental to a Christian's final justification in the end before God.

There will be a judgement of works which makes the whole subject an interesting one as far as how eschatology and theology correlates to our soteriology. Some don't view faith as a receiving act, which allows us to be in Christ's righteousness alone for justification but insist that the obedience of our faith (faithfulness) is the way our eventual justification is received. According to this view, the final justification will be granted only to those who have maintained their justification by persevering in obedience.

Are we saved?

Believers need to know for sure if they are saved already or if their salvation depends on their own future acts of obedience or disobedience to things, we see written down in scripture for us to do. If the justification of believers is based on their own future works after being forgiven and this final justification is based either in whole or in part on works, then believers can never know for sure that they are irreversibly right with God in the present. If Christ being crucified once and for all on their behalf and his righteousness is not the sole ground for our acceptance with God, both now and at the judgement seat of Christ, then believers cannot be sure that they will inherit eternal life until that great and final day of judgement.

Keeping the score

The idea of a future justification or condemnation because of works would mean that God is keeping a score sheet. It also means that we cannot be certain that God will continue to give us unmerited favor.

But we did not merit our unmerited favor in the first place and that would mean that it at least sounds contradictory to lose grace by demerit. Whenever we look at the final judgement as the last stage of justification it means that we ultimately believe that we will be justified and declared righteous in the end based on grace plus works! What should be the character of justification in our eschatological doctrine of the last things?

Definition of Justification

In Christian theology, the doctrine of justification by faith alone is God's righteous act of removing our guilt and final condemnation in the end, and the penalty of sin, by his grace, while, at the same time declaring the unrighteous to be righteous, through the faith in his atoning sacrifice. The doctrine of justification by faith alone concerns God's grace is giving a judicial verdict in advance of the day of judgement, pronouncing us sinners, who have turned to trust the work of Jesus Christ, forgiven, acquitted of all charges and righteous in God's sight! Paul described this wonderful news to the by saying, "But to him that worketh not, but believes on him that justifies the ungodly, his faith is counted for righteousness" (Romans 4:5).

This involves the removal of sin and the imputation of the righteousness of Christ (Romans 4:6-8). Imputation is when you are given credit based on someone else's merit or account. Sin is no longer reckoned to the account of the believers. The righteousness of Christ is credited to the believer but is not infused into his nature at justification. This happens over time during stages of sanctification in life, which is a work performed by the Holy Spirit, but is not finalized until glorification takes place which happens in the next life.

Justification is not about a change in nature, but we know that a believer repents when he turns to Christ in faith. Christ will change corrupt natures in his final act of salvation with our glorification. However, it's not our works or obedience to his commands that gives us a righteous status before God, rather it is about the righteous status that results from the righteousness of Christ being credited to us. Paul says it like this to the Church of Rome, "For what does the scripture say? Abraham believed in (trusted, relied on) God, and it was credited to his account as righteousness (right living, right standing with God). Now to a laborer, his wages are not credited as a favor or a gift, but as an obligation (something owed to him). But to the one who does not work (that is, the one who does not try to earn his salvation by doing good) but believes and completely trusts in him who justifies the ungodly, his faith is credited to him as righteousness (right standing with God)" (Romans 4:3-5, Amplified Bible).

Justification is not based upon the Spirit's work of regeneration and renewal. Our progress made in sanctification is not what justifies us either. It's not based on the progress we think we've made in our walk with God in our sanctification, but entirely on the person and work of Christ. The guilt of the people was transferred to him, and he paid the price by receiving the punishment due, likewise his righteousness was imputed to them and they are counted as righteous because of imputation (Isaiah 53:5-6,11). Christ took our sins and gave us his righteousness.

God gives a full pardon for all of time to the ungodly based on Christ's death. God saw our sin as belonging to Jesus Christ, his Son, who was without sin. As Paul said it to the Church of Corinth, "God made him who knew no sin to be sin for us, that we may be made the righteousness of God in him" (2 Corinthians 5:21). This entails giving the believer credit for righteousness based of Christs merit and transferring a man's guilt to Christ based on the sinner's guilt, but one time and for all of his debt to God for his entire lifetime. The Hebrew writer said it like this, "For by one offering he has perfected forever them that are sanctified" (Hebrews 10:14).

IMPUTATION

A billionaire can open up a secondary credit card in a poor friend's name and extend the credit earned from his good name to a friend. The friend is given credit based on the kind and generous payment that the billionaire has agreed to make or has already secured by the money in his account. This is the idea behind the doctrine of imputation that is taught in scripture. Imputed righteousness is a Protestant Christian doctrine that was taught by the Lutherans and the Calvinists during the Protestant Reformation.

Imputation is taught in the scripture and it's the doctrine that the sinner is declared righteous by God based solely on God's grace (unmerited favor) through faith in Christ, but also that they are given this credit for being righteous based on Christ's merit and worthiness, rather than their own merit or worthiness. The righteousness of Christ is imputed or credited to the account of the believer. Imputation teaches that God legally credits the believer with the righteous acts that Christ performed on the earth. Luther called it a "fortunate exchange" and we often call it today "the great exchange" when we speak of justification by faith and being declared righteous based on imputation.

I have some good news. This goes into the mind and heart of God. The Word of God says, "For whom he did foreknow, he also did predestinate to be conformed to the image of his Son, that he might be the firstborn among many brethren. Moreover, whom he did predestinate, them he also called: and whom he called, them he also justified: and whom he justified, them he also glorified" (Romans 8:28-30). Predestination is about God knowing you and deciding to love you and bring you to him in love in the end. Calling is about God acknowledging you and bringing you to himself once you arrive here on the planet. Justification is about God forgiving your entire debt of sin based on his love for you which was manifested by the sacrifice of Christ at the cross. Glorification is God completing his work to save you in the next life by giving you an immortal body with an incorruptible nature. It is God finishing the work he started to sanctify you apart from your sinful nature and the corrupt world with its influences and demons. Glorification is the Christ's final act of salvation, and it is done by Jesus Christ himself.

The Apostle Paul said these words to the Romans after he explained that our faith counts as our righteousness, "Blessed is the man to whom the Lord will not impute sin" (Romans 4:8). The Amplified puts it like this, "Blessed and happy and favored is the man whose sin the Lord will not take into account nor charge against him" (Romans 4:8, Amplified Bible). The doctrine of imputation teaches that in the doctrine of justification, God imputes or credits the righteousness and suffering of Jesus Christ to those who believe and trust in him, but also that God imputes all the sins of the believer to Christ. What is ours becomes Christ's and what is Christ's becomes ours. Adam's sin was imputed to all humanity as if we were there. We were born under the curse of sin and death because of Adam's sin. The Christian's sin and guilt was imputed to Christ and Christ's righteousness was imputed to us!

What is interesting about all of this is that God saw us as being in Christ in the same way that he saw us as being in Adam when Adam sinned in the garden. Long before we were born, we were judged and condemned to sin and to die because of what Adam did in the garden as our representative. But now Christ's believers are constituted as righteous because of his works, and he represented us by what he did (Romans 5:18-19). Faith is the instrument that God uses to justify us and not our works. Paul says it like this to the Church of Ephesus, "For by grace are you saved through faith, and that not of yourselves, it is the gift of God. Not of works lest any should boast" (Ephesians 2:8-9). Remember, God does not justify us because he sees our faith as being something virtuous within ourselves, but because of who our faith is in and the works which he performed for us to save us. Salvation is a gift that's not based on our works or worthiness!

This is a judicial act of God who renders a verdict that we are not guilty. Paul says it like this in the book of Titus, "Not by works of righteousness which we have done, but according to his mercy he saved us, by the washing of regeneration, and renewing of the Holy Ghost; which he shed on us abundantly through Jesus Christ our savior; That being justified by his grace, we should be made heirs according to the hope of eternal life" (Titus 3:5-7).

A man can only repent and believe if God regenerates him to give him life in the spirit by the Holy Ghost. Everything we do to come to God is because of God and what he did to bring us back to himself. Jesus said, "No man can come to me unless the Father who sent me draws him; and I will raise him up at the last day" (John 6:44). We see Paul saying here in the third chapter of the book of Titus that we are justified by his grace. Grace is God's unmerited favor.

Christ as Surety

When we ponder the biblical teaching about imputation, we keep in mind that the scriptures teach in the book of Hebrews "Christ is our surety of a better covenant" (Hebrews 7:22). A surety is a sponsor. A surety is someone who guarantees that they will perform whatever someone else has failed to perform. This is someone who undertakes the responsibility of another who is primarily liable. This is one who makes himself liable for the default or miscarriage of another or for the performance of some act on his part such as a payment of a debt, appearance in court, and the performance of deeds. A good example of a surety would be someone who signs a loan on behalf of the person who is primarily responsible for paying the debt, but if the primary borrower defaults it means that the surety pays off the debt!

Whenever people need to borrow more than their credit allows, they appreciate surety. Mankind is in debt to God and owes him performance of good works to merit eternal life. Jesus made this clear in his conversation with the rich and young ruler. He told him to keep the commandments in order to merit eternal life. The rich man mentioned that he had kept all the commandments from his youth. Christ then asked him to sell all his possessions and give them to the poor. The rich man then walked away sorrowful when he found that he had to sell all his possessions and give them to the poor in order to have eternal life

(Matthew 19:16-22). Money was his idol of the rich young ruler and his idolatry broke one of the Ten Commandment of God.

He left sorrowful and departed from Jesus because he realized he had not lived the life that he thought he had for God! The Word of God says these profound words, "The wages (reward) for sin is death, but the gift of God is eternal life through Jesus Christ our Lord" (Romans 6:23). Salvation is a free gift to those that put their full trust and confidence in Jesus Christ for their salvation. Trusting in our works will reveal to us that our works come short of God's expectations and hopes of what they ought to have been. We see this reality in the story of this rich and young ruler.

Eternal death and damnation are the penalty for sins in the lake that burns with fire and brimstone to those who have no surety to cover their sin debt that is owed to God (Revelation 21:8). The list of sins that put people in the lake of fire and brimstone that is mentioned in Revelation 21:8 and over in Revelation 22:14-16 would make all men guilty and hopeless! As Paul said to the Romans, "All have sinned and come short of the glory of God" (Romans 3:23). He also mentioned in his systematic theology, "The law was given that every mouth be stopped and that the whole world stand guilty before God" (Romans 3:19). All men are guilty if sin and doomed to spend eternity in the lake of fire and brimstone without a surety that will cover their debt for them. The debt has to be paid off and cancelled for man to be free of paying off his debt on his own.

What Christ being our surety teaches us is that he has paid all of the debt we owe to God off for us. Christ tasted death for every one of his children to deliver them (Hebrews 2:9-17). He fulfilled the righteousness required of the law on our behalf (Romans 8:3-4), so that we are righteous in God's sight with his perfect obedience (Ephesians 5:25-27, Colossians 1:21-22). Jesus Christ paid the penalty of sins by his death for us (I Peter 2:24). so that there are no more sins against or charges when we stand before him (John 1:29; Hebrews 1:28). Since Jesus is our surety, God does not withhold blessing from us (Romans 8:32). His death reconciled us to God.

Justified because of his works

The best way for me to explain this truth may very well be from the book to the Romans. Paul says in Romans 5:1-9, "Therefore, since we are justified (acquitted, declared righteous, and given a right standing with God) through faith, let us (grasp the fact that we) have (the peace of reconciliation to hold and to enjoy) peace with God through our Lord Jesus Christ (The Messiah, the Anointed One). Through him also we have our access (entrance, introduction) by faith into this grace (state of God's favor) in which we (firmly and safely) stand.

And let us rejoice and exalt in our hope of experiencing and enjoying the glory of God. Moreover (let us also be the full of joy now!) let us exult and triumph in our troubles and rejoice in our sufferings, knowing that pressure and affliction and hardship produce patient and unswerving endurance. And endurance (fortitude) develops maturity of character (approved) faith and tried integrity). And character (of this sort) produces (the habit of) joyful and confident hope of eternal salvation. Such hope never disappoints or deludes or shames us, for God's love has been poured out in our hearts through the Holy Spirit who has been given to us.

While we were yet in weakness (powerless to help ourselves), at the fitting time Christ died for (on behalf of) the ungodly. Now it is an extraordinary thing for one to give his life even for an upright man, through perhaps for a noble and lovable and generous benefactor someone might even dare to die. But God shows and clearly proves his own love for us by the fact that while we were yet sinners, Christ (The Messiah, the Anointed One) died for us.

Therefore, since we are now justified (acquitted, made righteous, and brought into right relationship with God) by Christ's blood, how much more (certain is it that) we shall be saved by him from the indignation and wrath of God" (Romans 5:1-9, Amplified Bible). Did you see that? Christ died for us and the ungodly. When we believe this, his blood justifies us and saves us from the wrath of God to come! We should be happy about his when we think about just how far away from the Word of God we strayed. The prophet Isaiah said, "But we are all as an unclean thing and all of our righteousnesses are as filthy rags" (Isaiah 64:6). Our works cannot match his works that he did to save us!

The justified already possess of eternal life

Jesus Christ spoke of this by saying, "I assure you and most solemnly say to you, the person who hears my word (the one who heeds my message), and believes and trusts in him who sent me, has (possesses now) eternal life (that is, eternal life actually begins-the believer is transformed), and does not come into judgment and condemnation, but has passed from death into life" (John 5:24, Amplified Bible). Christ is saying that the believer has eternal life right now because of what Christ did for him when he believes! He doesn't have to go and try to earn eternal life. He is also saying that the judgment and condemnation for his sins has already been and was in Christ.

Jesus Christ had spoken, "For God so (greatly) loved and dearly prized the world, that he (even) gave his (One and), only begotten Son, so that whoever believes and trusts in Him (as Savior) shall not perish, but have eternal life" (John 3:16, Amplified Bible). Do you see the connection between believing and receiving the gift of eternal life? Jesus said, "Whoever believes in the Son has eternal life" (John 3:36). The believer "has" (present tense) this eternal life. The verb is present tense in the Greek. Eternal life is in the possession of the believer now. The death that Christ died for us and the blood that he shed pays off all debts that we owe to God for our entrance into the world to come. We cannot pay for this and even if we tried to work for it.

John puts it this simple, "God has given us eternal life, and this life is in his Son. Whoever has the Son has life; whoever does not have the Son of God does not have life" (I John 5:11-12). Jesus said these words about the justified with eternal life, "And I give them eternal life, and they shall never perish, neither shall any man pluck them out of my hand" (John 10:28). Did you see that? We possess eternal life if we believe, and we shall never perish! Never means never! The very word eternal means forever.

There is no way to undo what Christ has said or done for us. Christ didn't die to just make us savable. He died to save us. He did not die so that our sin can be put away by some effort of our own. He died to put it away for us so that we enter his kingdom to come. Jesus said these words, "I am the good shepherd: the good shepherd gives his life for the sheep" (John 10:11). But Christ also said, "For I came down from heaven, not to do mine own will, but the will of him that sent me. And this is the father's will which sent me, that of all which he hath given me I should lose nothing but should raise him up at the last day" (John 6:38-40).

It's not God's will that Christ loses any of his sheep and Christ came to do his Father's will. He'll lose none of them. Christ said that his sheep shall never follow a stranger's voice but will run from him (John 10:5). Do you trust that Christ will do his Father's will and not lose any of his own sheep? Is it possible for Christ to lose someone that the Father chose for him and gave to him based on his divine foreknowledge of all future events (I Peter 1:2, Ephesians 1:4, Romans 8:28-30)?

The ransom that Christ paid for us has covered the entire debt that we owe to God! Christ said these words when he hung on the cross, "It is finished" (John 19:30). The word comes from the Greek word, "tetelestai" which means paid in full". Often it was used in an accounting term, which indicates a debt was paid in full. Now if you are one of his sheep this is good news because your entire debt that could condemn you to be thrown into Hell has been paid off by Jesus. Jesus came to finish God's work of salvation by paying in full, the entire debt, for our sins in the past and for sins to come. When someone pays your debts off it means that you can't default on a payment that becomes due.

There is no other way for the door of heaven to be opened to us other than by the forgiveness of our sin, through Christ's payment as our surety on our behalf. Here is how Paul brought this up to the

Church of Rome, "Who shall bring any a charge against God's elect? It is God who justifies. Who is he that condemns? It is Christ that died, and furthermore is also risen, who is even at the right hand of God, who also makes intercession for us" (Romans 8:33-34). You are now and shall be acquitted on the day of judgement if you are a true believer in Christ's work to save you and have repented of sin in your heart!

9

The difference between
Sanctification and Justification

A believer cannot be more justified than they are presently with a sanctification, but we shall be more sanctified, and during after our glorification in the next life we'll be perfectly sanctified! Justification and sanctification are different from each other. There is no justified believer that is not also being sanctified by the Holy Ghost. Justification is an act of God's grace, while sanctification is a work of God's grace through us to set us apart from sin having dominion over our lives.

This means that, justification is a one-time, definitive, legal declaration in God's courtroom in which we are "counted righteous." God pronounces the verdict now that a person believes in Christ for his salvation. Sanctification is an ongoing and progressive work in the life of the believer. Justification is presently perfect, but sanctification is presently imperfect while developing and growing toward perfection. We have also discovered that we have and possess a positional sanctification that is permanent based on what Christ achieved for us.

Justification removes all of the guilt of sin, but sanctification helps us by the Holy Ghost to overcome the addiction of sin and sin's activity dominating our lives. Justification is because of the imputation of the righteousness of Christ. Sanctification is due to the Holy Ghost moving us by God's grace to become inwardly more like Christ in righteousness in terms of how we live our lives out. There is no justification that causes us to become less saved because we are imperfectly sanctified and there is no sanctification that make us more saved than what we are with justification.

Sanctification is the work of God in a human being to make him more righteous in the practical sense of the word. God works repentance in our heart. The Grace of God turns us around and helps him or her to overcome things that he or she could not do in his or her own strength. So, sanctification doesn't earn anything from God because it is only God that works this process out through the believer by the power of the Holy Ghost.

It needs to be remembered that Sanctification starts with God transferring a person from the reign of the law and sin to a reign and control of grace. The sinner has no ability to do any spiritual good. We can neither come to God on our own, convert ourselves, nor keep ourselves! Sanctification is God bringing us to himself by his grace and developing us over time to be more and more like Christ. Paul says, "He who has begun a good work in you will perform it until the day of Jesus Christ" (Philippians 1:6).

There is also a balance taught in the scripture about sanctification. We know that God does this work, but he encourages us to be active and willing participants. As Paul said to the Philippians, "Work out your own salvation with fear and trembling" for it is God who works in you, both to will and to work for his good pleasure" (Philippians 2:12-13). Did you see that? We are commanded to work out our salvation with fear and trembling, but it's God who works in us to give us the ambition and desire or will to do the work that is pleasing to him so that we can get the work done!

Paradoxically, because God works in us, we must and will work out our salvation. The grace of God teaches us to live lives of godliness (Titus 2:11-12). How do we do these things? We repent of sin that springs up in our lives and we come to God confessing in prayer asking him to forgive us and to cleanse us from all unrighteousness (I John 1:8-9). This verse in John's writing teaches us that if we say that we have no sin that we have deceived ourselves. God keeps us clean by his blood when we confess the reality of what we know is sin and sincerely repent. Repenting is not just a change of mind about us being sinful. It is acknowledging that our own works can't justify us as we had originally thought that they could. Repenting is a radical change in our own philosophy that our works can somehow justify us before God! It's a change of mind about our sinfulness, but also a change of mind about how we can be made right with God!

Repentance is a divine gift that comes from God too and so is faith (Acts 5:31, Acts 11:18, Ephesians 2:8, Philippians 1:29). This is agreeing God's Word and God's way. It is the believer's responsibility to repent again and again if he has sin in his life after he has experienced justification. He shall do the same if he has the grace of God working in his heart with salvation to do it. Because God works through him, he'll have delight to do these things. He shall engage in a battle with the world, the flesh, and the devil. It he doesn't desire to engage in a battle it means that God is not working through him to fight. Why would that be?

He will keep his joy of justification because he knows that Christ has won the battle over sin and death by his sacrifice for him. He knows that Christ will finish this work in his life (Philippians 1:6). But he also knows that all sin shall not be completely eradicated out of creation and from his fallen nature until the consummation of salvation during glorification (I Corinthians 15:51, Romans 8:22-25). Paul describes to the Romans in this text that the creature was created subject to vanity and that the entire creation is in bondage to decay, corruption, sinfulness and depravity. He mentions how that we are saved by hope, but that hope which we can see isn't hope. He speaks of how the body itself will be saved and redeemed in the future, but that the body isn't saved now.

This idea parallels to his statement about his own struggle with sin in Romans 7:14-25 where Paul explained that he sometimes did what he hated and that it was no longer him, but sin that dwelt within his nature that acted at times. However, in many other passages he says that he was also delivered and that we too can overcome if we walk and yield to the operation of the Spirit instead of the nature and actions of the sinfulness in our flesh.

10

What is Holiness and
how does it relate to Justification

Much more could be said about sanctification. But remember
these words of the Hebrew writer, "Follow peace with all men
and holiness, without which no man shall see the Lord" (Hebrews
12:14). Holiness is a fruit that is produced in the lives of the believer.
This is the believer being set apart in terms of how his lives his life
out on the earth and who he lives his life for. He is not longer a servant of Satan.

Holiness is not what justifies a man on the day of judgment, but our
justification was completed by Christ at the cross. Holiness is a result
of the work of the Holy Ghost in the life of the believer. When Christ
saves someone, he'll produces fruit in their lives that identifies them as
belonging to him and being set apart on earth for his use.

Though his sanctification shall be imperfect until his glorification,
he or she shall have a life that is renewed as a new creature in Christ and
their works shall show this. Sanctification or "holiness" begins with a
change in Lordship. Jesus asked a very profound question to his disciples and said, "Why call me Lord and do not the things that I say" (Luke
6:46). Men and women who haven given their lives to Jesus will have a
strong ambition to lives their lives on earth for Jesus Christ.

Can a justified believer lose his or her salvation?

One thing that it's good to remember when we start pondering thoughts that one of God's sheep could lose salvation is whether or not The Word of God teaches that a born-again believer can practice sin as a lifestyle habit. The Word of God teaches the reality that his new birth by the spirit has rendered habitual practice of deliberate sin as an impossibility. He may fall. He may stray away. He may confess and need to be restored again.

But the true believer can never practice sin as a born- again spirit. John said it like this, "Little children, let no man deceive you: he that does righteousness is righteous, even as he is righteous. He that commits sin is of the devil; for the devil sinneth from the beginning. For this purpose, the Son of God was manifested, that he might destroy the works of the devil. Whosoever is born of God doth not commit sin; for his seed remains in him; and he cannot sin, because he is born of God. In this the children of God are manifest, and the children of the devil; whoever doeth not righteousness is not of God, neither he that loveth not his brother" (I John 3:7-10).

These verses teach that the born- again man cannot sin. This can have a few possible different interpretations that can be true. First, the Word of God teaches that sin cannot have dominion over us because we are no longer under the law, but under grace in Romans 6:14. This means that we cannot sin because the law that could condemn us in no longer in force to convict us in this dispensation. We also find also in Colossians 2:14 that Christ took every handwriting of charges and ordinances that was proven against us and nailed it to the cross!

What does that mean? Scholars know it can only mean that sin has been wiped out and done away with completely for the believer because of imputation, justification, and the forever effect of positional sanctification that is described in Hebrews 10:14. Sin is no longer real just as Lucifer is no longer real. Sin has changed its identity into being nothing. This means that God in no longer putting actual sin into our record book or charging it against us as we have described. Paul said, "Blessed is the man to whom the Lord shall not impute sin" (Romans 4:8).

The other two possibilities also could be and are likely true about this verse. John is not talking about the natural man that we know can sin. John is talking about the born-again spirit that is a new creation in Christ. The born-again spirit cannot sin as a born-again person, but the fleshly nature of a man can sin and does. Are these two different realities? We have heard that even Paul admitted that he did what he hated. Nevertheless, he described that it was no longer him, but sin that dwelt within him (Romans 7:14-25). John was only talking about the man that is born again, but not the flesh that is not born again. Paul mentioned in (Romans 8:29-32) that the body is still waiting for redemption and salvation.

The last theological possibility is that John is talking about sin as a lifestyle habit and not a fault that someone is overtaken with. Whichever perspective that we have is true based on a scripture that can be found somewhere. But the whole argument that a born- again believer can be damned in the end because of sin is thrown out of the entire debate room by these verses alone! Sin cannot be in a believer's life just like Satan is here but is no longer Lucifer. His identity changed. He is not Lucifer. He was Lucifer. He doesn't have the position he had in heaven to exist as who and what he was! In the seventh chapter of the book of Romans, Paul explained that our relationship with the law is the same as a widows' relationship with a husband that is deceased. He said that the widow is free to remarry and that she has not committed any adultery if her husband is dead. He then explains that we are delivered from the law that could count us as transgressors.

I'll give you an illustration. A man who does mass murder because of his hatred of a specific group of people as we have recently seen in America is considered a murderer. He goes to the Lake of fire and brimstone based on Revelation 21:8. The people who do these things do not belong to Christ at all and they may profess it, but it's a false profession. Christ said, "They are of their Father the devil and they'll do the lusts of their father. He was a murderer from the beginning and a liar" (John 8:44). There are specific types of acting out that Christians cannot do.

Aside from believers not being able to do the most horrific and terrible crimes against society, they cannot live their lives upon the earth for Satan. He cannot even have an attitude of hatred toward other people, Our works don't justify us or save us, but works still show whether we belong to Christ or the Devil! John also said these words, "Whoever hates his brother is a murderer and we know that no murderer has any eternal life abiding in him" (I John 3:15).

What the Holiness preacher is saying

There will be a radical difference between the life of a Christian and that of an unbeliever or someone who isn't born again. The Holy Ghost will set the believer apart. Jesus said, "Let your light so shine before men that they see your good works and glorify your Father in heaven" (Matthew 5:16). The believer's works don't save him, but they are the fruit that the Holy Ghost produces in his life. His works shall reveal that he has been justified! God shall sanctify those that he justified. This sanctification shall be imperfect in this life, but he shall be perfectly sanctified at glorification. Christ himself shall acquit him on that day, but he shall also announce to the world what the believer's works are to showcase to all what he manifested in their lives to reveal that they belonged to him!

Justified by faith and not by works

A person is justified, when he is approved of God as free from guilt of sin and it's deserved punishment, as having a righteousness belonging to him that entitles him to the reward of eternal life. The Judge accepts the justified person as having both a positive righteousness belonging to him and looks on him as not only free from any obligation to punishment, but also as just and righteous and so entitled to a reward. This is the meaning of the word.

The believers' justification not only implies the removal of sins, or the acquittal from the wrath due to it, but also an admittance to a title to that glory which is the reward of righteousness. Paul makes this evident when he says, "Therefore being justified by faith, we have peace with God through our Lord Jesus Christ, by whom also we have access into this grace wherein we stand and rejoice in hope of the glory of God" (Romans 5:1-2). We have peace with God and hope of glory because our faith in his body that was nailed to the cross for us took our sins away.

Paul says it like this to the Church of Rome, "But to him that works not, but believes on him that justifies the ungodly, his faith is counted for his righteousness" (Romans 4:5). This justification is given to a man that is considered ungodly. The same law that counted men as transgressors is the law that wipes your sin out of existence when the blood of a perfect sacrifice is shed for him or her. He takes the entire list of charges that were proven against them and nails it to the cross (Colossians 2;14).

The Amplified Bible puts it like this, "But to the one who does not work (that is, the one who does not try to earn his salvation by doing good) but believes and completely trusts in him who justifies the ungodly, his faith is credited to him as righteousness (right standing with God)" (Romans 4:5). Once God has removed the guilt and wrath of God away from the sinner, he won't leave the sinner in his condition. God promises, "I will put my laws in their hearts, and I will write them on their minds" (Hebrews 10:16). God works on the inside of an individual's heart to start the process of remodeling his life. He is justified by faith alone, but he will change in terms of how he conducts himself and behaves. He lives a lifestyle that emulates his faith in Christ and his love for God!

11

The paradox in Paul's dissertation

Paul did not retract any of his statements or any of these contradictory positions throughout his ministry. He was aware of the
inconsistency. The letter to the Romans was carefully constructed and
put together by Paul when he was mature in ministry. These widely
different perspectives on such a serious matter as standing before God
must somehow synthesize with one another. The Word of God reveals
to us as to how this cohesion occurs.

When we seek synthesis of any paradox, we must listen to all of the
biblical revelation and make sure that we avoid either one side of Paul's
teaching on the issue. Both statements that was cited are issues that God
will deal with on the day of judgment. Keep in mind that the Protestant
Reformation was about the Reformers coming to an agreement that
believers shall stand at the final judgment by a righteousness given by
faith alone as a gift. The righteousness that saves us is the righteousness
of Christ that is imputed to us as a gift at conversion. The Lutherans
and the Calvinist broke from Catholicism and taught what Augustine
taught that justification is the work of God alone by teaching, "If salvation is by grace, it is no longer by works, otherwise grace, is no longer
grace" (Romans 11:5). Paul was the primary scriptural witness to this
truth as taught by the Reformers.

We will look at the tension between two different schools of thought
and how one can wrestle with the relationship between "justification by faith" and a final judgment according to works. The idea is to

understand the message of the scriptures in its fullest without taking either side of a doctrine without accepting the truth about the other. This is an effort to see how the scriptures affirm the thesis of both and how the scriptures show the resolution of what was thought to be an apparent contradiction. The solutions are in Paul's letters, but it encompasses the whole of scriptures too. We find that other elements of the biblical witness as taught by Jesus and the other apostles affirm Paul's teaching, but they also reveal more about the eschaton.

Rewards at the final judgement

Paul mentioned, "God shall judge the secrets of men according to my gospel, through Christ Jesus" (Romans 2:16). Paul had spoken of a final justification according to works within his gospel of justification apart from works. We, therefore, cannot escape the tension within these thoughts. How do we look or interpret those passages which indicate that the believers who practice certain things shall not inherit the kingdom of God?

We see Paul teaching two thoughts. He taught, "Knowing that a man is not justified by the works of the law but by faith in Jesus Christ, even we believed in Christ Jesus, that we might be justified by faith in Christ and not by the works of the law; for by the works of the law no flesh shall be justified" (Galatians 2:15, King James Version). The verse is teaching that it doesn't matter how great your works are with keeping the rule of God's laws that you cannot be considered just and righteous by doing so.

Paul also taught, "For this you know, that no whoremonger, nor unclean person, nor covetous man, who is an idolater, hath any inheritance in the kingdom of Christ and of God. Let no man deceive you with vain words: for because of these things comes the wrath of God upon the children of disobedience" (Ephesians 5:5-6). Can you see how that it's by the faith of Jesus and not the keeping God's law that justifies us, but also how the scriptures teach that if one does not do the works that the wrath of God comes on the disobedient? How do we reconcile the two? Could it be that the disobedient were not born-again or that God sees the believer different pertaining to his law than the unbeliever? Is it possible that a righteous lifestyle follows our faith after repentance and that if it doesn't that this means that we were not converted?

A solution to the great paradox

One attempt to solve the great mystery is to draw a distinction between final salvation and reward. Final salvation is secured by Christ for the believer once and for all. The latter is dependent on us obeying God. In this scenario all of the biblical texts that speak of justification being by faith alone keep their validity. The texts that speak of judgment by works also keep their full force as we learn yet another lesson taught in the scripture. The judgement of works that Paul spoke of entails reward for faithful service, but also a passing through fire to burn up the deplorable works.

Paul referenced to the one saved "yet as through fire" in I Corinthians 3:10-17 which shows that he was aware of deficient service within the church, which will be exposed and consumed at the final judgment, ending in the bare salvation of some after having their works burned up. He mentioned how that some had built wood, hay, and stubble on the foundation. He said that others had built gold, silver, and precious stones on the foundation.

This scripture teaches us that men shall have a judgment of works and that works which are not approved of shall be tested by fire and burned up, but the final salvation of the believer shall stand. Paul said it like this to the Church of Corinth, "Every man's work shall be made manifest: for the day shall declare it, because it shall be revealed by fire; and the fire shall try every man's work of what sort it is. If any man's work abides which he has built thereupon, he shall receive a reward. If any man's work shall be burned, he shall suffer loss: but he himself shall be saved; yet so as by fire" (I Corinthians 3:13-15). Did we see that? God saves the individual but burns up his unsatisfactory works instead of giving him a reward for them!

Scholars may not all agree on whether Paul is talking about the works of Christian leaders in this text or of all believers, but we know that all believers shall appear to have works judged at the judgment seat of Christ. Paul described this by saying, "For we all must appear before the judgement seat of Christ; that everyone may receive the things done in his body, according to that he hath done, whether it be good or bad" (2 Corinthians 5:10). The works that Paul is referring to is work of ministry or any other work that men have done in the body.

Paul did not make such distinctions about the final judgment in other passages and left the details undefined. In some passages he made it clear that people who practice certain things shall not inherit the kingdom of God. He indicated in some passages that there was a danger of final condemnation for empty labor or works that did not to a practical righteousness and a lived- out holiness. We find Paul saying in Ephesians 5:5-6 that we know that no whoremonger, nor unclean person, nor covetous man, who is an idolater, hath any inheritance in the kingdom of Christ and God. Let no man deceive you with vain words and that the because of these things the wrath of God comes on the children of disobedience!

Could it be that Paul is talking about the unsaved that are lost that were not forgiven or the professing believer that never actually got saved or born again? We find that all believers appear before the judgement seat of Christ and that the works of believers that are not pure will be burned up, but they'll be saved. We can also find an entire thesis spoken of by Jesus and Paul of people in the visible church the profess Christ who are among true believers, but Christ said about the false professions of faith that he never knew them and that their end is a furnace of fire (Matthew 7:21-24, Matthew 13:24-30). Paul mentioned that there was false apostles and deceitful workers, transforming themselves into the apostles of Christ. But also, that Satan transformed himself into an angel of light and his ministers as the ministers of righteousness, but that their end would be according to their works in 2 Corinthians 11:13-15. These are apostles and prophets that never belonged to him.

Justification and final judgement

The original paradoxical juxtaposition of forgiveness secured by sacrifice and the requirement for absolute obedience reappears throughout the New Testament. We find that the biblical demand and the biblical promise have been fulfilled in one person. The Son offered up his body as a sacrifice, once and for all. Paul explained by saying, "For by one offering, he has perfected forever them that are sanctified" (Hebrews 10:14). In him, and in Christ alone, this tension within the scriptures finds it's coherence and unity. We find the resolution between justification by faith alone and the final judgment according to works in Christ alone. Let us dig deeper to see the synthesis in Christ.

The truth revealed in the Book of Hebrews

The Hebrew writer said, "For by one offering he hath perfected forever those who are being sanctified" (Hebrews 10:14, King James Bible). What did he mean? He meant that in Christ we are sanctified because of his work by being crucified for us at the cross! This is the way that God sees us as being perfected before him. It's our faith. Everyone who has trusted Christ as Savior has been set apart by God through what he did at the cross. The key word in this verse is the word one. The one sacrifice of Christ was to atone for all sin of all time! The same law that required obedience also made it law those sins were obliterated when blood was shed for them.

The Hebrew writer mentioned in this chapter that the sacrifices made by the priest in the Old Covenant happened every year and that they did not make the sinners perfect. However, that Christ's made one sacrifice once and for all (Hebrews 10:10). The one sacrifice of Jesus Christ for our sins was for all of time and for all of the sin of his sheep to come. Christ paid the price for all of time- and wiped-out sin completely so that we can have a full pardon of all sin.

The words "perfected forever" speaks of the permanent status that believers have once they are forgiven. The pardon was not just for sins that are past, but for everything for every year of their lifetimes. This is what his sacrifice did! Sin has been completely wiped out as something that can be charged against the true believer in Christ and that is how he perfected them forever by his one sacrifice at the cross! How could they be condemned or sentenced to Hell?

We could never have been sanctified and made holy through our own good works or merit. However, this doesn't change God's immutable holiness which expects the same of all. God did not forgive us and then count us as holy and sanctified through our own vain efforts to keep the requirements of the law or because of our tradition to be sanctified. We are set apart, consecrated, and sanctified for God by Christ's substitutionary offering, made one time at the cross to put away all sin and forever. Our positional sanctification is permanent. Forever means forever!

Let's look at this 10th chapter of the Book of Hebrews closer. Many have used it to explain how one of God's sheep could lose his salvation. Does this chapter even teach that this is this even possible? In Hebrews chapter one and verse one it mentions that the sacrifices in the Old Testament that were made year by year could never make the sinners perfect. We find in verse 2 that the sacrifices did not cleanse the conscience of the sinner.

The writer mentions in verse 3 that there was a remembrance of sins made by the offerings each year and in verse 4 we'll find that it wasn't possible that the blood of bulls and goats could take away sins. Keep in mind as we read this that God is going to do away with sin by his plan to bring his Son to earth to do what the sacrifices of bulls and goats could not do! Christ is coming to take sin away! We find in the book of Hebrews in chapter 10 and verse 5 that Christ is saying that a body was prepared for him to come into the world to take sin away!

We find in verse 7 that Christ came to do the will of God. Why is this important to know? We need to know what God's will is when it comes to taking sin away. He takes sin away by the sacrifice made to satisfy his justice and his wrath for the sin in order that he may throw the guilt, condemnation, and record of sin away. What satisfied God? God is the one who has to say that you are not guilty and holy before him? What is the basis for him making that declaration and viewing us as his holy ones? Could it be that our progress toward a practical holiness in this life is only the beginning and that our progress was never intended to achieve what Christ has already achieved?

The Hebrew writer says these words about the sacrifice of Jesus for us at the cross, "And by that will we are sanctified through the offering of the body of Jesus Christ once and for all" (Hebrews 10:10). The sacrifice that Jesus made for us was "once" and for all sin for all of time. He views his believers as being sanctified and holy because of the death and blood of his son that has set them apart from the reality that sin can be charged against them.

They receive a full pardon for all sin because of the one offering of Christ that took away sin once and for all of time. There is no other sacrifice of anyone of anything that will need to be made next year or during any year to take any sin away again. Therefore Jesus said at the cross, "It is finished" (John 19:30). This is a term that means that something is paid in full.

We can now look again at verse 14 that says, "For by one offering he hath perfected forever them that are sanctified" (Hebrews 10:14). What Christ did for us cannot be undone. All sin has been removed and thrown away and that's why God sees us as being perfected forever and sanctified or set apart. Please notice what he says in verse 17, "There sins and iniquities will I remember no more" (Hebrews 10:17). God no longer holds a score sheet to count or charge the believer of a sin. Therefore it's not possible to sin. He took the laws that proved us a sinner and nailed them to the cross with the charges against us (Colossians

2:14). Some say it wasn't the law and only the charges, but others say it was both. In either case it still means that sin is gone.

But since God still wants us to do righteousness, he has done something different to help us that he had never did before. He says, "I will put my laws into their hearts, and in their minds will I write them" (Hebrews 10:16). Men who are believers don't sin. But they can and will do righteousness because God has written his law within them. This is his work and his doing and not that of our own. He is the potter, and we are the clay. We are the work of his hand. The pot cannot shape itself.

Now we can come to verse 18 and this says, "Now where remission of these is, there is no more offering of sin" (Hebrews 10:17). God has permanently removed all of guiltiness and condemnation for sin away by nailing the entire list of ordinances proven against us to the cross. The Colossians author put it like this, "He canceled the record of charges against us and took it away by nailing it to the cross" (Colossians 2:14, New Living Translation). Keep in mind that the Hebrew writer had declared that we have been perfected forever and sanctified by his offering at the cross. Therefore, no other sacrifice for sin is needed for any future sin. He paid our entire debt of sin off once and for all (Hebrews 10:10). The one sacrifice was for everything that you would do and there would be no need for him to be sacrificed again or for any other sacrifice made.

Why do we go to heaven? Look at the next verse. The Hebrew writer says, "Having therefore, brethren, boldness to enter into the holiest by the blood of Jesus" (Hebrews 10:18). It is his blood that gives us the right to enter by prayer into the holiest place to communicate with God. But it's only by his blood that we can be justified before God on that day. Again, "Being now justified by his blood, we shall be saved from wrath through him" (Romans 5:9).

Now let us come to one of most misunderstood or misinterpreted scriptures in the Bible. Look at verse 26. The Hebrew writer says, "For if we sin willfully after that we have received the knowledge of the truth, there remains no more sacrifice for sins, but a certain fearful looking for judgment and fiery indignation, which shall devour the adversaries" (Hebrews 10:27-27). What was the author talking about? Why is there no more sacrifice for sin, but only a looking for judgment if a person does willful sin? What type of willful sin is the author talking about?

The author explains the interpretation of his statement in the next verses. But looking back at the chapter it's clear that he is talking about the specific type of willful sin that entails rejecting Christ's offering and his sacrifice as the only way for one to be forgiven and saved. We know this because of the context of the entire chapter. He says, "We are sanctified through the offering of the body of Jesus once and for all" (Hebrews 10:10). He says that this is a permanent sanctification based on the finished works of Christ when he says, "For by one offering he hath perfected forever them that are sanctified" (Hebrews 10:14). What part of being perfected forever by Christ's offering could be so difficult to understand?

Why then does the Hebrew writer say that if we sin willfully that there remains no more sacrifice for sins? Why does he mention that the willful sinner can only look forward to judgment for the adversaries of Christ? The Bible explains in the next verses by saying, "He that despised Moses' law died without mercy under two or three witnesses. Or much sorer punishment, suppose ye, shall he be thought worthy, who hath trodden under foot the Son of God, and has counted the blood of the covenant, wherewith he was sanctified, an unholy thing, and hath done despite the spirit of grace" (Hebrews 10:27-29). The willful sin is described as someone rejecting Christ and his blood as the only offering and counting his sacrifice for them as being some-thing unholy!

The author is describing the willful sin of people who reject the sacri-fice of Christ and his blood. However, he also explains that the Hebrews that he addresses the letter to are not those people. He explained that they are not the ones who draw to a way like this. Consequently, you should not think that God's people are. He says, "Now the just shall live by faith: but if any man draws back, my soul shall have no pleasure in him. But we are not of them who draw back unto perdition; but of them that believe to the saving of the soul" (Hebrews 10:38-39). The author explains that there are some who do draw back into the perdition of being damned in the end, but that they as Hebrews were not of them who did draw back! Keep believing that you are sanctified by the blood of Jesus! He died once and for all of your sins (Hebrews 10:10).

The Believer and Paul's thesis about the Final Judgment

Paul understood that the gospel had the power to save because the righteousness of God had already been revealed in it. The day of judgment has been brought into the present from a future reality. Christ has been crucified and risen. He was crucified for us and our transgressions. He was raised from the dead for our justification on the day of judgement (Romans 4;25). For those who believe in Jesus, God has come to us from the day of judgement to vindicate his charge against us. Christ is the justifier of him who has faith in Jesus (Romans 3:26). God's righteousness is ours through Christ by faith (Romans 1:17, Romans 3:22). The justification of the sinner is also the justification of God in his wrath against the sinner. The penalty for his sin was laid on Jesus Christ at the cross.

For the believer judgment has already passed even though it is yet to come. Paul spoke of Christ's cross in this way, 'For through the law died to the Law. I have been crucified with Christ. I live, but it is no longer I, rather Christ lives in me. What I now live in the flesh. I live by faith in the Son of God, who loved me, and gave himself for me" (Galatians 2:19-20). Our obedience to Christ as believers presupposes that our old life has been judged and condemned at the cross. Paul was not saying that the eschaton or glorification had come, but that Christ's resurrection is projected and attributed to our present: "We have been buried with him through baptism into his death so that just as Christ was raised from the dead, so we might walk in a newness of life" (Romans 6:4). Christ came out of eternity and into time when he wrapped himself up in a human body. He brought condemnation and judgement that we deserved in an eternity to come into a past to give his sacrificial death an eternal impact on the eternity of believers.

When Paul spoke of newness, he has in view the entrance of the age to come into the present world. Paul mentioned, "If any man be in Christ, he is a new creature and old things have passed away with all things having become new" (2 Corinthians 5:17). The newness of life in which believers walk is a reality that comes from beyond the final judgment, from the life of the age to come. The works of a believer cannot be reduced to a condition of obtaining entrance into the age to come. His or her works are the reality of the age to come that have penetrated through their flesh into the present in and by Jesus Christ. The righteousness of Christ in us that was given to us as a gift does the work, but our own work doesn't work the work. As Paul put it, "Being confident of this very thing, he that has begun a good work in us will perform it until the day of Jesus Christ" (Philippians 1:6).

Justification is a judgment and eschatological verdict

Does it matter if we are justified based on Christ's work and our faith in it or based on a future justification by works? Does justification have two stages that entails an initial justification based on the righteousness of Christ alone and a future justification based in part on good works? If such a distinction of justification is required, how can we avoid the conclusion that the present justification of believers is a form of probation and that our final justification is based on a future event in which God's justifying verdict is announced based on our lifetime of works? If the justification of believers is based on a future justification by works, then believers can never be assured now or know for certain that they are irrevocably right with God. If the grace of God and the righteousness of Christ is not the exclusive reason for our acceptance with God, now and for the future, then believers cannot know for sure that have eternal life in Christ.

Acquitted

The idea of a future justification or condemnation based on works undermines that God will have unmerited favor or grace. A final judgment that is the believers' final stage of justification is the equivalent of saying that we shall ultimately be justified by grace plus works. Nevertheless, this undermines the eschatological character of justification. Paul said it like this, "Much more then, having been justified by his blood, we shall be saved from wrath through him" (Romans 5:9).

Paul mentioned that since we were reconciled to him by the death of his son while we were God's enemies, how much more, having been reconciled, shall we be saved through his life (Romans 5:8, 5:10). Paul reiterated the point here that in Christ we are justified, but this means also that we are acquitted and shall be saved from the wrath of God to come! Keep this in mind. Paul is teaching that our justification before God is based on the blood of Jesus Christ that was shed for us and that because of that we'll be saved from the wrath of God to come!

What shall the final judgment disclose

Whenever someone views the final judgment as the final stage of the believer's justification it amounts to saying that believers will be justified by grace plus works. However, the scriptures reveal a language that does not speak of a justifying verdict in the end which ultimately determines that we are declared right with God based solely or in part by our own works of righteousness. The Word of God does not suggest that the assurance of God's favor in Christ is merely provisional and will depend on merit, nor that it is not yet secure or certain. The final judgment openly manifests to all what is already known to believers by faith: The Judge, Jesus Christ, who acquits them for all of their known sin in the final judgment has already been judged in their place and he is their righteousness before God.

The resurrection of Christ confirmed the sufficiency and perfection of his atoning sacrifice for sin, but he will also open acquit believers at the final judgment by publicly confirming their free justification by faith in Christ alone. Paul said it to the Romans like this, "He was raised because of our justification" (Romans 4:25) This indicates that our judgment broke out of eternity and into the past and was laid on Christ at the cross! Paul says to the Church of Rome, "Who shall bring a charge against God's elect? It is God who justifies. Who is he who condemns? It is Christ that died, and is risen, who is even at the right hand of God, who also makes intercession for us" (Romans 8:33-34, New King James Version).

The final judgement will also have an open acknowledgement of those whose faith in Christ was not a dead faith or a faith without works. We see in James 2:14-26 that faith is accompanied by good works. On the day of judgment, the open acknowledgement of believers includes granting them rewards according to or in proportion to their good works. It is to be remembered and understood that the works that we eventually walk in were prepared by Christ himself beforehand for us to walk in them (Ephesians 2:10).

God is giving us more grace by acknowledging our works with rewards because he had foreordained things for us to be able to do the good works that we do. Many scriptures reveal a final judgment of works for the believer, but they never acknowledge or reveal that the works shall be the cause of their justification (Matthew 12:36, 2 Corinthians 5:10, Revelation 20:11-15). Paul said it like this to the Galatians, "Knowing that a man in not justified by the works of the law but by the faith of Jesus Christ, even when we believed in Christ Jesus, that we might be justified by the faith in Christ and not by the works of the law; for by the works of the law no flesh shall be justified in his sight" (Galatians 2:16).

God will reward the imperfect works of believers, but this reward depends on a fundamental truth that believers are already made right with him based on the perfect righteousness of Christ. The reward that is granted is not the gift of eternal life. Believers that have repented already have eternal life now! The judgment will confirm that although faith is why God justifies them that their faith is not alone but is always accompanied in time by works through those whom he also sanctifies. Know this, "For he hath made him to be sin for us, who knew no sin; that we might be made the righteousness of God in him" (2 Corinthians 5:21). Christ was made sin for us, and we are declared righteous and not guilty because he wiped out all our of debt of sin and was crucified to pay the penalty as our surety or guarantee (Hebrews 7:22).

Separating the sheep and the goat

The Grace of God can be seen in Christ's parable of how he'll separate the sheep from the goat at the final judgment. He says to his sheep, "Come, you who are blessed of my Father, inherit the kingdom prepared for you from the foundation of the world. For I was hungry, and you gave me food, I was thirsty, and you gave me drink, I was a stranger, and you took me in and welcomed me, I was naked and you clothed me, I was sick and in prison and you came to me" (Matthew 25:34-36). Jesus compared this final judgement to a King who gathers his flock to separate the sheep from the goat. The sheep are identified and rewarded for the works they did and how they treated the least of them. They enter his kingdom, but the goat who did not do these things go into everlasting fire that was prepared for the devil and his angels.

Foreordained inheritance

This may look like a judgment of works until we read these words, "Come, you blessed by my Father, inherit the kingdom prepared for you from the foundation of the world" (Matthew 25:34-36). Jesus noted that their inheritance of the kingdom was prepared for them from the foundation of the world in Matthew 25:34. God knew who these sheep were and sent his Son to die for them in time. This type of language is also taught by Jesus in other parts of the book of Matthew where Jesus taught that his servants enter his kingdom by God's grace and forgiveness, not by their own merits or accomplishments (Matthew 5:3, Matthew 6:12, Matthew 18:23-25, Matthew 19:25).

Let's take the parable of the servants that owed their King a debt and could not pay him as our example. The servants worked for the King, but their works did not add up to everything that they owed him, and they only entered the kingdom because he forgave their debts. When Jesus spoke that parable, he makes the point that it was a parable about the kingdom of heaven. The fact that the kingdom was prepared for the sheep in advance of the foundation of the world being laid indicates divine favor and a blessing that was determined beforehand. The was due to both divine foreknowledge and divine sovereignty. This was also due to an everlasting love that God said that he loved us with (Jeremiah 31:3). Jacob was picked for his inheritance before he or his brother Esau was born and prior to them deciding to do good or evil, but so that the doctrine of election would stand to be based on him who calls us (Romans 9:9-13).

We also find Paul explaining the predestination of grace to Timothy, "Who saved us and called us with a holy calling, not according to works, but according to his own purpose and grace which was given to us in Christ Jesus before the world began" (2 Timothy 1:9). God gave us the gift to be who and what we turn out to be in this life and in the next one, but before he lays the foundation of the world! Over time we will become what he intended for us to be. This is our responsibility, but don't forget that God is in control and working out things in us and through us (Phil 2,13, Phil 1:6).

Even though the final judgment rewards the sheep and the goat in this passage according to their works, the statement of Jesus about how the kingdom was prepared for them beforehand mitigates against the idea that he meant this passage to mean that the sheep are saved based on their works. The big difference between the sheep and the goat lies in their relationship to Jesus. By showing the love and kindness to the least of Jesus' brothers, the sheep showed by their works that they had love for him. They did not do what they did out of fear of punishment or the promise of a reward for Christ!

They asked him as to when did they show him such love and kindness. God's people may do many things and forget them, but the works were not prompted out of fear of a final condemnation or a promise of reward from Jesus. The deeds of the sheep simply confirmed their confession that Jesus was their Lord by their works it showed who they belonged to. Jesus said these words, "Let your light so shine before men that they may see your good works and glorify your Father which is in heaven" (Matthew 5:16).

The relationship between justification and a final judgment show that believers will have their works tested in the fire and even if he suffers loss, he will himself be saved. He will be acquitted based on Christ being judged and condemned for him at the cross. The believers' confidence that there is now no condemnation for them that are in Christ as stated in Romans 8:1 should not be shaken by the reality of the final judgment. In this day of judgement, believers who trust in Christ alone for their righteousness will be openly acquitted before God. The open acknowledgement and reward of the believers' work shall reveal to all the genuine nature of their faith. Faith will always produce the fruit of good works, but the good works don't save them or justify them on that day. Christians are encouraged to know that their good works and faithfulness will be rewarded one day when Christ shall say to them, "Well done, good and faithful servant, thou hast been faithful over a few things, I will make you ruler over many things. Enter into the joy of the Lord" (Matthew 25:21).

The letter to Rome was carefully designed and put together by Paul in his maturity. These two different perspectives on the issue of us standing before God to be judged by works and being justified by faith alone can cohere with each other. How do they exist with each other? Solomon spoke of the judgment by saying, "For God shall bring every work into judgment with every secret thing, whether it be good, or whether it be evil" (Ecclesiastes 12:14). It looks like that God will judge men based on their works in this text.

What will this judgment look like for the believer? I think we have just satisfied the question. Works shall be tried by fire and burned up, but leaving the believer saved after losing a reward. Rewards will be granted due to faithfulness of works. Rewards will be lost at the judgment of works, but he himself shall be saved. The final acquittal of the true believer that is born again shall take place. A public showcase of the good works of true believers will be manifested before all. Many different types of crowns will also be given for different aspects of faithfulness in works to the believer that did not suffer loss!

The Five Heavenly Crowns for believers

The believers that do not suffer a loss of reward will receive one of five different types of crowns for faithfulness. The New Testament explains that these are the crown of glory, the crown of rejoicing, the crown of righteousness, the imperishable crown, and the crown of life. The Greek word translated for crown is *stephanos* (the source of the name Stephen) and it means a badge of royalty. This was a prize in a public game and a symbol of honor. This was placed on the victors' head as a symbol of a reward for winning an athletic contest.

An entire book could be written about the five heavenly crowns, but I want to briefly explain what the crown of righteousness is awarded for. It's not about us having our own righteousness. The scripture says, "There is none righteous, no, not one" (Romans 3:10. We also find these words written in scripture, "The law was given that every mouth be stopped and so that the whole world stands guilty before God' (Romans 3:19). How or why then is the crown of righteousness awarded?

Paul said these words, "And be found in him, not having my own righteousness, which is from the law, but that which is through the faith in Christ, the righteousness of God by faith" (Philippians 3:9). Paul only saw himself as being righteous because of his faith in Christ being crucified for him which wiped out his entire debt of sin that he owed to God. Christ paid the penalty for his sin, and he also kept the conditions of the law during his lifetime as his surety.

Paul said these words when he spoke to the Corinthian Church, "For we all must appear before the judgment seat of Christ; that everyone may receive the things done in his body, according to that he hath done, whether it be good or bad" (2 Corinthians 5:10). Jesus said these words, "And behold, I come quickly; and my reward is with me, to give every man according as his work shall be" (Revelation 22:12). Will Christ reward good and bad works?

Christ said these stern words to the Church of Thyatira, "And I gave her space to repent of her fornication; and she repented not. Behold, I will cast her into a bed, and them that commit adultery with her into great tribulation, except they repent of their deeds. And I will kill her children with death, and all the churches shall know that I am he which searches the reins and hearts: and I will give unto every one of you according to your works" (Revelation 2:21-23). This is tough! He also said to the Church of Laodicea, "I know your works, that you are neither cold nor hot. So then, because you are lukewarm, and neither cold nor hot, I will vomit you out of my mouth" (Revelation 3:15-16).

Christ then says to the same church that although they had a testimony that they were rich and increased with goods that they did not know that they were wretched, pitiful, poor, blind, and naked. He then advised them to buy from him gold that was refined in the fire in order to become rich and white clothes to wear to cover the shame of their nakedness with something to put on their eyes so that they could see. He then says to them, "As many as I love, I rebuke and chasten be zealous therefore, and repent" (Revelation 3:19). Why did Christ rebuke this church and why did he tell them that he would vomit them out of his mouth? Was this a judgment based on works or a scolding based on how they were doing things? We may not know for sure, but we know what he told them to do. Repent!

Paul explicitly includes a final justification according to works within his gospel of justification apart from works. Nevertheless, in seeking a biblical synthesis, we must be sure to listen to all of the biblical evidence and avoid diluting either of the Pauline statements we have cited or any other revelation in the scriptures. Paul later affirmed that justification is a gift given to faith, which prompted the Protestant reformation. The Reformers, whether Lutheran or Calvinist, came to understand that believers shall stand at the final judgment by a righteousness given to faith alone as a gift. In other words, the righteousness that saves us is found outside of us in Jesus Christ, incarnate, crucified for us, and risen. This departed from Catholic tradition that the initial gift of justification had to increase and grow internally into satisfactory works for the believer to attain a final salvation in the end.

Paul often spoke of how that the men who are justified do not practice certain things and warned that the that the ones who did practice certain things would not enter the kingdom. This paralleled also to things that Jesus said. Paul says, "For this ye know, that no whoremonger, nor unclean person, nor covetous man, who is an idolater, hath any inheritance in the kingdom of Christ and of God" (Ephesians 5:5). The book of Revelation says, "Blessed are they that do his commandments, that they may have right to the tree of life and may enter in through the gates into the city. For without are dogs, and sorcerers, and whoremongers, and murderers, and idolaters, and whosoever loveth and makes a lie. I, Jesus, have sent mine angel to testify these things in the churches. I am the root and offspring of David, and the bright and morning star" (Revelation 22:14-16)

We must accept the truth about the reality of us being justified and declared righteous as a free gift from God based on grace alone, but also that Christ wants to church to know the types of people that will not enter through the gates into the city of heaven. Could it be that because the men or women who did these things had their sins forgiven and blotted out that they are now perfected forever because of that one sacrifice of the body of Jesus? (Hebrews 10:14) Can we look at this last thing from this last chapter in the Word of God and ignore that Christ himself was saying that certain types of people cannot enter heaven?

Keep in mind that the sin that the believer would commit in his lifetime has been judged and condemned already at the cross! Jesus said it like this, "He that believes on him that sent me has everlasting life and shall not be condemned but has passed from death to life" (John 5:24). How can we be acquitted at the final judgment and pronounced "not guilty" because of Christ's sacrifice for us and still be in jeopardy of a final condemnation if we don't have the works?

What do we mean when we say that the believer is justified by faith alone? What is the scriptural basis for this doctrine? The word justification means to declare and pronounce righteous or just and not guilty of being a lawbreaker. Paul says to the Romans, "For when we were without strength in due time Christ died for the ungodly" (Romans 5:6). Why did Christ die for us? Paul goes on to explain how and we are justified, "But God commended his love to us, in that while we were yet sinners, Christ died for us. Much more then, being now justified by his blood, we shall be saved from wrath through him" (Romans 5:8-9). Did you notice here that Paul said that we are justified by his blood! When Christ was crucified, he paid for our debt of sin by shedding his blood for us. He did this to justify us before God and to acquit us of sin! Did you notice that Paul stated that we are saved from the wrath of God because we are justified by his blood?

Justification in the Word of God is a forensic act by which a believer is declared righteous. Justification is not a process by which a person is made righteous in the practical sense. He is not justified because his works have been righteous enough for God to see him as being righteous based on his own meritorious works of righteousness. "Forensic" means legal and involves the image of a courtroom. Justification involves a change in our status before God, but not a change of our nature!

Imputation of Righteousness

The cause of justification is the active righteousness and obedience of Christ to the law and his death and shedding of his blood which blotted out our entire record of sin. This is not righteousness that is poured into us of somehow infused in us, but righteousness that is imputed or reckoned to our account. Justification is an act of God and because it is based on the finished work of Christ, we can have assurance that we are saved.

Justification is also oriented toward the future. It is acquittal on the day of judgement because of what Christ did. Justification is the assurance in the present that the final verdict will be in our favor because of the blood of the Lamb! Paul said it like this to the Corinthians, "For he hath made him to be sin for us, who knew no sin; that we may be made the righteousness of God in him" (II Corinthians 5:21). Did you see that? Christ was made sin for you when he hung at the cross in your place! He was declared guilty at the cross for you! You are now declared righteous as a declaration by God! It's a divine exchange of his righteousness being transferred to your account in heaven and your record being nailed to him at the cross!

The Apostle Paul also mentioned that he did not have his own righteousness which came from keeping the law, but a righteousness based solely on the faith of Jesus. He said to the Church of the Philippians, "And be found in him, not having mine own righteousness, which is of the law, but that which is through the faith of Christ, the righteousness of God by faith" (Philippians 3:9). Paul knew that he could not be considered justified or righteous before God based on keeping the law, but that God declared men righteous based on their faith in Jesus being their justifier when their sin was nailed to the cross with him! Paul said to the Romans, "Blessed is the man to whom the Lord will not impute sin" (Romans 4:8) What does it mean that the Lord does not impute sin to a man? So according to theologians and the Bible God can lay or charge and reckon to our account whatever he chooses and however he chooses! God's thought makes is so! God is the arbitrator of the universe, and he decides whether to count sin against your record or to count your sins as being on Christ when he hung at the cross!

Our feeling that we are righteous one day and not righteous the next does not matter. What does matter is what God thinks! In the judicial and the theological sense of the word, to impute is to attribute anything to a person or persons, upon adequate grounds, as the judicial or meritorious reason for a reward or a punishment. You are blessed when God says that you are not guilty because of Christ crucified for you and that you are righteous on the basis of his righteousness given to you as a free gift! An even better example of imputation may be to think of something as belonging to someone else. As stated, when God thinks of us as righteous in Christ, his righteousness belongs to us in his sight. The Word of God says, "My thoughts are not your thoughts. As the heavens are higher than the earth, so are my ways higher than your ways and my thoughts than your thoughts" (Isaiah 55:8-9).

We cannot we establish our own righteousness

Many have continued to believe that somehow, we will need our own righteousness based on us keeping laws for God to see us as being just and righteous before him. Paul says these words to the Romans, "For I bear them record that they have a zeal of God, but not according to knowledge. For they being ignorant of God's righteousness, and going about to establish their own righteousness, have not submitted themselves to unto the righteousness of God. For Christ is the end of the law for righteousness to everyone that believeth" (Romans 10:2-4).

What does all of this mean? God doesn't impute sin to us. He doesn't count us a lawbreaker once we have the faith in Christ Jesus. It's God who decides if or when he will count something as sin in his record book. God decided that the New Covenant would simply be that he counts us a having met the requirements of the law pertaining to righteousness when we believe Jesus Christ died and rose for us and then trust him for our salvation!

So, by now we can see why the Reformers taught that we are justified by faith alone. It wasn't to suggest that the Holy Ghost doesn't work the work of sanctification in our lives. We know that the believer will live a new life in Christ empowered and led by the Spirit. We also know that sanctification is the work of the Holy Ghost, and a radical transformation will take place in this life. However, the saint will not merit has salvation based on his sanctification.

His works shall follow his faith and they'll be the evidence that he loves God and has a relationship with Christ. But his works that arise out of the work of the Holy Spirit in him to sanctify him doesn't justify him or make him righteous enough to earn eternal life or heaven. Paul said it like this to the Galatians, "I do not frustrate the grace of God: for if righteousness came the law, then Christ is dead in vain" (Galatians 3:21). If it were possible for us to be just or righteous to God based on our own merit or our own work of sanctification, then Christ is dead in vain. Keep in mind too that the Word of God teaches that we are holy and sanctified in Christ based on the works of Christ at the cross. As the Hebrew author said it, "For by one offering he has perfected forever them that are sanctified" (Hebrews 10:14).

Paul says to the Romans in his dissertation to them, "For all have sinned and come short of the glory of God. Being justified freely by his grace through the redemption that is in Christ Jesus. Whom God has set forth to be a propitiation through faith in his blood, to declare his righteousness for the remission of sins that are past, through the forbearance of God; to declare, I say, at this time his righteousness: that he might be just, and the justifier of him which believes on Jesus" (Romans 3:23-26).

Did you notice here that God is satisfied by faith in his blood for the removal of sins that were done which is how he justifies him that believes on Jesus? Paul says it like this in the next chapter when discussing justification, "But to him that works not, but believes on him that justifies the ungodly, his faith is counted as his righteousness" (Romans 4:5). We both may think someone is wrong about something and we may be right, but God justifies the ungodly based on their faith in his blood to remove their condemnation and grant to them eternal life! A person is justified, when he is approved of God as free from the guilt of sin and its deserved punishment and having that righteousness belonging to him that entitles him to the reward of eternal life. Sin was taken away in the body of Jesus and put on the cross. John the Baptist says this when he saw Jesus, "Behold the Lamb of God that takes away the sin of the world" (John 1:29).

12

The Marriage Supper of the Lamb

Remember, "As it is written, there is none righteous, no not one" (Romans 3:10). We won't be able to enter heaven on the basis of our own righteousness or our own garments that we wear to the marriage, but only by the robe of righteousness that he furnished and provided to the guests to wear to the supper (Matthew 22:2-14, Revelation 19:6-9). This is the faith of Jesus as we've seen. The Revelator says, "And to her was granted that she should be arrayed in fine linen, clean and white: for the fine linen is the righteousness of the saints. And he saith unto me, Write, blessed are they which are called unto the marriage supper of the Lamb. And he saith unto me, these are the true sayings of God" (Revelation 19:8-9).

How is the bride of Christ clothed in fine linen that is white? What is the righteousness of the saints? Notice why the robes where white earlier in this book. John says, "And I said unto him, Sir, thou knowest, And he said to me, These are they which came out of the great tribulation, and have washed their robes and made them white in the blood of the Lamb" (Revelation 7:14). As you ponder what all of this means keep in mind a parable that Jesus spoke about the kingdom of heaven and the King that forgave his servants. The servants did not have what was owed to the King and only escaped him wrath because they were forgiven (Matthew 18:23-35). What was to basis of their justification and their acquittal? It could not have been their works of righteousness if they were in debt as servants and didn't have the ability to pay what was owed!

In the Roman Catholic view, believers are always liable to the loss of justification through the commission of mortal sin, for those who "shipwrecked" through mortal sin, the only remedy for restoration to a state of grace is in the sacrament of penance. An example of penance would be to publicly try to make up for your misdeeds. Penance is an act of humility or devotion voluntarily to show sorrow for a sin or wrongdoing. This may include confessing the sin to a priest, acceptance of punishment, and absolution. It's a form of self-punishment intended to right a wrong or serve as a reparation for an act. You try to earn your forgiveness with penance. It's trying to make up for misdeeds by works.

Protestant theologians have also proposed similar distinctions between different stages of justification—past, present, and future. Writers have become proponents of a "new perspective on Paul," believers "get into" salvation by grace, but "stay in" and are ultimately vindicated by their works. These theologians teach Romans 2:14-16 and many other passages of scripture including Jesus' own parables to mean that our "future justification" will be based on a lifetime of faithfulness. Others teach that the works that Christians produce are in some way instrumental to a Christians' final justification. Instead of viewing faith as the instrument God's uses to justify us because of what Christ did to save us, they insist that the obedience that comes after faith is the way our justification is received and that these works of obedience makes us righteous and just. According, they teach that justification pronounced at the final judgment will be granted only to those that maintained a just standing by persevering in obedience.

Before I review the the final judgment according to works again, we should ask ourselves some tough questions. Does a final judgment of the believer that is based on works mean that his salvation is based on grace plus works or at least in part due to his own works of righteousness? Is the future justification of the believer on the day of judgment based on the meritorious works of the person justified? Is it possible for the believer to have works that are non-meritorious of salvation, but that are a cause for him to be the recipient of some other reward or acknowledgement on that day?

If the justification of believers is ultimately based on his works in his lifetime that justifies him on a future day of judgment, believers can never know for sure that they are definitely and irrevocably right with God. If the righteousness of Christ and him living the life as our surety and being crucified to justify us is not the exclusive ground for our acceptance with God, now and forever, then believers cannot know for sure that they do have now and will have then their inheritance of eternal life in Christ! The concept of a future justification or condemnation on the basis of our works would mean that we cannot know for sure that God will continue to have favor toward us and that his favor on that day depends on what we do and what our works actually are. If we view the final judgment of works as the final stage of the believers' justification it is the equivalent of saying that we are saved and justified by grace plus our works.

The final judgment of works does not suggest that the believer's present assurance of God's favor is not secure or certain. However, the final judgment manifests what is already known to believers by faith! Jesus is the Judge that acquits them in the final judgement, and he has already been judged in their place and he is their righteousness before God! The resurrection of Jesus Christ confirmed the sufficiency of his atoning sacrifice for sin, so the open acquittal of believers in the final judgment will publicly confirm their free justification by faith in Christ alone. As Paul put it, "But to him that works not, but believes on him that justifies the ungodly, his faith is counted as his righteousness" (Romans 4:5).

The final judgment will disclose more. The final judgment also includes an open acknowledgement of those whose faith in Christ was not a dead faith without works but accompanied by good works that true and authentic faith produces (James 2:14-26). Jesus spoke of an open acknowledgement of believers that includes him granting them rewards according to or in proportion to their good works (Matthew 25:21,23; I Corinthians 3:10-15; 2 Timothy 4:8) This reward will be granting by grace and not according to merit, however, it will show that God's acknowledgement of what believers have done in grateful service to him (Hebrews 6:10).

God will be adding grace to grace when he acknowledges and rewards the works of the believers! God himself prepared these works beforehand and foreordained that they would walk in them (Ephesians 2:10). Jesus spoke of his sheep that fed the hungry and that clothed the naked or visited the sick and those in prison. He said that the goat did not do these things and that we treated him the way we treated the least of them. But the scriptures say, "And he shall set the sheep on his right hand, but the goat on his left. Then shall the King say unto them on his right hand, Come, ye blessed of my Father, inherit the kingdom prepared for you from the foundation of the world" (Matthew 25:33-34). Christ knew these sheep before the foundation of the world and had prepared for them his kingdom. They are special!

The New Testament speaks of the final judgment of believers that will be according to their works (Matthew 12:36, Matthew 16:27, 2 Corinthians 5:10, 2 Timothy 4:1, Revelation 20:11-15) These scriptures do affirm that God will reward believers for their works. But they do not teach that the works of the believer is cause or reason for their justification before God. That is because it is written, "Therefore by the deeds of the law there shall no flesh be justified in his sight: for by the law is the knowledge of sin" (Romans 3:20). We also find Paul saying to the Galatians, "Knowing that a man is not justified by the works of the law, but by the faith of Jesus Christ, even we have believed Jesus Christ, that we might be justified by the faith of Christ, and not by the works of the law: for by the works of the law shall no flesh be justified" (Galatians 2;16).

God will reward the imperfect works of the believer. However, the believers are already acceptable to him because of the righteousness of Christ and their sins having been judged and condemned at the cross.

The reward granted to the believers on this day is not the gift of eternal life, but it's a kind acknowledgement of how the life of the believer was used by him and for him based on the works of the Spirit of the Lord in them. The works in the life of the believer are based on scriptures that teach our faith alone justifies, but whom he justifies he'll also sanctify and set apart from following Satan.

We see Jesus rewarding his sheep in Matthew 25:31-46. He rewards them based on their works. They fed the hungry. They visited the sick. They gave clothes to the naked. They visited those in prison. They took in strangers. Christ rewards them for their works and punishes the goat after describing them as not doing the same! However, Christ did not teach this to mean that salvation is by works. First, before saying anything about the good deeds of the sheep, Jesus says that their inheritance of the kingdom was "prepared for them from the foundation of the world" (Matthew 25"34). This shows that Christ gave this to them before they had any works of their own! That makes it Grace! This is God's work and based on his determination to have his elect as his own! Christ also taught that those who enter into the kingdom will do so only because of God's grace and forgiveness, but not because of their own accomplishments. The kingdom of heaven is like a King who had servants that owed him, but he forgave his servants of their debts (Matthew 18:1-35) The servants can only enter in because of his grace and forgiveness.

The final judgement will confirm that the justified were acquitted by Christ because of his works, but that the believers were not devoid of any fruit. They shall be rewarded for their works. A few conclusions should follow a discussion of the relationship between justification by faith alone and the final judgment of works. The believer should still have faith that there is no condemnation for those that are in Christ Jesus (Romans 8:1). But also, those that trust in Christ alone as their righteousness shall be openly acquitted and have their faith vindicated. Also, the believer will have an open acknowledgement and a reward for good works which shall be the evidence of the authentic nature of their faith. True faith is always accompanied by the fruit of works. There shall also be evidence in the life of the believer that he repented of sin. The believer will rejoice when Jesus says to them: "Well done, good and faithful servant. Enter into the joy of the Lord" (Matthew 25:22-23).

I stress, as does Paul, that sinners are justified by faith, apart from than works of the law (Romans 3:28, Romans 5:1). Paul himself said that he had no righteousness of his own which came from obeying the law, but that his righteousness was by the faith of Jesus (Philippians 3:9). He taught to the Romans that we are justified (declared right before God) by his blood and that we'd be saved from wrath through him because of the blood of Christ (Romans 5:9). The Church was purchased by the blood of Christ (Acts 20:28). Paul thus says, "But to him that works not, but believes on him that justifies the ungodly, his faith is counted as his righteousness" (Romans 4:5). God see the believers and declares that he is not guilty of sin because of Christ's work at the cross. The believer is also declared just and righteous as a gift from God "forensically" because Christ fulfilled the law on their behalf.

Paul never retracts that both realities are true. How could it be that we need to keep the law to be saved and that we are considered saved and just without keeping it? He was aware of the inconsistency. The letter was constructed and put together by the Apostle in the most developed stage of his ministry. He was led by the Holy Spirit. We must consider as to how could these two different positions could possibly cohere with one another. How can we seek synthesis without diluting either one of these true statements which I just cited?

We know that the Protestant Reformation, Lutherans and the Calvinist, understood that believers would stand at the final judgment by a righteousness given to us through faith alone as a gift. As Paul put it to the Church in Ephesus, "For by grace are ye saved through faith-and this is not from yourselves: it is the gift of God: not of works lest that man should boast" (Ephesians 2:8-9). Justification is the act of God as Judge proceeding according to the law, declaring that someone is righteous and just, informing all that the law does not condemn him, but that the law of God acquits and pronounces him or as her "not guilty" and deserving of eternal life.

Attempts have been made to reconcile things and solve the paradox. James taught, "I shall show you my faith by my works" (James 2:18). This thesis is correct. A person who has faith in Jesus Christ will produce a lifestyle of good works which are the evidence of his faith. However, James also speaks of not only a justification by faith that is demonstrated by works, but also of a justification by works. Many other New Testament passages indicate the same. Jesus, too, regarded obedience to the law as necessary to entrance into the kingdom of heaven, as evident in his response to the rich young ruler (Mark 10:17-22). Keep the commandment to get eternal life is what Christ said to him!

Why would Jesus tell the rich young ruler that keeping the law correlated to him receiving eternal life? Keep in mind too that an entire list is given in Revelation 22:14 and we find John saying that they who are blessed are the ones who have faith in Jesus that kept the commandments, but also that because of this they'll have the right to the tree of life. He goes on to say in Revelation 22:15-16 that the types of people that will not be allowed to enter the kingdom are dogs, sorcerers, liars, whoremongers, idolaters, and murderers.

He wrote that the abominable, murderers, whoremongers, liars, sorcerers, idolaters, and murderers would have a part in the Lake of Fire in Revelation 21:8. The citation of John in Revelation 22:16 indicate that Jesus sent his messenger to let these things be known in all the churches! Who then can enter heaven? Paul says, "The law was given that every mouth be stopped so that the whole world stands guilty before God" (Romans 3:19). We also find it written, "There is none righteous, no, not one" (Romans 3:10). We also see too that, "All have sinned and come short of the glory of God" (Romans 3:23). The Apostle John said these words, "If we say that we have no sin, we deceive ourselves and the truth is not in us" (I John 1:8).

Nevertheless, Paul identifies justification in Christ and his saving work by saying, "Much more now being justified by his blood, we shall be saved from wrath through him" (Romans 5:9). God revealed to Paul that it's the blood of the Lamb that justifies us by wiping out our entire debt of sin, but also that we are considered righteous on the basis of the merit of Christ alone. We have a gift of righteousness by a forensic declaration because of the obedience of Christ alone!

Paul understood that the gospel has the power to save because of the righteousness of God has been revealed through it. The day of judgment has been brought into the present in Jesus Christ who was crucified for us and risen from the dead. It was for us and our justification as being righteous that he was raised (Romans 4:25). God justifies the one who has faith in Jesus (Romans 3:26). God's righteousness is ours through Christ by faith (Romans 1:17, Romans 3:22). Jesus said it like this, "Whoever believer on him that sent me has everlasting life, and shall not be condemned, but has passed from death unto life" (John 5:24). Did you see that? Because you believe on Jesus as the Son of God you shall live forever, and you shall not be declared guilty and sentenced to Hell! You have already passed from death to life and your judgement has already passed although it has not yet come! It's called being acquitted before the trial! Our old life and all our sins were judged and condemned at the cross!

At the moment of conversion, in response to our faith, God justifies us (Romans 3:26-28, Romans 5:1, Galatians 2:16). Justification is the instant and legal act of God in which he forgives our sins and sees the righteousness of Christ as belonging to us. He declares us righteous in his sight at this time based on the testimony of the New Testament.

The Greek verb "dikaioo" most commonly means "to declare righteous" (Luke 7:29, Romans 4:5). Paul used the verb in a legal sense in Romans and says, "Who shall lay anything to the charge of God's elect? It is God that justifies! Who is he that condemns? It is Christ that died and has risen to sit at the right hand of God making intercession for us" (Romans 8:33-34). How could you, me or anyone pronounce that anyone is guilty of sin that Christ had taken away and wiped out forever by having that sin nailed to the cross with him?

When God justifies us, he declares us righteous in his sight. We no longer have any penalty to pay for any sin. There is no condemnation for those that are in Christ (Romans 8:1, 33-34). We are righteous in God's sight because of the works of Christ alone! God has fully forgiven our sins (Romans 4:6-12), and he has put his own righteousness on us (Isaiah 61:10, Romans 3:21-22, 4:3, 5:19). Keep in mind too that the robe that was furnished by the King for those invited to his supper was not their own garment, but it was a robe that was furnished by the King himself (Matthew 22:1-14). The robe of righteousness is a robe that Christ furnished for us to wear based on our faith that our sins were wiped out by his death at the cross, burial, and resurrection from the death for us and our justification!

God imputes or imparts Christ's righteousness to us. He thinks of it as belonging to us. God knew your entire life story and gave our sins to Christ

at the cross and before you were born! Paul says it like this to the Church of Corinth, "He that knew no sin, became sin for us, that we may be made the righteousness of God in him" (I Corinthians 5:21). Christ was not guilty of any sin, but Christ declared him guilty at cross! We are not actually righteous by keeping the law, but God declared us righteous because of the life that Christ lived for us! Justification is not taught to make us good based on our own intrinsic goodness or virtues. Sin to one degree or another remains with us and Paul himself described how that he sometimes did the things that he hated (Romans 7:14-26). Paul spoke of God's gift of righteousness and eternal life as a gift of grace (Ephesians 2:8-9, Romans 5:17, Romans 6:23).

No one will ever be able to accomplish justification before God through his works of righteousness; it is a gift (Romans 3:20-24). God justifies us because of our faith in Jesus Christ (Romans 3:23-26; 5:1; Galatians 2:16). Faith is about the attitude and the heart toward believing the gospel which is the exact opposite of depending on ourselves and what we can actually do to perform good enough. Paul says, "There is none righteous, no, not one. None good, no, not one" (Romans

3:10). When we come to Christ for salvation, we are saying I give up! We acknowledge that we will not depend on ourselves and our own good works any longer! We trust Jesus to forgive us and to wipe our sins away and we acknowledge that we cannot do it on our own. We trust him to give us a righteous standing before God because we know that we cannot!

The things that Christ did was what he did alone, but we are said to have done it with him (Galatians 2:20, II Timothy 2:11, Colossians 3:3, Romans 6:4, Colossians 2:12, Colossians 3:1, Ephesians 2:5-6). How could this have been and why? It's because God in his wisdom, eternity, justice, love, grace, lawgiver, and creator saw us as being in him because he represented us with who he was and what he did. We were said to be there although we weren't there as we were said to have been in the garden in Adam although we weren't there. However, the curse of sin and death came on us because of Adam's sin just as the verdict that we inherit eternal life and justification

Who on earth is good or righteous?

The whole idea of a man being considered righteous and just by God due to his moral excellence and from his good works or righteousness that comes from keeping the law is inconsistent with the entire testimony of the scripture. Paul's dissertation to the Romans puts it like this, "All have sinned and come short of the glory of God" (Romans 3:23). He says again, "There is none righteous, no, not one. There is none that understands, there is none that seeks after God. They are all gone out of the way, they are altogether become unprofitable; there is none that doeth good, no, not one" Romans 3:10-12).

The Apostle teaches that the law was given to prove that man is not righteous and that he is not just, but only guilty and deserving of punishment. He says, "Now we know that whatever the law says, it says to those that are under the law, that every mouth may be stopped, and all the world may become guilty before God" (Romans 3:19). God's law only proves that the whole world is guilty of sin and worthy of punishment. John says, "If we say that we have no sin we only deceive ourselves and the truth is not in us" (I John 1:8).

All men have broken God's law and cannot be considered righteous based on his works or by keeping the commandments. The prophet Isaiah says it like this, "But we are all as an unclean thing, and all of our righteousnesses are as filthy rags; and our iniquities, like the wind, have taken us away" (Isaiah 64:6). What does mean that the righteousness of every man is like a filthy rag? I think that it means that a man cannot justify himself before God based on his lifestyle in the past or the present. He may think he is righteous on his own, but he is not! He is a sinner.

Why then does Jesus and the entire New Testament say that the believer is justified? Why is he saved? What happens when he is judged? What about all of those passages that teach the believer will be judged based on his works? How is he justified now or on the day of judgment if he is guilty of sin? Are there different stages of justification-past, present, and future. Some believe that men get into salvation by grace, but that they only "stay in" and are ultimately vindicated by their works. Some others teach that if the believer doesn't sanctify himself and live the life of holiness that he can lose his salvation and no longer be justified when he is judged on that day of the final judgement. This position has a person who was once justified and saved being condemned and thrown into Hell at the end of his life.

None are righteous

I want you to understand today as to "why" this doctrinal truth is important, but before defining what it means and before diving into the meaning of it. Most religions upon the face of the earth including many Christians believe that we can somehow earn our trip to heaven or at least have a measure of righteousness on our own which will somehow tilt God's favor toward us. The idea that many believers have is that our works or our performance of doing righteousness becomes the basis for us being considered just to God and that this righteousness of our own is ultimately why God saves us from his own wrath on the day of judgment.

There are some scriptures that seem to support this theology on the surface. God does want his people to do right. Some passages teach that the man that is born again will not continue to practice sin as a lifestyle habit. We are commanded to be holy and to live a life that is righteous. God wants us to repent and to turn away from sin.

The book of Revelation says this, "And behold, I come quickly; and my reward is with me, to give every man according as his work shall be. I am Alpha and Omega, the beginning and the ending, the first and the last. Blessed are they that do his commandments, that they may have the right to the tree of life and may enter in through the gates into the city. For without are dogs, and sorcerers, and whoremongers, and murderers, and idolaters, and whosoever loveth and makes a lie. I, Jesus, have sent mine angel to testify these things in the churches. I am the root and offspring of David, and the bright and morning star" (Revelation 22:12-16).

What are the commandments that Christ said that men must obey? I will name a few. He said to love God. He said to love our neighbors as we do ourselves. Jesus began his public ministry by saying to repent and to believe the gospel. He said to get baptized. He said to take the Lord's supper. Love is the new law in the gospel. God puts this love in our heart for others. He writes his statute in our hearts on his own. He spoke about the Good Samaritan that helped the man that wounded and left half-dead. He taught us about his sheep that enter the kingdom that were also rewarded for feeding the hungry and clothing others who were the least of them at their point of need.

The command to repent is simple. We have a godly sorrow in our hearts about our sin. We confess our sins to God and ask him to help us to overcome. He taught us to pray that we are not led into temptation and that we are delivered from evil. Repentance is also about no longer trusting in our works and our goodness to justify ourselves before God on that great day and believing the gospel.

The gospel is all about us receiving Christ and the gift of eternal life which includes the forgiveness of sin and the removal of guilty with its damnation after it based on Christ's live and his death, burial and resurrection for our acquittal. Good news is good news. The Baptism that Christ commanded only symbolizes the reality that we identify ourselves with him in his death at the cross and burial which washed our sins away.

But also, that we identify with his new creation in eternity based on his resurrection as well. The Lord's supper that Christ commanded is done in remembrance of the sacrifice he made with his own body at the cross to save us from our sins. We can no longer be number as one of the sinners that cannot enter his kingdom because we've obeyed his commandments and believed.

As we read the last paragraph, we'll have to conclude that Jesus himself is saying that he will reward men based on their works upon the earth! The problem is that Christians, have done within their lifetimes, things that exclude them from entering into the city that was prepared for them! How or why then can anyone go to heaven? Paul says to the Church of Rome, "There are none righteous, no, not one" (Romans 3:10). What did Paul mean by this statement? How can we prepare and be ready for the day that we see the Lord in person. The Word of God says, "For it is appointed to men once to die, but after this the judgment" (Hebrews 9:27).

Repent! Pray! Believe the gospel message! Live a holy life with the help of the Holy Spirit. Christ said that he will separate the wheat from the tares and the sheep from the goat! Do the things that Jesus Christ taught us to do and get ready to meet the Lord himself!

Remember these words of Christ, "Not every one that says to me, Lord, Lord shall enter into the kingdom of heaven. Many shall say to me in that day, Lord, Have not a prophesied in thy name, cast out devils, and done many wonderful works. Then I will profess to them-I never knew you. Depart from me thou workers of iniquity" (Matthew 7:21-24). Why were people who thought they had "wonderful works" told by Christ that he never knew them? Were they trying to justify themselves based on their wonderful works?

Finally, remember these words as your hope, "Much more then being now justified by his blood, we shall be saved from wrath by him" (Romans 5:9). Remember too these words, "If you openly declare that Jesus is Lord and believe in your heart that God raised him from the dead, you will be saved" (Romans 10:9). This is wonderful news! Paul said these words to the Galatians and they are still a great reminder for us as to who and what to put our trust in, "Knowing this, that a man is not justified by the works of the law but by faith in Jesus Christ, even we have believed in Jesus Christ, that we might be justified by faith in Christ and not by the works of the law; for by the works of the law no flesh shall be justified" (Galatians 2:16, King James Version). Confess all sins to God! Repent of sins! Believe the gospel about what Christ did to accomplish and finish your salvation! Live a life that is holy and submit to the Holy Ghost as you grow and mature in grace!

Mount up with wings as an eagle

Mount up with wings as the eagle! This is about moving with God and his spirit to a place where you cannot go on your own! The Lord is our salvation and our strength. He is our help to overcome our enemies and the world. We must pray and seek his power and strength until it becomes our own!

The Acts of the Apostles records, "Ye shall receive power after the Holy Ghost has come upon you" (Acts 1:8). The gift of the Holy Ghost was a promise to every believer in the 14th chapter of the gospel of John. We find Luke explaining that the Holy Ghost gives us power in the book of Acts and here in chapter one and verse 8.

Some years ago, a man was in the hospital and in a coma. The Medical Doctors told his family that he would be dying and that they could take him off the life support machine. I was asked by this family as to what I thought about it. I said that I would come to the hospital and pray for him in Jesus' name to be raised out of his coma. I came to the hospital and prayed for his healing, and he came out of his coma and was discharged from the hospital!

This was God doing what modern medicine and science could not do! The scripture says, "And these signs shall follow them that believe; In my name shall they cast out devils; they shall speak with new tongues; they shall take up serpents; and if they drink any deadly thing, it shall not hurt them; they shall lay hands on the sick, and they shall recover" (Mark 16:17-18).

This miraculous doing was that of Jesus Christ. We mount up with wings like an eagle with supernatural help. We can do nothing on our own! Believe it! The Word of God says, "With men this is impossible; but with God all things are possible" (Matthew 19:26).

I found out that a man had died. I was walking through a facility in Milwaukee with Evangelist Griger. The paramedics had been called. Firefighters and paramedics could not revive him. I asked how long he had been dead, and the firefighters said that he had been gone for ten minutes. I looked at Evangelist Griger and told him that if I simply thought for him to rise that he had to come back to life. Mike prayed and I bent over to touch his foot in faith, and he immediately came back to life. Jesus Christ brought this man back to life and to Christ alone be the glory!

Man cannot raise the dead. God has used men to heal the sick, raise the dead, cast out devils, divide the Jordan, call fire out of heaven, and many more supernatural things. The most important wonder of all is that God has saved souls from Satan's hand and Hell's certainty and brought them into the kingdom of God by the preaching of the gospel. Let us mount up with wings like the eagle. Walk in supernatural victory and power. Overcome the world. Defeat Satan. Walk in the spirit.

Soar above and beyond the storms that try to discourage us and get us to quit or go back to our former lives!

Trust the Lord. Climb higher. Do greater works by sharing the gospel of the Lord Jesus Christ to all! Yes! It is possible! It is possible with the Holy Ghost and help from God to overcome the sins that war against our souls! Mount up with wings as an eagle! You shall run and not be weary! You shall want and not faint! Believe it! Go from one degree of glory to the next. Never stop believing that you are already sanctified and holy because of the finished work of Christ at the cross!

Ask God to fill you with the same power of the Holy Ghost that fell on and in believers in the early church age! Get ready to walk in supernatural victory and God's anointing. Believe that as God was with Moses or the prophet Elijah and Elijah that he can be with you. Let the glory of God manifest in your life and be transformed into the image of Christ from one degree of glory to another. Wait on God to finish what he started with you. It's God's power! It's God that works through us to overcome! Finally, "Let us therefore come boldly to the throne of grace, that we may obtain mercy, and find grace to help in the time of need" (Hebrews 4:16). Keep praying. Keep believing. Wait on the Lord and then you shall renew your strength!

13

The Shroud of Turin & Historical proof of the Resurrection

I want to open by saying the Bible is not only inspired by God, but it is a historically reliable book based on the same tests used for the credibility of ancient history. The historical reliability of the scriptures is tested by the same criteria that all historical documents are tested. The three basic principles of historiography are the bibliographical text, the internal evidence test, and the external evidence test. (Sander, IRE, 143 ff.). We can examine the New Testament to determine its reliability as an accurate source for the historical events it reports.

The bibliographical test evaluates the copies that we have and the time interval between the original copy made and the currently existing ones. In other words, since we do not have the original documents, how reliable are the copies we have in regard to the number of manuscripts and that number compared to the time interval between originals. E.E. Peters states that "on the basis of manuscript tradition alone, the works that make up the Christians' New Testament were the most copied and widely circulated books of antiquity." (Peters, HH, 50). Consequently, the vast number of manuscripts alone gives credibility to the text.

We have with us more than 5,686 Greek manuscripts of the New Testament. Don't forget about the more than 10,000 Latin Vulgate and the 9300 other versions of (MSS). We have about 25,000 manuscript copies of the portions of the New Testament. Now let us talk about history for a moment. No other document of ancient history is even close to the credibility of the New Testament based on the bibliographical test for ancient history. In comparison, Homer's Iliad comes in second place and that is the poem wrote by the poet Homer, which recounts some of the events of the final weeks of the Trojan War. Homer's Iliad has only 643 manuscripts that still survive.

There are currently a total of 5,686 Greek manuscripts of the New Testament and 19,284 manuscripts from other languages. John Warwick Montgomery stated, "to be skeptical of the manuscript text of the New Testament books is to allow all of classical antiquity to slip into obscurity, for no documents of the ancient period are as well attested bibliographically as the New Testament" (Montgomery). No other ancient text comes close to this type of credibility for in a bibliographical test.

Sir Frederick G. Kenyon, who is second to nobody on issuing statements on the bibliographical test regarding time intervals in particular states, besides the number, the manuscripts of the New Testament differ from those of classical authors. In no other case is the interval of time between the composition of the book and the date of the earliest manuscripts so short as in the earliest extant copies of the New Testament. (Kenyon, HTCNT,4).

Kenyon continues in *The Bible and Archaeology:* "The interval between the dates of the original composition and the earliest extant evidence doubt that the Scriptures have come down to us substantially as they were written has now been removed. Both the authenticity and the general integrity of the books of the New Testament may be regarded as finally established," (Kenyon, BA 288).

We are also aware that the first century Roman historian, Tacticus is considered one of the more accurate historians of the ancient world. He wrote about Pontius Pilate and the Christians as well as their belief.

Josephus (c. A.D. 37-c.A.D. 100) was a Pharisee and a Jewish historian, working under Roman authority. He wrote two major works, *Jewish Wars (A.D. 77-78)* and *Antiquities of the Jews* (c. A.D. 94). Josephus made many statements that verify the historical truth of the

New Testament, and he was not a Christian at all. Thallus wrote around A.D. 52 and none of his works are extant. The Talmudic writings about the historical Jesus were compiled between 70 A.D. and 200 A.D. The Babylonian Talmud documents historical facts about Christianity and the miracles Jesus performed during his life before his execution by a Roman crucifixion.

All of the that being said and more that could be said, The Apostle Paul said these words in the New Testament, "For I delivered to you first of all that which I received, how that Christ died for our sins according to the scriptures; And that he was buried, and that he rose again the third day according to the scriptures: And that he was seen of Cephas, then of the twelve: After that, he was seen of above five hundred brethren at once; of whom the greater part remain until present, but some have fallen asleep. After that he was seen of James: then of all the apostles. And last of all he was seen of me also, as one born out of due time" (I Corinthians 15:3-8).

The empty tomb was a historical fact, but it was Christ's post-resurrection appearances that caused them to believe. Winfried Corduan writes on the certainty of the empty tomb, "If ever a fact of ancient history may count indisputable, it should be the empty tomb. From Sunday on there must have been a tomb, clearly known as the tomb of Jesus, that did not contain his body. This tomb is beyond dispute: Christian teaching from the beginning promoted a living resurrected Savior. The Jews strongly opposed this teaching and were prepared to go to any length to suppress it. Their jobs would have been easy if they could have invited potential converts for a quick stroll to the tomb and there produced Christ's body. This would have been the end of the Christian message. The fact that the church centering around the risen Christ could come about demonstrates that there must have been in empty tomb, (Corduan, NDA, 222).

William Lane Craig stated, "The simple fact that the Christian fellowship, founded on belief in Jesus' resurrection, came into existence and flourished in the very city where he was executed and buried is powerful evidence for the historicity of the empty tomb. (Craig, DJRD, as cited in Wilkins, JUF, 151-52). The Jews or the Romans knew his burial site and could have produced his body to stop the spread of Christianity and destroy the testimony of eyewitnesses to his resurrection. The silence of the Jews and the Romans speak as loud as the proclamations of eyewitnesses to his resurrection from the dead. The apostles could not have successfully proclaimed the resurrection in the same time and place where he was crucified and had it believed if he had not arose and been seen alive.

King Tut was the 12th Pharaoh of the 18th Egyptian dynasty. He was in power from 1332 until 1323 B.C.E. King Tut was the Egyptian pharaoh made famous for his tomb, discovered intact in 1922. He is entombed in Egypt's Valley of the Kings. His golden death mask was made over 3300 years ago from 24 pounds of beaten gold. It is probably the most recognizable artifact from antiquity. Over a million tourists have went to visit the mummy of King Tut in the Valley of the Kings. The burial site of Jesus Christ was also known over 1300 years after the death of King Tut. Jesus Christ is famous not only because of his miracles and teachings, but because of his empty tomb. The tomb of Christ was empty on the third day following his crucifixion by the Romans. He had foretold his death and his resurrection on the third day while alive and he was later seen alive by hundreds of eyewitnesses after his death by crucifixion and burial. The eyewitnesses refused to change their stories when facing the death penalty from the Roman government and they all kept their testimonies before being put to death.

We can prove that King Tut reigned in Egypt and that he was buried in Egypt's Valley of the Kings. We have his mummy. We can prove based on authentic evidence that Jesus Christ walked the earth, died from a Roman crucifixion to be buried in a borrowed tomb, and rose again from the dead three days later as he foretold in advance. There are historical records, hundreds of eyewitnesses, the empty tomb, changed lives, in towns and villages with the supernatural spread of Christianity throughout the region during that same time and place based of the fact of the resurrection which would have been easy to disprove at that time or later if it weren't true.

Did you know that Confucius, the Chinese philosopher was on September 28, 551 B.C. and later died in 479 B.C. which was almost 500 years before Christ was born. The body of Confucius is still buried in China with over 100,000 followers in the same cemetery. The burial site of Jesus Christ was also known and his empty tomb on the third day was too notorious to be denied. The disciples did not go to Athens or Rome to proclaim the resurrection. They went right to Jerusalem, where, if the teaching were false, the falsehood would be evident because others could have went straight to the tomb to see for themselves or have produced his body. The body was never produced by anyone and hundreds of eyewitnesses paraded the streets of Jerusalem and Rome proclaiming that they saw him alive. They could have never proclaimed the resurrection successfully and had it believed under the circumstances had it not occurred.

The crucifixion had silenced any hope of disciples that Jesus was God in the flesh or the Messiah. The resurrection is what made Christianity come alive and flourish. The disciples would have been crushed and defeated without it. The cross was a sad and scary end of his career. The disciples denied that they knew who Jesus was when they carried him away to put him to death, but they became bold as lions to proclaim his resurrection days later. What could have possibly happened?

Jesus rose from the dead as he said that he would. He foretold that his tomb would be empty on the third day after his death, but when he was alive. The scriptures teach us, "If you openly declare that Jesus is Lord and believe in your heart that God raised him from the dead, you will be saved" (Romans 10:9, NLT). Jesus was the embodiment of God's love on earth, dying for us to satisfy justice and save us from sin. Christ said, "God so loved the world that he gave his only begotten Son that whosoever believes in him should not perish but have everlasting life" (John 3:16). When you believe the truth, you will receive the gift of eternal life. Christ said, "Look, I stand at the door and knock, if you hear my voice and open the door, I will come in and we will share a meal together as friends" (Revelation 3:20, New Living Translation).

The New Testament has more copies of original manuscripts closest to the time of actual events happening than any other ancient text. The bibliographical test for the reliability of the New Testament gives us 24,970 documents written in various languages since the resurrection of Jesus Christ from the dead. F.E. Peters states that "on the basis of manuscript tradition alone the works that make up the Christians' New Testament were the most widely circulated books of ancient antiquity." (Peters, HH,50). We know more about Jesus Christ than any other man that walked the face of the planet.

John Warwick Montgomery says that "to be skeptical of the resultant text of the New Testament books is to allow all of the classical antiquity to slip into obscurity, for no documents of the ancient period are as well attested bibliographically as the New Testament." (Montgomery, HC, 29). Kenyon continues in the Bible and Archaeology: "The interval between the dates of the original composition and the earliest extant evidence becomes so small as to be in fact negligible, and the last foundation for any doubt that the Scriptures have come down to us substantially as they were written now has been removed. Both the authenticity and the general integrity of the books of the New Testament may be regarded as finally established." (Kenyon, BA, 288).

God came to earth as a man. He foretold his death as a man by crucifixion and of his resurrection from the dead on the third day. One reason that we men ought to believe is simply that we can verify these things from the historical records alone. Historians recorded the history of the lives of Alexander the Great, King Tut, Confucius, many others, and Jesus Christ. Cornelius Tacitus was the greatest Roman historian that lived from the era. He was an unbeliever and a pagan. Cornelius Tacticus (c. A.D. 55-120) was a Roman historian who lied through the reigns of over a half dozen Romans emperors. He has been called the "greatest historian" of ancient Rome, an individual generally acknowledged in the academic world of scholars for his integrity and goodness" (Habermas VHCELJ,87). Tacticus' most acclaimed works are the *Annals* and the *Histories*. The Annals cover the period from Augustus's death in A.D. 14 to that of Nero in A.D. 96." (Habermas, VHCELI.87).

Cornelius Tacticus spoke of the Christ being put to death by Pontus Pilate and alluded to the conviction of the early church that the Christ who had been crucified had risen from the dead. No serious scholar has attempted to postulate that Jesus Christ did not exist in history. No historian has refuted that the tomb of Christ was empty on the third day as Christ foretold. Cambridge lecturer Markus Bocmucehl notes that Tactitus' comments provide us with testimony during the days of Christ by the leading Roman historian of his day, "independent confirmation other than the Bible that Jesus lived and was formally executed in Judea in the reign of Tiberius and during Pontius Pilate's office as procurator (A.D. 26-36). These facts disprove every notion of any idea that Jesus Christ never existed or walked the earth at this time; and secondly, this is a profound rebuttal that he did not actually die by the duly administered Roman death penalty." (Bockmuehl, TJMLM,10,11) The Old Testament prophecies foretold every detail of his Jesus' life hundreds of years beforehand and see how the prophecies came to pass centuries later. It becomes evident that God planned the events and orchestrated the details of his life story and brought to pass as planned. Why? It was God's way of satisfying his love and his justice to save sinners. Love assumed the nature of that which offended God's justice when God became a man. He died to satisfy God's love and his justice. As Christ said, "God so loved the world that he gave his only begotten Son that whosoever believes on him should not perish but have everlasting life" (John 3:16).

Christian Hershel Moore, professor at Harvard University, said, "Christianity knew its Savior and Redeemer not as some god whose history was contained in a mythical faith, with rude, primitive, and even offensive elements. Jesus was a historical not a mythical being. No remote or foul myth obtruded itself of the Christian believer; his faith was founded on positive, historical, and acceptable facts." (Moore as cited in Smith, GCWC,48). As John R. W. Scott has said, "the silence of Christ's enemies is an eloquent of proof of the resurrection as the apostles' witness" (Scott, BC, 51). The silence of the Jews on the subject speaks louder than the Christians, or as Farbbairn notes, "The silence of the Jews is as significant as the speech of the Christians" (Fairbairn, SLC, 357).

Josephus, a Jewish historian writing at the end of the first century A.D. has this writing in his historical document in Antiquities, 18.3.3: "Now there as about this time Jesus, a wise man, if it be lawful to call him man; for he was a doer of wonderful works, a teacher of such men as receive the truth with pleasure. He drew over to him many Jews, and also many of the Greeks. This man was the Christ. And when Pilate had condemned him to the cross, upon his impeachment by the principal man among us, those who had loved him from the first did not forsake him, for he appeared to them alive on the third day, the divine prophets hang spoken these and thousands of other wonderful things about him. And even now, the race of Christians, so named from him, has not died out. (Josephus, AJ, 18:3.3).

All historians, Jewish officials, Romans, and scholars who have studied the history of times including the first century, agree that the tomb of Jesus was empty on the third day. As Wilbur Smith put it: "Let it simply be said that we know more about the details of the hours immediately before and the actual death of Jesus, in and near Jerusalem, than we know about the death of any other one man in all of the ancient world." (Smith, TS, 360). But know too that if he had not risen, the Romans would have gone to the tomb of Jesus and paraded His body throughout Jerusalem to silence the disciples and prevent the spread of Christianity. They viewed Christianity as a threat to their empire. They further acknowledged that Jesus had predicted the resurrection would occur prior to His death on the cross, which is why the Roman governor put Roman soldiers around his tomb to guard it overnight and on the third day. Matthew, Mark, Luke, and John were not only believers, but eyewitnesses to the resurrected Christ and historians.

The truth has been collaborated for centuries by historians and the radical transformation of people's lives who believed Christ and trusted him for their salvation. Jesus died on a Friday afternoon. Friends quickly placed His body in a tomb cut into a rocky hillside and blocked the entrance with a great stone. (It is said that the stone took 10 strong men to move it.) Guards were sent to secure the stone with a seal. Breaking the seal or moving the stone meant death by execution from the Roman government. People feared breaking the seal, but the seal was broken on the third day with Roman guards gone and an empty tomb. Hundreds of witnesses later saw him alive. The Roman government never went to the tomb to parade his body around to prove he hadn't risen on the third day, but they executed believers for their continued proclamation of and witness to the resurrection.

In the 1974 edition of the *Encyclopedia Britannica*, the contributor writing about Jesus Christ took twenty thousand words to describe him, more space than what was given to Aristotle, Cicero, Alexander Julius Caesar, Buddha, Confucius, Mohammed, or Napoleon Bonaparte. The author concludes: "The independent secular accounts of Jesus of Nazareth prove that in ancient times even the opponents of Christianity never doubted the historicity of Jesus, which was disputed for the first time on inadequate grounds at the end of the 18th and 19th century," (EB, 145). The non-Christian sources provide collaboration that Jesus was a historical person. They prove that Jesus lived in Palestine in the first century and that he was crucified by the Romans under the governorship of Pontius Pilate. They also prove that his ministry was associated with healings and wonders.

Edwin Yamauchi, professor of History at Miami University, asserts that we have more and better historical documentation for Jesus than for any other religious founder (e.g., Zoroaster, Buddha, or Mohammed). From the non-biblical sources testifying of Christ, Yamauchi concludes: Even if we did not have the New Testament of Christian writings, we would be able to conclude from such non-Christian writings as Josephus, the Talmud, Tacitus, and Pliny the younger that Jesus was a Jewish teacher. Secondly, that many people believed he performed healings and exorcisms, third, he was rejected by Jewish leaders, fourth, he was crucified under Pontius Pilate in the reign of Tiberius, fifth, despite his shameful death, his followers who believed he was still alive, spread beyond Palestine s that there were multitudes of them in Rome by A.D. 64; sixth, all kinds of people from the city to the countryside-men and women, slave and free-worshipped him as God by the beginning of the second century. (Yamauchi, JUF, 221-222).

Simon Greenleaf (1783-1853) was the famous Royal Professor of Law at Harvard University and succeeded Justice Joseph Story as the Dane Professor of Law in the same university upon Story's death in 1846. H.W.H. Knott says of this great authority in jurisprudence: "To the efforts of Story and Greenleaf is to be ascribed the rise of the Harvard Law School to its eminent position among legal schools in the United States," (Knott, as cited in Smith, TS, 423).

Greenleaf produced a famous work entitled, "A Treatise on the Law and Evidence that is still considered the greatest single authority on evidence in the entire literature of legal procedure." (Smith, TS,423). In 1846, while still professor of law at Harvard, Greenleaf wrote a volume entitled An Examination of the Testimony of the Four Evangelists by the Rules of Evidence Administered in the Courts of Justice .The professor of law examined the value of the testimony of Matthew, Mark, Luke, and John as historians with their testimony to the resurrection of Jesus Christ. The professor of law stated as a jurist the following, "It is impossible that the disciples could have persisted in affirming the truths they have narrated , had not Jesus actually risen from the dead, and had they not known this fact as certainty as they know any other fact" (Greenleaf, TE, 28-30). The man who wrote the book on the Law and Evidence for Harvard University has already stated that his examination of the history wrapped into legal procedure inevitably leads us to the fact of the resurrection of Jesus Christ from the dead.

Dr. Thomas Arnold was the professor of history at Oxford University. Thomas Arnold, was the author of the famous three-volume History of Rome, appointed to the chair of modern history at Oxford, and acquainted with the value of evidence in determining historical facts. The chair of modern history said the following: "The evidence for our Lord's life and death and resurrection may be, and often has been, shown to be satisfactory; it is good according to the common rules for distinguishing good evidence from the bad Thousands and ten thousands of persons have gone through the evidence piece by piece, as carefully as every judge summing up on a most important cause. I have myself done it many times over, not to persuade others but to satisfy myself I have been used for many years to study the histories of other times, and to examine and weigh the evidence of those who have written about them, and I know of no one fact in the history of mankind which is proved by better and fuller evidence of every sort, to the understanding of the fair inquirer, than that great sign which God hath given us that Christ died and rose again from the dead. (Arnold, as cited in Smith, TS, 425-26).

Wilbur M. Smith concludes: "If our Lord said, frequently, with great definiteness and detail, that after he went up to Jerusalem he would be put to death, but on the third day he would rise again from the grave and this prediction came to pass, then it has always seemed to me that everything else that our Lord ever said must also be true." (Smith, TS, 419). It is further stated by W. J. Sparrow-Simpson, "If it be asked how the resurrection of Christ is proof of him being the Son of God, it may be answered, first, because he rose by his own power. He had power to lay down his life, and he had power to raised it again, John 10:18 This is not inconsistent with the fact taught in so many other passages, that he was raised by the power of his Father, because what the Father does the Son does likewise; creation, and all other external works, are ascribed indifferently to the Father, Son, and Spirit. But in the second place, as Christ had openly declared himself to be the Son of God, his rising from the dead was the seal of God to the truth of that declaration. If he had he continued under the power of death, God would thereby have disallowed his claim to be the Son. But as he raised him from the dead, he publicly acknowledged him by saying, "Thou art my Son, this day have I declared thee such." (Sparrow-Simpson, RCF,287-88).

When an event takes place in history and there are eyewitnesses who are alive at the time who participated in or observed it, and when the information is published throughout the world, one is able to verify the validity of the historical event by the circumstances. Professor Kevan points out: "As the church is too holy for a foundation on rottenness, so she is too real for a foundation of myth." (Kevan, RC,4-5). Professor Kevon also says about the epistles of the New Testament, "For the embellishment of an alleged historical fact no documents are esteemed to be more valuable than contemporary letters." (Kevan, RC, 6). Read the eyewitness accounts of the resurrection in your Bibles. Know too that historians that were not Christians spoke about the empty tomb in the first century. Josephus was the prominent Jewish scholar that spoke about it.

Professor Kevon says of the epistles of the New Testament, "There is the unimpeachable evidence of the contemporary letters of Paul the Apostle. Those epistles constitute historical evidence of the highest kind. The letters addressed to the Galatians the Corinthians, and the Romans, about the authenticity and date of which there is little dispute belong to the time of Paul's missionary journeys, and may be dated in the period of A.D. 55-58. This brings the evidence of the resurrection of Christ still nearer to the event: the interval is the short span of twenty-five years. Since Paul himself makes it plain that the subject of his letter was the same as that about which he had spoken to them when he was with them, this really brings back the evidence to a still earlier time. (Kevan, RC,6).

William Corduan wrote about the undeniable fact of the empty tomb of Jesus Christ by saying, "If ever a fact of ancient history may count as indisputable, it should be the empty tomb. From Easter Sunday on there must have been a tomb, clearly known as the tomb of Jesus, that did not contain his body. This much is beyond dispute: Christian teaching from the very beginning promoted a living, resurrected Savior. The Jewish authorities strongly opposed this teaching and were prepared to go to any lengths in order to oppose it. Their job would have been easy if they would have invited potential converts for a quick stroll to the tomb and there produced Christ's body. That would have been the end of the Christian message. The fact that the church centering around the risen Christ could come about demonstrates that there must have been the empty tomb. (Corduan, NDA, 222).

When therefore the disciples began to preach the resurrection in Jerusalem and people responded, and when religious authorities including the Roman government stood helplessly by, the tomb must have been empty and they knew he had risen. It was too easy to produce the body to stop the movement. The single fact that Christianity flourished in Jerusalem with over 3000 people getting baptized on the day of Pentecost when Peter reminded them that the tomb was empty in the very city where he was executed and buried is powerful evidence of the historicity of the empty tomb with the reality of his resurrection. Peter's sermon on the day of Pentecost that led to their conversions was the proclamation that his tomb was empty and the fact that Jesus Christ is a risen Lord and Savior.

It was Christ's post-resurrection appearances that assured his disciples that he had risen from the dead. It is also the millions of testimonies by people today that are alive now that assert that Jesus Christ has come into their hearts to change their lives. The empty tomb is a historical fact, verifying the appearances as being nothing less than Jesus of Nazareth, resurrected in flesh and blood. (Hastings, DCG, 506). J.N.D. Anderson, lawyer and professor of oriental law at the University of London said, "There was no point in arguing about the empty tomb. Everyone, friend and opponent, knew that it was empty. The only question worth arguing about were why it was empty and what its emptiness proved." (Anderson, RJC,4-9).

In other writings, Andersons says: "It is a matter of history that the apostles from the very beginning made many converts in Jerusalem hostile as it was, by proclaiming the glad news that Christ had risen from the grave-and they did it within a short walk from the grave. Any one of their hearers could have visited the tomb and come back again between lunch and whatever may have been the equivalent of afternoon tea. Is this conceivable, then that the apostles could have had this success if the body of the one they proclaimed as risen Lord was all the time decomposing in Joseph's tomb? Would a great company of priests and many hard-headed Pharisees have been impressed with the proclamation of the resurrection at all, but a mere message of spiritual survival couched in the misleading terms of a literal rising from the grave? (Anderson, CWH, 95-96). The converts lived during that time and could walk to the burial site. They could not have been converted after he was nailed to the cross if he had not risen from the dead with eyewitnesses!

Dr. Frank Maier and many other prominent professors of ancient history have mentioned that no shred of evidence has yet to be discovered in literary sources, epigraphy, or archaeology that would disprove that the tomb of Jesus was empty on the 3rd day when Christ said he would rise from the dead. Many tourists have visited the mummy of King Tut over in Egypt in that place they call the valley of the kings. Confucius is a Chinese philosopher that is still buried over in China with over 100,000 followers since 479 B.C. These men lived before Christ was born. Christianity was founded on the empty tomb which Jesus prophesied before his death and on the hundreds of credible eye-witnesses to his resurrection from the dead! Christ distinguished himself as Lord over death and the grave with his resurrection which he foretold in advance of his death. Christians have hope of eternal life when they believe that God loved them and sent his Son to die for them so that they can have everlasting life (John 3:16).

Why is the resurrection of Jesus Christ one of the most important doctrines taught by Evangelists and Pastors? The scriptures teach, "That if thou confess with thy mouth the Lord Jesus and shall believe in thine heart that God has raised him from the dead, thou shalt be saved. For with the heart a man believes unto righteousness, and with the mouth confession is made unto salvation: (Romans 10:9-10).A man must believe he is the Son of God and that he rose from the dead in order to be saved. A man's faith saves him from the wrath of God to come. Wilbur M. Smith, noted scholar says: "No weapon has ever been forged, and none ever will be, to destroy rational confidence in the historical records of this epochal and predicted event. The resurrection of Christ is the very citadel of the Christian faith. This is the doctrine that turned the world upside down in the first century, that lifted Christianity pre-eminently above Judaism and the pagan religions of the Mediterranean world. If this goes, so must almost everything else that is vital and unique in the Gospel of the Lord Jesus Christ: "If Christ be not risen, then is your faith vain" (I Corinthians 15:17). (Smith, SR, 22). Witnesses throughout the world today are still sharing that Jesus Christ came into their hearts and changed them into a new creature with a new heart. Christ said after his resurrection, "All power in heaven and earth is given unto me" (Matthew 28:18-19).

On Sunday when two women, one named Mary Magdalene and the other called Mary were visiting the tomb, they felt a great earthquake. They saw an angel come and roll the giant stone from the entrance of the tomb. The guards were so frightened they shook in terror and fled. The angel told the women not to be afraid, and that Jesus was not there, and that He had risen, which meant that He was alive and arose again from the dead. He told them to go quickly and tell Jesus' friends that He was alive. No government has ever produced the body and the burial site was known. King Tut, Confucius and the prophet Mohammed are still buried in their graves today and we know the location of their tombs. Millions of tourists have saw their mummy or burial sites and they died long before Christ was born. God came to earth as a man! He rose from the dead as he promised and is now back in heaven sitting on his throne!

Mary Magdalene was crying and grieving after Jesus died. The angel told her on the third day after His death, *"Do not cry, He, Jesus is alive and not dead"*. When Mary and Jesus' friends saw him they rejoiced for they knew what the angel said was true. On their way back, Jesus met them and said, *"Do not be afraid. Go and tell my brothers to go to Galilee and there they will see me"*. And just as Jesus had promised, He rose from the dead on the third day after His death! Jesus is alive!

Jesus had now made a way for us all to have eternal life and to go to heaven with Him. We have all sinned and come short of God's glory and deserve damnation in hell and eternal death. However, God so loved the world that He gave us Jesus, His only Son, that whoever would believe Him would not perish and spend eternity in hell but have everlasting life. Our sins, lying, stealing, adultery, fornication, idolatry, gossiping, and more had separated us from God and made us His enemies and doomed us to hell.

However, Jesus loved us, died for us on the cross of Calvary and shed His blood for us to pay the price for our sins. He set us free from the curse of sin and death and the wrath of God by what he has done for us, but only if we believe Him. We have eternal life when we repent of sin, confess our sins to God, believe that Jesus died for us and rose again from the dead with all power in heaven and earth. He is the way, the truth, and the life, and no man can come to the Father but by Him.

Jesus Christ was wounded for our transgressions, bruised for our iniquities, and the Lord laid on Him the iniquities of us all. He is merciful and just. Repent of your sins with a godly sorrow for offending God by changing your mind and confessing all sins to Jesus. Tell Him that you are sorry. If you are sincerely sorry then you will repent with a godly sorrow about your sins and ask Christ to forgive you. Believe that he paid the penalty of your sins when He shed His blood for you on the cross so that you will not have to spend eternity in hell.

Ask Jesus to forgive you for all of your sins, come into your heart, and become the Lord and Savior of your life. Ask Him to set you free from any former sin, addiction, stronghold, bad habit, or wrongdoing, and to give you the strength to live godly. Christ said, "Behold, I stand at the door and knock: If any man hear my voice, and open the door, I will come in to him, and will sup with him, and he with me" (Revelation

3:20). Peter said it like this, "Repent and be baptized every one of you in the name of Jesus Christ for the remission of your sins, and you shall receive the gift of the Holy Ghost" (Acts 2:38). The resurrected Savior will enter into our hearts and make us a new creature if we want his help and if we are willing to open the door of our hearts.

The same power that raised Jesus up out of the grave will now come into your heart and life and help you to live a godly lifestyle once you have surrendered your life to Him. Never give up on yourself or God because Jesus loves us and is always willing to pardon us, but he can give us more grace and another chance. He is patient, merciful, and longsuffering. He can fill us with his promise of the Holy Ghost which gives us power in Acts 1:8.

He is not willing that any of us should perish but that we all come to repentance. (II Peter 3:9) Jesus wants you to deny yourself and lay down your self-will and allow him to live his life through you. Open up your heart and receive him and ask him to forgive you and to become the Lord and Savior of your life today! The fact that Jesus rose from the dead proves that He is the Creator, Lord and Savior of the world. He can do things in your life with you that seem impossible. He can save you from your sins.

Men must repent for the sins committed such as lying, stealing, not being kind to others, and other bad things you have done to hurt the heart of God. Only Jesus can raise you up out of any problem, sin, failure, or sickness just as he himself was raised up out of death and the grave. He loves you and He voluntarily died in **your** place for you. God so loved this world that he gave his only son so that whoever believes in him would have everlasting life (John 3:16).

Jesus rose from the dead. The power that raised Jesus from the dead can live in you. In Acts 2:38 Peter said, *"Repent, and be baptized every one of you in the name of Jesus Christ for the remission of sins, and ye shall receive the gift of the Holy Ghost"*. The Holy Ghost is a promise that Jesus made to come to the believer to comfort him and give him a peace that the world could not give (John 14:16-26). We also find

Christ informing his disciples that they would receive power after that the Holy Ghost had come upon them in Acts 1:8. We find throughout the book of Acts that apostles healed the lame or the sick and raised men from the dead. This is real power!

John the Baptist had promised that the Holy Ghost would purge his floor in Matthew 3:12. It is the Holy Ghost that does the purging or cleansing of men and women from sin. We cannot sanctify ourselves and walk in a holy lifestyle in our own strength simply because we were taught the truth about issues. People often fall to the same issue again and again and will return to it after they quit it again and again. But God helps us with his supernatural gift to purge his floor! Samson took the jawbone of a donkey and whipped a thousand men with his bare hands all by himself (Judges 15:16). This was not his own strength, but the gift of supernatural strength and God's power working through him. The Holy Ghost is the power that raised Jesus Christ from the dead that is living inside of every born again believer (Romans 8:11).

The Chair of Modern History at Oxford University

Thomas Arnold was for fourteen years, the Headmaster of Rugby, author of the famous three-volume set, *History of Rome*. He was appointed to the chair of modern history at Oxford, and the most acquainted man with the value of reliable evidence in determining historical facts. This great scholar said the following on the evidence for Christ's resurrection:

"Thousands and ten thousands of persons have gone through the historical evidence piece by piece, as carefully as every judge summoning up the most important cause. I have myself, done it many times over, not to persuade others but to satisfy myself. I have been used for many years to study the histories of other times, and to examine and weigh the evidence of those who have written about them, and I know of no one fact in the history of mankind which is proved by better and fuller evidence of every sort, to the understanding of a fair inquirer, than the great sign, which God has given us that Christ died and rose from the dead." (Arnold, as cited in Smith TS, 425-26.)

Medicine

An article in the Journal of the American Medical Association concluded from the Gospel accounts that Jesus certainly died before He was moved from the cross. An eyewitness saw blood and water come out of His pierced side in John 19:34-35. The evangelist that recorded this would not know what medical doctors know today. A semi-solid red clot seeps out of the body followed separately by a slow, watery serum if you are cut and the heart is no longer pumping blood. Blood gushes out with every heartbeat if the heart is pumping blood. No water flows out after the blood.

The Harvard Professor of Law

Dr. Greenleaf, the Royal Professor of Law at Harvard University, was one of the greatest legal minds that ever lived. He wrote the famous legal volume entitled, *A Treatise of the Law of Evidence*, considered by many the greatest legal volume ever written. Dr. Simon Greenleaf believed that the resurrection of Jesus Christ was a hoax. He also determined once and for all, to expose the "myth" of the resurrection. After thoroughly examining the evidence for the resurrection, Dr. Greenleaf came to the exact opposite conclusion! He wrote a book entitled, *An Examination of the Testimony of the Four Evangelists by the Rules of Evidence Administered in the Courts of Justice*. He stated the following in his book:

"It was impossible that the apostles could have persisted in affirming the truths they had narrated, had not Jesus Christ actually risen from the dead..." (Simon Greenleaf, *an Examination of the Testimony of the Four Evangelists by the Rules of Evidence Administered in the Courts of Justice*, p. 29). Dr. Greenleaf concluded that according to the jurisdiction of legal evidence, the resurrection of Jesus Christ was the best supported event in all of history! What changed the mind of Dr. Greenleaf and many others?

Professor E.M. Blaiklock

"I claim to be an historian. My approach to Classics is historical. And I tell you that the evidence for the life, the death, and the resurrection of Christ is better authenticated than most of the facts of ancient history..."

A mob of people arrested Jesus in the Garden of Gethsemane and brought Him to Pilate. The people spit upon Him, cursed, laughed at Him, beat Him with a whip, called Him names and accused Him of blasphemy. He was sentenced to die by crucifixion. Mark 14:50 says, *"And they all forsook Him, and fled"*. They were afraid that the same thing would happen to them.

Peter had boasted just days earlier, *"Though I should die with you, I will not deny you"*, in Matthew 26:35. After Jesus was dead and crucified one of the women saw Peter and said, *"You were one of them; you were with Jesus of Nazareth"*. The Bible says he began to curse and swear, saying, *"I know not this man of whom you speak"* in Mark 14:71. Three times Peter denied the Lord, cursing and swearing, *"I know not this man"*.

They all forsook Him and fled because they were frightened for their own lives and humiliated. They had seen Him walk on water and heal the sick. They had seen Him raise others from the dead. They were both humiliated and frightened. Something happened, because after Jesus was buried they later went back to Jerusalem boldly preaching, even at the threat of death, that Jesus was alive!

Peter said in Acts 2, *"You men of Israel hear these words; Jesus of Nazareth, a man approved of God among you by miracles and wonders and signs...you have taken, and by wicked hands have crucified and slain...this Jesus that*

God has raised up, whereof we are all witnesses" (verses 22, 23, 32).

How could such confused and frightened men become so outspoken and courageous when they knew they could face the death penalty?

Peter also said in Acts 2:29, *"Men and brethren, let me speak freely to you regarding David, he is dead and buried and his grave is with us this day"*. Peter was informing them that the grave of old King David was still with them and they could go and visit the grave. However, he could proclaim the resurrection of Jesus successfully to the Jews on the day of Pentecost because if Jesus had not risen, everyone would be able to go to the place where He was buried and find Him. And that would never happen because He arose from the dead and left the grave. Nobody in history has ever even claimed to have His body, nor to be able to produce it to silence the disciples to stop the truth regarding His resurrection from being known. The disciples later died a horrible death for continuing to proclaim the truth regarding the resurrection of Jesus.

Proof of the Resurrection

1   If the resurrection were a lie, the Jews or the Romans would have been able to produce Jesus' body and nipped the superstition in the bud to end the tale. The place as to where He was buried was known. They never went to the tomb to silence the disciples because He rose from the dead just as He said. The body did not stay in the grave.

2   Unarmed disciples could not have overpowered armed Roman soldiers who faced the death penalty if they allowed the body to be stolen. It is a known historical fact that Roman soldiers were put to death and executed if they allowed anyone to escape

while on guard duty. How could his body have vanished? The empty tomb proves the resurrection.

3   The disciples fled and forsook Him and feared for their lives, so no motive existed for stealing the body. The disciples could not have successfully proclaimed the resurrection in Jerusalem during the same time and place where the resurrection had taken place among so many eyewitnesses and had it believed if it was not the truth. The disciples wrote down what happened as historians and it was impossible to fabricate events. Under the circumstances, they could have never successfully proclaimed the resurrection and had people believe it, had it not actually occurred.

4   The empty tomb is the proof. The disciples did not go to Athens or Rome to preach the resurrection; they went directly to Jerusalem, where if the teaching were false, the falsehood would be evident because they could go right to the tomb and the place where He was laid. That empty tomb was too notorious to be denied. The truth about Jesus and His resurrection was an easy fact to prove due to the empty tomb. Peter's sermon on the Day of Pentecost in Acts 2 informed everyone that the tomb of David was still with them, and they knew the place where He was laid. He also told them that Jesus was not at the place where He had been laid, but that God had raised Him up from the grave and from hell, and that it was not possible for Him to stay in the realm of death.

5   This sermon had credibility because it was an invitation for everyone to go to the grave of Jesus for themselves to see with their own eyes as to whether or not the tomb was truly empty. Jewish and Roman historians all admit to the empty tomb. All the Romans or the Jews had to do to silence the disciples during

those days and in centuries to come was to go to the tomb and get His corpse (dead body) and prove that He had not risen from the dead. That never happened. Therefore, thousands of people, in fact 3000 Jews were baptized and converted on the Day of Pentecost after Peter's declaration that He had risen.

6   The Gospel was successfully proclaimed and drew many followers from the beginning because of the empty tomb, plus the fact that everyone knew that he rose from the dead. No other explanation exists for how the vast majority of the Jews, the disciples who had denied him prior to the crucifixion, and thousands of others would have started to follow him so soon after the resurrection was proclaimed on the streets of Jerusalem. The tomb was empty and they knew that the Roman soldiers were guarding it and the seal had been broken. They had heard that the Roman soldiers fled and were also aware that Jesus said before His death that he would rise again three days later. They knew He was Lord and God and that He had come to visit us on the earth to reveal Himself to us, and he proved it.

7   Jewish and Roman historians all admit to the empty tomb. Josephus, the Jewish historian who wrote about Jesus and was not a disciple, nor a Christian did. Tacitus, the Roman historian for the Roman government also admitted that the tomb was empty. The large stone moved. History teaches us that such stones would weigh about two tons. The stone would have been too much for unarmed disciples to move it. The stone was moved, however, and it looked as if it had been picked up and carried away. How could unarmed peasants have done that?

8   The Roman Guards ran away. History teaches us that if Roman guards allowed anyone to escape, they were put to death. A guard unit was made up of four to sixteen men. They paid close

attention to doing their jobs. A Roman soldier was stripped of their clothes and burned alive in fire until death for leaving the place of responsibility. They would have never run away from the gravesite of Jesus knowing that they would be put to death. Would you quit your job or skip a class if you knew that you would be put to death? No! But the soldiers ran from the gravesite and fled their duty knowing they would be put to death for doing so. They saw the angels that night as the Bible states that told them Jesus had risen from the dead.

9   The Broken Seal is undeniable. The Bible says that after a stone was rolled over the grave's entrance they placed the Roman Seal on the stone. The seal is like a warning, "Do not enter", or a "No trespassing sign", and under Roman law you were put to death if you broke the seal. The Roman Seal was much like the yellow tape that you use to mark a crime scene. And anyone who broke the seal, the penalty was torture and crucifixion upside down. Breaking the seal in an effort to get inside of the tomb was a suicide mission and a death request. People feared breaking the seal just as people fear standing as a target for someone to shoot them on a rifle range. The seal was broken, the Roman soldiers ran and the tomb was empty on the third day. Jesus rose from the dead.

10   Over 500 eyewitnesses saw him alive. The apostle Paul told the people that there were over 500 people that saw Jesus, and Paul said it so that everyone could question them if they doubted what he had said. The things recorded by Matthew, Mark, Luke, and John are also recorded by other historians such as Josephus and Tacitus. The miracles such as casting out devils, raising others from the dead, healing the sick, and the empty tomb are all matters of history that Jewish and Roman historians have also documented.

11   The Psychology of Truth is real. People do not die for what they know to be a lie if all they had to do is tell the truth and live. The disciples proclaimed that Jesus had risen from the dead in Jerusalem and in Rome, knowing that they would face the death penalty if they did not stop proclaiming that they saw Him alive.

12   There was no motive for storytelling. Lies are always told for some selfish advantage such as for money or for love, or to get a job, or to save your life. The disciples proclaimed the resurrection of Jesus and the fact that they saw Him alive while knowing they would be hated, scorned, persecuted, imprisoned, tortured, crucified, boiled alive, roasted, beheaded, disemboweled, or fed to the lions. Lying would not have occurred to get this torturing and hatred from people including execution by the government. They told the truth and we know it. Hundreds of people are not going to any government today, such as the one in China where they will shoot you on the spot for a crime, and confess to them crimes they did not commit, if they know they will lose their lives. No one. Not even you and I would put our lives on the line for what we know to be a lie that was invented.

13   Lives have been transformed by Christ for centuries. Jesus has changed the lives of cities, towns, villages, states, and countries. Millions of people have testified during Biblical days and do testify as witnesses today that Jesus has touched their lives and turned them around, healed them, saved them, and performed many other miracles. People have been raised up out of addictions, poverty, health problems, and many other oppressions by the same Spirit that raised Jesus out of the grave. The same Spirit that raised Jesus up from the grave is the Holy Ghost and

He can raise us up out of any circumstance, sin, trouble, tragedy, sickness, disease, etc.

John 2:19 says, *"Jesus answered and said unto them, Destroy this temple, and in three days I will raise it up"*. **And the tomb was empty on the third day.**

John 10:18: *"No man takes it from me (My life), but I lay it down of myself. I have power to lay it down, and I have power to take (raise) it (up) again. This commandment have I received of my Father".*

The resurrection of Jesus sharply distinguishes Jesus from all other religious founders. The bones of Abraham and Mohammad and Buddha and Confucius and Lao-Tzu (the Father of Taoism), and Zoroaster (who was considered) a philosopher (also known as Zarathustra), an ancient Persian prophet (who founded the first world religion Zoroastrianism) are still here on the earth. Jesus' tomb is empty! William Lane Craig on the importance of the empty tomb: "The empty tomb is proof of the resurrection. The notion that Jesus rose from the dead with a new body while His old body still lay in the grave is a modern concept/idea and is not true. Jews would not have accepted the idea of a division of two bodies.

Even if the disciples would have failed to check the empty tomb, the Jewish authorities could not have been guilty of such an oversight. When the disciples began to preach the resurrection in Jerusalem and people responded, and when religious authorities stood helplessly by, the tomb must have been empty. The simple fact that the Christian fellowship, founded on belief in Jesus'   resurrection came into existence and flourished in the very city where He was executed and buried is powerful evidence/proof for the historicity of the empty tomb." (Craig, "DJRD," as cited in Wilkins, JUF, 151-52.)

Englishman Frank Morrison comments, "In all the fragments and echoes of this far off controversy which have come down to us, we are nowhere told that any responsible person asserted that the body of Jesus was still in the tomb. We are only given reasons why it was not there. Running all through these ancient documents is the persistent assumption that the tomb of Christ was vacant. Can we fly in the face of this cumulative and mutually corroborative evidence? Personally, I do not think we can. The sequence of coincidences is too strong". (Dr. Frank Morrison, "Who Moved the Stone?" page 116.)

The church was founded on the resurrection and disproving it would have   destroyed the Christian Movement. However, instead of any such disproof, throughout the first century, Christians were threatened, imprisoned, stoned and killed because of their faith. It would have been much easier to have silenced them by producing Jesus' body, but this was never done. Think about that for a moment. Where was the body of Jesus if he did not rise? Why didn't the Roman government go right to the tomb and produce the body to silence the outbreak of Christianity throughout Jerusalem and Rome? The silence of Christ's enemies and the lack of evidence to disprove the resurrection proves the resurrection just as much as the apostles' witness. If he had not arose they would have went to the tomb and produced his body.

Millions of people in history transformed by Jesus Christ

John R.W Stott say: "Perhaps the transformation of the disciples of Jesus is the greatest evidence of all for the resurrection." (Stott, BC,58-49). The lives of men and women have also been transformed by Christ for the over nineteen hundred years. Changed lives is subjective evidence that bears witness to the objective fact. Paul Little points out that the church, which was founded around A.D. 32, did not just happen, but had a definite cause. It was said of the Christians at Antioch in the early days of the church that they turned the world upside down

(Acts 17:6). The cause of this influence was the resurrection. (Little, KwhyB,62).

H.D.A Major, principal of Ripon Hall, Oxford, (cited by Smith) says: "Had the crucified Jesus ended his disciples' experience of him, it is hard to see how the Christian church could have come into existence. The church was founded on faith in the Messiahship of Jesus. A crucified Jesus was no Messiah at all. He was one rejected by Judaism and accursed of God It was the Resurrection of Jesus, as St. Paul declares in Romans 1:4, which proclaimed him to be the Son of God ith power." (Major, as cited in Smith, TS, 368) The fact of the resurrection of Jesus transformed the lives of his disciples and of men and women throughout history. Any shred of evidence presented to disprove the authenticity of it would have stopped Christianity in its place. The changed lives can only be explained by the fact of the resurrection. Jesus must be alive and able to change the lives of those who follow Him.

The Fact of the Church in History

The church has survived as an institution for over 2000 years, based upon the preaching of the resurrection of Christ from the dead on the third day. A fact of history to disprove this event would have destroyed the church if it were true and could be proven. The resurrection was established as a real event in time and space within history as stated in the Bible.

> Acts 2:23-24 says, *"Him being delivered by the determinate counsel and foreknowledge of God, ye by wicked hands, have crucified and slain; whom God has raised up, having loosed the pains of death, because it was not possible that He should beholden of it".*

Scholars have studied the history of many decades and events including the days of Julius Caesar, Alexander the Great, Confucius, and many others. They all agree that the resurrection of Jesus is the most widespread and easily proven fact of history. Repent and believe the gospel. Jesus died for your sins and rose from the dead on the 3rd day. He was the creator of everything and laid down his life because he loved you and was raised from the dead. No shred of evidence has yet been discovered in literary sources or archaeology that would disprove that the tomb of Jesus was empty on the morning of the first Easter.

Dr. Frank Morrison (a rationalistic lawyer) decided to take three years off from his law practice in order to disprove the resurrection of Jesus Christ. After three years of intense study he found that the sheer weight of the evidence compelled him to conclude that Jesus Christ rose from the dead, and as a consequence he wrote the famous book, "Who Moved the Stone?"

Think about this, all historians agree that the large boulder was placed by the Romans over the tomb before the armed Roman guard unit watched the grave site. Whoever moved the stone would have faced the death penalty under Roman law for treason. They would have also had to have enormous strength and have been able to overpower the guard unit, which was typically 4-16 men. Unarmed disciples who fled as cowards and denied that they knew Him before the crucifixion were not equipped for such a feat, and no historical data corroborates the premise.

Professor Josh McDowell, according to a recent survey, is one of the most popular speakers among university students today. He has spoken on more than 650 university and college campuses to more than seven million people in seventy-four countries during the last twenty-four years. A student at the University of Uruguay said to him, "Professor McDowell, Why can't you refute Christianity?" For a very simple reason he answered, "I am not able to explain away an event in history, the resurrection of Jesus Christ!"

After Peter's famous sermon on the Day of Pentecost about the resurrection and the Lordship of Jesus with the public challenge to verify the truthfulness of the good news of the resurrection, the Jews wanted to know what they needed to do to be saved. Peter said to them, "Repent, and be baptized every one of you in the name of Jesus Christ for the remission of sins, and ye shall receive the gift of the Holy Ghost" in Acts 2:38.

Have you repented today? Have you been baptized in the name of Jesus Christ? Have you been filled with the gift of the Holy Ghost? Jesus is alive and he is real, and because the resurrection is true, everything else that Jesus said is proven to be the truth! And His name is Jesus. Because these things are true we have a lot to look forward to after this life once we are in heaven and in the New Jerusalem. The scripture says, "Neither is there salvation in any other: for there is none other name under heaven given among men, whereby we must be saved" (Acts. 4:12).

Thomas Arnold said, "Thousands and ten thousands of persons have gone through the historical evidence piece by piece, as carefully as every judge summoning up the most important cause. I have myself done it many times over, not to persuade others, but to satisfy myself. I have been used for many years to study the histories of other times, and to examine and weigh the evidence of those who have written about them, and I know of no one fact in the history of mankind which is proved by better and fuller evidence of every sort, to the understanding of a fair inquirer, than the great sign which God has given us that Christ died and rose from the dead. (Arnold, as cited in Smith, TS, 425-26.)

We can be saved from eternity in hell because of faith in His death, burial, and resurrection! As we clearly see, his resurrection is a fact of history. It is very comforting to know that we have hope of everlasting life due to His death on the cross for us, if *we confess, repent, and believe*. *The Bible says, "For God so loved the world that He gave His only begotten son, that whosoever believes in Him should not perish but have everlasting life"* (John 3:16).

Did you know that people travel each year to Mecca to pray at the place where the prophet Mohammad was and still is buried today? Not so with Jesus Christ because He rose from the dead on the third day! The Islamic prophet Mohammad is buried and his remains are still with us today in the A-Masjibal-Naban (Mosque of the Prophet) in the city of Medina. I have heard so many people say that they follow Mohammad and that Jesus was just a prophet. However, Jesus Christ is God in the flesh. He was God and man. He was human and divine. He was and is called from the Old Testament scriptures "Wonderful, Counselor, The Mighty God, The Prince of Peace, and the Everlasting Father" (Isaiah 9:6).

Did you know that Confucius, the Chinese philosopher was born on September 28, 551 B.C. and that he died in 479 B.C., which was 479 years before Jesus was born? The place where the body of Confucius was buried and where his bones remain is still in his hometown of Qufu, Shandong Province China. What remains of the body of Confucius is lying in a large cemetery today, and more than 100,000 of his followers are buried in the same cemetery. The burial site and tomb of Jesus Christ was empty on the third day and all historians are well aware of it! He is the Lord God and we know it. He told the people during his life that if you destroy this temple (referring to his body) that in three days he would raise it up again. Believe in Jesus today, and trust Him for your salvation.

Repent of your sins today. Ask Him to forgive you, save you, and to fill you with his Holy Spirit. Jesus is coming back soon. The believers were filled with the Holy Ghost on the day of Pentecost and God is still baptizes believers with the Holy Spirit today. Keep in mind too that the first missionary to the gentile world said, "Now if you confess with your mouth the Lord Jesus and believe in your heart that God has raised him from the dead you shall be saved. For with the mouth a man believes to righteousness and with the mouth confession is made to salvation" (Romans 10:9-10).

The Shroud of Turin

What is The Shroud of Turin?

The shroud of Turin is the linen cloth that is believed to be the linen cloth that was wrapped around the body of Jesus in the tomb. The Bible describes this linen cloth in the gospel of John, chapter 20 and verses 5-7. The shroud is currently located in Turin, Italy.

The Shroud has been studied by many scientists and scholars

The Shroud of Turin is the most studied artifact in human history and more than 150,000 man hours which have been invested in investigating this linen cloth. Scientists, physicists, chemists, radiologists, botanists, medical doctors, and other scientists and scholars from various professional fields who have studied the shroud for decades.

A scientific miracle may prove the authenticity of the shroud:

- The technology to create the 3 dimensionally encoded photonegative image on the Shroud of Turin does not exist today.
- The shroud has the photonegative images of a man crucified by a Roman crucifixion from first century A.D. that fits the description of the historical Jesus of Nazareth as described by the four gospels.
- The laser technology does not exist and the shroud cannot be replicated or reproduced by any of our most advanced scientific instruments today.

The shroud was studied by medical doctors and forensic pathologists and they identified the shroud as the likely burial cloth of the historical Jesus of a first century Roman crucifixion. Medical doctors and forensic pathologists have proven the following:

- According to Professors of Medical Pathology, the lashes or stripes were that were made was consistent with the instruments used by Roman soldiers in the 1ˢᵗ century for crucifixion.
- The red color of the blood has been proven to be post-mortem. (after death) The wrists and ankles had nails driven through them and were nailed to the cross.
- The scourges are all over the back and lower legs.
- Heavy bleeding occurred from the wounds in the scalp from the crown of thorns and from the feet that were nailed to the cross. The crown of thorns identifies that the victim of this crucifixion is Jesus.
- The bible indicates that a crown of thorns was placed on his head which is described in the gospel of Mark, chapter 15, and verses 15-18.
- The weight of the body was supported on the cross by nails through the palms.
- The shroud shows that the nails were driven through the wrists through a small point known as the despots point.
- The weight of the body was supported on the cross by nails through the palms.
- The nails passed directly through the wrists through the Carpal Tunnel, causing great pain.
- There was a post-mortem wound to the chest. (Consistent with a Roman solider piercing him in the side as stated in the bible.
- There was a skin wound in the chest areas produced by a spear.
- Forensic Pathologists say the spear went through the 5ᵗʰ and 6ᵗʰ rib.
- The post-mortem wound to the chest caused blood and water the flow from
  the heart and onto the cloth which is consistent with the biblical record of blood and water flowing from his heart and out of his back after being pierced by the Roman soldier.

The plants identified on the shroud was from Jerusalem.

Research reveals that of the 28 plants found that 20 are known to grow in Jerusalem and the other 8 grow around the Judean desert or the Dead Sea area. We know from biblical history that Jesus lived and traveled in the Judean desert and near the Dead Sea. The plants are not located anywhere else in the world. The plants which were identified in images on the shroud is more evidence that it was the burial cloth of Jesus.

The pollen identified on the shroud was from Jerusalem.

Botanists discovered pollen and spores on the linen of the Shroud and the pollen has been researched in laboratories. The pollen found originates from 58 different plants that originate nowhere else in the world but in Jerusalem. The evidence that this was the burial cloth of Jesus grows with each item discovered on or within the miraculous shroud.

The dirt on the cloth is from the roads of Jerusalem and Golgotha

Dirt was found near the nose, left kneecap, and both heels. It has been determined that the dirt on the nose and the left kneecap came off the road as He fell under the weight of the cross beam tied over His shoulders. The dirt on the heel area likely came from the area near Golgotha according to researchers. The dirt was compared to the dirt with limestone from ancient Jerusalem tombs and it was concluded that there may be some other places in the world where this type of dirt can be found, but that it has not been found as of today anywhere else in the world. Consequently, they have concluded that it's unlikely it came from anywhere else but Jerusalem.

The coins placed over the eyes are from the days of Pontius Pilate

As scientists viewed the image of the crucified man in the shroud, they noticed coins over the eyes of the victim. The coins which have the name of Pontius Pilate on them are from the years 29 A.D. 30 B.C. and 31 A.D. Jesus was crucified in 33 A.D. and the coins were still in use during His crucifixion. The coins give overwhelming proof that the crucified man lived and was crucified after the dates inscribed on the coins. Again, the crown of thorns on his head identifies him as Jesus Christ based on the biblical record. Coins were placed over the eyes of the dead by Jews to keep the eyes closed. The victim bled from his head directly beneath the shroud according to forensic pathologists and the Medical Doctors who studied the shroud.

Scientists profess they have proved that the shroud was deliberately encoded.

- Scientists have proven that the shroud had to come from a 3 dimensional person, which proves it was not a painting or something fabricated.
- The shroud is the only 3 dimensional subject on the earth with encoded information from technology or science that we don't have.
- The known laws of physics would have to be violated to replicate or reproduce anything like it.
- The shroud was made by light radiation that deliberately formed a 3D image onto the burial cloth that was deliberated encoded with information.
- The image is a photographic negative only possible if light and darkness are reversed but dimensionally encoded.
- No technology is on the earth today that is capable of reproducing the shroud or anything like it.
- The Shroud reveals that a supernatural intelligence not of earthly origin deliberately encoded the shroud with information.

Evidence from NASA

NASA discovered that a photograph of the shroud produced a 3D image when placed under a V8 computer. The discovery proved that the shroud had distance-imaging information embedded in the image, which proved that the shroud was dimensionally encoded. Scientists have concluded all of the following:

- The Distance imaging information was encoded within the image on the Shroud at its formation.
- The body was 3 dimensional.
- This is the only 2D property on the earth with this quality.
- The image is a topographic image. The closer the cloth to the body the more the image was highlighted. The image acts as a photonegative with light and darkness reversed but dimensionally encoded deliberately.

- The V8 analyzing computer discovered 3D information deliberated encoded.

The world- renowned scholar Dr. Dame Piczek, a Hungarian trained particle physicist explained the following:

- She explained that the body was suspended in mid-air versus lying flat on the rock when the images were projected on the shroud as a quantum hologram which does not conform to any known law of physics.
- The phenomenon of the body hovering while in mid-air while traveling in an upward direction while laser-light radiation made the image, if further proven by the fact that a perfect picture of both the front and back side of the crucified man, Jesus, appears on both sides of the shroud.

- The physics behind the image in the shroud is complicated physics. Scientists discovered that "Quantum time" collapsed to absolute zero (time stopped moving) in the tomb of Christ.
- The event horizon, in relativity is a boundary of space and time most often near an area surrounding a black hole. Light emitted from beyond the horizon can never reach the observer and anything that passes through the horizon from the observer's side appears to freeze in space; A suspension of gravity.
- According to the physics of event horizons, the dead body must have left the image on the 2 surfaces of the horizons at the time of the explosion or when time stopped, the images were ejected onto both sides of the cloth with the body hovering parallel to the event horizons. <u>(which proves the body raised up off of the flat rock which he was laid on in the dark tomb)</u> .

In other words, scientists have proven that in the tomb of Jesus Christ that the body at some point was not lying flat on the rock but was suspended in the air under the shroud while moving in the upward (resurrection) direction. Light traveled from the body while it hovered in the middle of the air in an upward direction and encoded three-dimensional information on a two- dimensional surface as a quantum hologram, scientifically impossible. Dr. Dame Piczek, particle physicist, stated that we have the beginning of a new universe inside of the tomb of Jesus Christ. Physicists say that the same power responsible for the origin of the universe previously known was inside of the tomb of Jesus Christ. Moreover, Jesus is described as the creator of all things in the gospel of John in chapter number one.

The light could be compared to the light at the transfiguration of Christ when time stopped and Moses and Elijah appeared at the Mount with the disciples as light shown from Jesus when He was transfigured. Visible light that shined from the body of Jesus is only one form of electro-magnetic radiation. You have radio waves, ultraviolet light, gamma rays, and more. Only particles that are extremely hot or ones that travel at high rates of speed can create gamma rays. Visible light, X-rays, Gamma rays are all part of the Electromagnetic Spectrum, but they travel at different velocities. It has been proven that the light in the dark tomb traveled through both sides of the body and to the shroud to produce the images. We were told at the transfiguration of Jesus that His face shone like the sun and his clothes became white as light. Jesus' whole body changed from His normal body to a body radiating light at the transfiguration. A light from within His face became as bright as the sun. The Bible also says that God is light. Jesus said, He was the light of the world. The image in the shroud is a photograph but it is more, it is a hologram. It could only have been made in the tomb of Christ with darkness and a flash of light. A holograph is an intermediate photograph that contains information for reproducing a 3D image by holography technology.

The words, "The Lamb" are also in the shroud not too far from the beard of the man crucified and are in Aramaic not far from the coins dated 29 and 31 A.D. Jesus was called "the Lamb of God" that takes away the sins of the world by John the Baptist. Many scholars from the scientific community believe that the Shroud of Turin proves the resurrection of Jesus Christ scientifically. As an Evangelist and a Pastor I want to say that your belief that Jesus died for your sins and rose from the dead is essential for you to receive the greatest gift, eternal life, from Jesus Christ and the forgiveness of your sins.

We must believe that He is the Son of God and that he died for our sins and rose again from the dead. The book of Romans says in chapter 10 and verse 9, that "if you confess with your mouth the Lord Jesus, and shall believe in your heart that God has raised Him from the dead, thou shall be saved". Moreover, Faith comes by hearing and hearing by the Word of God. "How shall they call on him in whom they have not believed? And how shall they believe in him of whom they have not heard? And how shall they hear without a preacher?" (Romans 10:14)

The Shroud (the cloth wrapped around the body of Jesus after His death and placed in His tomb) was not preached by divine inspiration as proof of the resurrection of Jesus from the dead during Biblical days. However, many scientists and atheists have become believers because of the shroud. It may have been left behind for skeptics and the scientific community as proof for those like doubting Thomas who needed physical evidence of the resurrection.

During biblical days and specifically on the day of Pentecost, Peter reminded everyone that the tomb of the patriarch King David was still with them in Jerusalem, and that Jesus' body was not in the tomb and that He had risen from the dead. Approximately 3000 Jews were baptized in the name of Jesus Christ on the Day of Pentecost after Peter's declaration to "Repent and be baptized every one of you in the name of Jesus Christ for the remission of sins, and you shall receive the gift of the Holy Ghost". The empty tomb on the third day after Christ's death was a fact that was too notorious to be denied, and it was the very truth that caused thousands to be converted to Christianity throughout Jerusalem and Rome. The Holy Ghost fell on them on Pentecost because they repented and believed the gospel preached by the Lord Jesus Christ. If you have not already been filled with the power of The gift of the Holy Ghost ask Jesus to send this important gift to you. The Holy Ghost is the spirit of Jesus Christ indwelling the heart, body and soul of the believer, leading him, teaching him, convicting him of sin, and working God's plan of sanctification (separation from sin) out in the life of the believer as he yield's to and is submitted to the Holy Spirit. The Holy Spirit gives us power and the same power living inside of us that raised Jesus from the dead. (Romans 8:11) The bible says in Acts 1:8 "But you shall receive power after that the Holy Ghost is come upon you and you shall be witnesses." Jesus saved us to do something! He saved us to witness the good news to others!

Hell is real. Jesus was surely the Son of God and was raised from the dead. Sin is the reason we all deserve to pay for our sins in hell. The Good news is that Jesus died for our sins and was raised from the dead on the 3rd day. Once we have repented and believed this good news we can be born again and filled with the Holy Spirit just as the Holy Ghost that fell on them in Acts chapter 2. Confess your sins to Jesus and repent and believe the gospel. He has promised us the gift of the Holy Ghost in John 14:17-26. The Holy Ghost is our comforter and shall teach you all things. In John 14: 27 Jesus said he has also left us with peace but not as this world gives and encourages us "Let not your heat be troubled and neither let it be afraid." He repeated this and had stated in John 14:1-3 "Let not your heart be troubled, ye believe in God, believe also in me. In my father's house are many mansions: if it were not so I would have told you. I go to prepare a place for you. And if I go to prepare a place for you, I will come again, and receive you to myself: that where I am you may be also."

14

The Gospel Message

The Atonement

The atonement is simply what Jesus did for us to accomplish our salvation by reconciling us back to God. Sin caused a barrier between us and God and Jesus tore down the barrier and built us a bridge. My hope is that after reading this book that you can comprehend the special love that God has for you as one of his loved, foreknown and chosen. Jesus died for the purpose of saving those whom he died for. This is the equivalent of saying that he died in order to save those to whom he would actually apply the benefits of his redemptive work to. The benefits include the inheritance of the kingdom. For centuries there have been various viewpoints about what Jesus accomplished for us with his redemptive work. It should be known, first of all, as a general rule, that the design and purpose of God cannot be frustrated and overthrown by the will of man. The purpose of saving a man or woman through the death of Jesus Christ cannot be derailed by the actions or inactions of man. The Sovereignty of God is his divine control as a King over each event that happens in the universe. God has a purpose for your life prior to your arrival on earth. Sometimes he will use angels, people, and our own gifts to reveal that purpose to us. God is able to keep us from falling and to present us faultless before him in exceeding joy (Jude 24). Will he keep all that he saves or can some fall away in the end and be lost?

Gospel of the Kingdom and Grace

The gospel message is simply that you can live forever in a perfect paradise in his kingdom with the God of love if you believe Jesus. He has prepared this place specifically for you and its mansions (John 14:1-3). The streets in the city that you inherited is paved with gold and the gates are made out of pearls. There shall be no more sorrow, death, pain, sickness, disease, famine, and crying. God shall wipe away all of your tears and his glory shall lighten the city (Revelation 21:1-27). You can have a new birth in your spirit and shall enter God's spiritual kingdom and live forever if you believe Jesus (John 3:3). Jesus can heal your mind or your broken heart and set you free from spiritual captivity if you believe (Luke 4:18-19). The sins which have enslaved us can be overcame because of our faith. The sins which make all worthy of a fate in Hell are forgiven when you believe Jesus and trust him for your salvation (Romans 5:1).

Believing Jesus means that we conclude that he is the Son of God and that he came to earth to die for us and that he rose again from the dead. We are saved from spending an eternity in Hell and from the wrath of God to come because we believe in our hearts that Jesus died for us and rose again from the dead (Romans 10:9). That is good news since we all deserve Hell for breaking his commandments. We believe his work on the cross was done for us to save us by securing our salvation and that his work was part of God's eternal plan for us that existed before the worlds were formed (Ephesians 1:1-4). Jesus said, "For God so loved the world, that he gave his only begotten Son, that whosoever believes in him should not perish, but have everlasting life. For God sent not his Son into the world to condemn the world; but that the world through him might be saved" (John 3:16). Jesus didn't come to earth to condemn us but to save us. Salvation comes by faith when we believe.

Believers of the gospel are divorced from the law and married to Christ (Romans 7:1-4). This is good news because the Old Testament laws prove that everyone is currently a transgressor and that they are standing guilty before God as sinners (Romans 3:19). Sinners cannot go to Heaven. However, The law cannot be used to condemn a believer to Hell or curse a believer for a violation of the Old Testament Commandments (Galatians 3:13). The laws that proved we were sinners was taken away and nailed to the cross with Christ for us when and if we believe (Colossians 2:14).We are no longer under the law but under Grace. God wiped away sin through his perfect offering at the cross for all those that believe him. The scripture says, "For by one offering he hath perfected forever them that are sanctified" (Hebrew 10:14). Righteousness is a free gift and he sees us a righteous because of what Jesus did. The Bible teaches, "For he hath made him to be sin for us, that we might become the righteousness of God in him" (2 Corinthians 5:21).

All of this means that once you believe that you are not required to keep a set of commandments or rules in order to keep eternal life and inherit the kingdom. It also means that after you are forgiven by God that you are not required to add good works to your faith to avoid being thrown into hell or damned. The scriptures teach, "Therefore, we conclude that a man is justified by faith without the works of the law" (Romans 3:28). God says that we are just and righteous because we believe. This is the substance of the New Testament which started when the blood of Jesus was shed. The Hebrew writer taught us, "In the case of a Testament (will) it is necessary to prove that the person who made it has died, for a Testament means nothing while the person who made it is alive; it goes into effect after his death" (Hebrews 9:16-17). God' will is for believers to inherit eternal life, heaven, blessings, and his love because of the death of the testator. The testator is Jesus and he is the "surety" of a better testament (Hebrews 7:22). A surety is the person who guarantees that the people chosen to receive the inheritance receives all of the promises contained therein.

You are no longer under a system of commandments or laws that you are required to follow to prove that you are worthy of God's acceptance and love or inheritance of the kingdom. The gift of eternal life that you receive by faith cannot be earned or merited. The beauty of the gospel message is that Christ died for you because he loved you. He knew you before he made the earth and chose you before he laid the foundation of the world (Ephesians 1:4-5). Jesus Christ died to justify us freely by his grace and to set us free from sin by removing the curse for disobedience to the commandments, blotting out the laws that prove we are transgressors, and ending the Old Covenant which we are no longer under (Galatians 3:13, Galatians 3:23). The Old Testament laws were designed as a tutor for us to prove that we were sinners that could not keep his standards. They lead us to see that we needed the new system which is designed to declare us righteous and holy simply because we believe Jesus (Galatians 3:23-25). When you believe that Jesus came to earth in the flesh as a man and lived a perfect life of obedience for you and then suffered, shed his blood, and died in your stead, your faith counts as perfect righteousness for you (Romans 4:1-5). That is good news! Why? People have discovered that they don't live up to all of the laws when they have tried to nor all of the time. The scripture teach, "For whosoever shall keep the whole law and yet offend in one point, he is guilty of all" (James 2:10). We have either kept the entire law or we broke it and the Bible says that all broke it and stand guilty before God (Romans 3:19) You have been estranged from Christ, you who attempt to be justified by the law (rules and regulations); you have fallen from grace" (Galatians 5:4). The one important thing to remember is that the kingdom will be established both within the hearts of men and as an actual place on earth. Christ will reign as the King of Kings. Jesus mentioned during the early stages of his earthly ministry, "Repent for the kingdom of heaven is at hand" (Matthew 3:2). When we believe the gospel we repent by changing our mind about our own lifestyle and conduct and we turn to Jesus to accept him as our King. We love him because he first loved us (I John 4:19-21).

Atonement

The atonement not only made salvation possible for the sinner, but secured salvation for the sinner. Who did it secure salvation for? Was this conditional security or unconditional security? Those are the questions. The Calvinists, Roman Catholics, Lutherans, and the Arminians differ in their interpretation of what Christ accomplished with his redemptive work. Some believe that Christ died for all and thus everybody will go to Heaven. It is true that the death of Christ meritoriously secured the salvation for those whom he died for. The big question is who are these people and how can they be identified or known. Was the purpose and design of the Atonement constructed for the benefits to be applied to all or exclusively for some? Does the Atonement save everyone? Did Christ die for all to apply the benefits of his redemptive work to all? Will God leave it up to individuals to thwart his purpose for their lives and his plan to save them or will he accomplish his goals with individuals in spite of their faults, inconsistencies, and moral failures?

The Atonement of Jesus Christ secures for those whom it was made a perfect judicial standing before God. This includes the forgiveness of sin, the adoption as children, and the right to eternal life with an inheritance. Eternal life never ends but is an everlasting state in bliss with God. The Atonement also secures a union with Christ through regeneration and sanctification. These works of the Holy Spirit gradually modifies the old man to put on a new man in Jesus Christ. The Atonement secures the final bliss of a believer with God through Jesus Christ in glorification and the enjoyment of eternal life in God's new creation and New Jerusalem. The Atonement makes salvation final and it starts the process of gradually transforming people into the image and likeness of the Son of God. Who did Christ do this for? If he did this for you it means that you will definitely be in Heaven unless for some reason he didn't do it for you or unless there is some unresolved paradox of epic and universal proportions. The simple truth has been revealed, "For God so loved the world, that he gave his only begotten

Son, that whosoever believes in him should not perish, but have everlasting life" (John 3:16).

What is the extent of the Atonement and who did Jesus complete this wondrous work for? All admit that the work of Jesus Christ was sufficient to save everybody. The truth is that the people who teach that his work was completed to be applied to every man do not believe that all men are saved and that all men will actually be saved in the end. Did God intent that the benefits of Christ's work be applied to everybody? Does the fruit of the death of Christ accrue the benefit of salvation for everybody? Did God in sending Jesus Christ and did Christ in coming to the world, to make atonement for sin, do this with the purpose of actually saving all men or just specific people? We can see from the paragraph above that God's purpose was to save those that would believe in him. I encourage you to believe that Jesus Christ did this to save you and that he did it to accomplish your final salvation for you. When you stand before God you will need to know that you can only enter into Heaven because of Christ's work for you. Eternal life is a free gift that Jesus promised to those that would believe in him and trust him for their salvation. The believers trust in him to save them from their sins. They know that his blood was shed in love for them to bring them to heaven. They realize that they cannot change themselves and depend on him to rescue them. They ask. He forgives them and comes to live in their hearts and souls.

God is omnipotent and sovereign and all theologians will admit that. He does his will among the inhabitants of earth and in heaven. God is in perfect control of what happens next in history and with all of our lives (Daniel 4:35-37). Everyone admits that only a limited number out of multitudes will be saved in the end. Why? God declared the end from the beginning and from ancient times things that are not yet done, saying, my counsel shall stand, and I will do all my pleasure (Isaiah 46:10). God will accomplish what he has purposed for your existence. The human will is free but God has a plan. Can man thwart the plan of God and overthrow his purpose or design? Has your destiny been determined in advance of creation or do you determine your own destination? God loves us with an unconditional love. It is a love that is not contingent upon our actions, failures, faults, and shortcomings. It is a love that endures. God knew about your failures in advance of your actions. God purposed before he laid the foundations of the world that Jesus would be his sacrificial lamb to die in your stead on the cross and save you. The scriptures testify, "Who hath saved us, and called us with an holy calling, not according to our works, but according to his own purpose and grace which was given us in Christ Jesus before the world began" (2 Timothy 1:9).

The thing that we must keep in mind is that Jesus Christ was specific in terms of who he was laying down his life for. Therefore, we all should rejoice and know that we are victorious and uniquely loved since he died for us. Those whom Jesus died for are called his sheep, the church, and his people, (John 10:11,15, Acts 20:28, Ephesians 5:25-27, Matthew 1:21). Jesus said he was laying his life down for his sheep and that he came to save his people from their sins. The author of the book of Acts stated that he purchased the church with his own blood. What about those that are not in Christ yet? I encourage all to come to Jesus and trust him for your salvation. Jesus promised that whoever believes in him shall not come into condemnation (John 5:24).

Keep in mind throughout this book that a doctrine that Christ died for the purpose of actually saving all men is what logically led men to the doctrine of universalism. Universalism teaches that all men are actually saved and will be saved in the end. Everybody goes to Heaven if Universalism is true. It is to a degree improbable that they for whom Christ has paid the price for all sins, past, present, and future, whose guilt he removed, should or would be lost because of guilt or transgression. We know based on scriptures that all men will not be saved. Therefore, the work of Christ was sufficient to save all but the benefits of his work and the application of it would only apply to and for those who would believe him. We find that people who profess him as Lord will be told by Jesus that he never knew them (Matthew 7:21-24). I'd think that if he had died for them and if he knew them in the sense that he knew his Elect or beloved ones that they would not have been called the workers of iniquity and told to depart from him. Could Christ purchase salvation for someone and not apply the benefits of it to them? Can they lose an inheritance that was bought for them by Christ? The benefit includes Heaven. The idea is that if Jesus died with the purpose of saving anyone in particular that this person is saved and will be saved on Judgment day. People will not be condemned on Judgment day for sin which Christ has suffered and died for already if they believe. That is Great news. He died for all sins, past, present, and future. We will not pay for the penalty of any of our own sins because he nailed them to the cross. When does these benefits apply to us? Do they apply only if we are obedient to Christ after we have been forgiven? Will they apply simply because he purchased the church with his own blood or must we follow rules, laws, and meet certain conditions thereafter?

We shall examine all theological views. Whom did Christ do this wondrous work for? What was his purpose and shall he accomplish it? That is the question. I will also share with you some historical theology to compare one theological system to the other. Be confident that you are secure and that you will be in Heaven, however, be cautious with concluding anything. Freewill is an enigma inside of a paradox wrapped up in a mystery. God has depths in his knowledge, wisdom and judgments that are unsearchable. His ways are past finding out and no man knows his mind to be his counsellor (Romans 11:33-34). God's thoughts and ways are transcendent to our own human thoughts and our finite ways (Isaiah 55:8-9).

The sacrificial work of Jesus Christ and his intercessory work are two different aspects of his atoning work, consequently, the entire scope of one cannot be broader than the other. Jesus Christ limited as to who he was praying for in his intercessory work when he prayed, "I pray not for the world, but for those whom thou hast given me" (John 17:9). It is very unlikely that he limited his intercessory prayer to those whom God had identified out of the world in advance if his sacrificial work was to pay to price for all to include those that would never believe on him. As you read this entire chapter you find that Jesus mentioned that he was praying for all of those that would believe on him in the future in addition to those that were already with him. Jesus Christ will not have a prayer that goes unanswered. He prayed in order that the benefits of his redemptive work on the cross would be applied to the lives of his chosen to save them. He will save them.

Some have concluded that the atonement is for everyone but that the application of it is particular. The theory is that Jesus only made salvation possible for all but actually saves a limited number. However, there is a connection that we cannot separate with the purchase of the benefits of salvation and the actual application of those benefits to those whom he died for. The atonement removed sin because of the blood and the sacrifice removed the guilt and condemnation. In the Old Testament typology it is true that whoever had the benefit of having the sacrifice made for them also had the benefits applied by the priest. The scriptures teach that the atoning work of Christ was not simply to make salvation possible, but to reconcile man back to God, and to provide for him or her eternal life and a salvation which many others would fail to obtain.

The Atonement also secures the condition that must be met in order for us to obtain salvation (Philippians 1:29, Romans 2:4, II Timothy 3:5-6). The conditional faith, repentance, and obedience are also works generated through us by the operation of the Spirit of God. Therefore, there are no conditions which we must meet on our own that has been left up to our own will or dependent on us as men, women, boys, and girls. It can be hard for many of us to let go of the idea that we still must work to do something ourselves to accomplish salvation for ourselves. Many good works are commanded and many exhortations abound that are only the means by which God accomplishes his plan of salvation by the operation of the Holy Spirit. God uses us and others as the instrumentality to work his work in us.

The Governmental Theory of the Atonement

The view holds that God and sovereign and it is his prerogative the pardon or relax the requirements of his justice. However, the view teaches that Christ's suffering were not punishment but an example of a determination to punish sin hereafter. The view holds that his suffering was not designed to satisfy divine justice, but to impress the public mind of a moral universe with a sin –deterring motive. The view was first held by Hugo Grotius (1645) and then by the Supernaturalists of the last age of Germany and in America by Jonathan Edwards, Jr., Maxey, Smalley, Dwight, Emmons, and Park. The cross is seen as an example of a punishment to deter men from sinning and to uphold God's moral government of the universe in order for it to be appropriate for him to pardon.

While this theory embraces truth, it fails the embrace the entire revelation in scripture regarding the purpose and design of the Atonement. Only a real bona fide punishment can be an example of a punishment, or proof of God's determination to punish sin. The view also ignores the reality that God cannot save a sinner if justice is not satisfied in a strict and legal sense. The view denies that Jesus suffered the full penalty of the law as God's justice required in order to have a legal effect judicially to fully satisfy God to save a sinner.

The Governmental theory sees Christ's suffering as a viable substitute for the punishment of sin but not as a punishment of sin. The view holds that God demonstrated his displeasure with sin by punishing his own obedient Son. Because his suffering and death served as a substitute for the punishment humans might have received it makes God able to extend forgiveness while maintaining divine order. The theory holds that Christ's death was a substitute for inflicting the penalty of sin on someone but not an actual penalty inflicted on him as a substitute for our penalty for breaking the law. Pardon is granted under this theory due to God relaxing the strict requirements of the law. The theory teaches that the penalty for us breaking the law was not suffered by Christ. The theory teaches that his substitution for us was only an example of God's divine displeasure with sin but not a legal substitution in our stead nor a penalty for our transgression to satisfy God's divine justice.

The Truth

What is the truth? How should the suffering and death of Jesus Christ be interpreted by sinners? Did Jesus suffer the full penalty of the law in our stead or did he simply suffer abandonment by God and some of God's divine displeasure with sin as a substitute for the full penalty of the law? Was this substitute a relaxing of God's law instead of the punishment of sin? Was his death only an example and display of God's love with an example of a punishment to substitute for a punishment or was it the suffering of a real punishment for sinners?

The sufferings of Jesus Christ were not a substitute for the infliction of a penalty of the law upon sinners in person, but they were the penalty itself executed on their substitute. This was a strict penal satisfaction, Christ being the person suffering as the substitute. This was not merely an example of a punishment nor an exhibition of showmanship of love. This was a punishment and love in action to save those for whom Christ died for. The motive was the love of God for us (John 10:15, Galatians 2:20).

Jesus Christ was fully God and fully man. As a man he assumed the legal responsibilities of his people under the conditions of a human being. Jesus obeyed as suffered as their substitute. The obedience and suffering of Jesus Christ was vicarious and in the stead of his people. The guilt and legal responsibilities of our sins, were imputed to him, charged to him, and he was punished for. Jesus did not suffer the same punishment in degree, kind, or duration that would have been inflicted upon us, but he did suffer that which divine justice demanded of him as a divine person standing in our stead. His sufferings were those of a divine person in a human body. The omniscience of God interpreted the degree of suffering that a divine and perfect person needed to suffer in order to render a full legal payment of our sin debt.

The cross was the result of God's love for us. It satisfied the justice of God. The Atonement removed the guilt of sin, and reconciled God to us. It secured the salvation of those for whom he died, purchased the gift of the Holy Spirit and grace thus ensuring the application of it with the consummation of salvation in the end. The benefits accrue to the recipients of his grace. It was also the execution of his strict justice and an example of punishment to the moral universe. The love shown left a profound moral impression to subdue rebellion to convince sinners. Jesus Christ did these things to accomplish salvation for his people and for all that would believe. The Bible declares that Jesus came to fulfill and not suspend or amend the law (Matthew 5:17-18, Romans 10:4, Romans 3:31). It is revealed to us that God will punish sin (Ezekiel 18:4, Romans 3:26). The law of God is declared to be immutable and thus unchangeable (Luke 16:17). The Jewish sacrifices were vicarious sufferings of the penalties in the stead of offenders that were types and shadows of the penalty Christ would suffer on our behalf. Christ affirms that all of the law as well as the prophets spoke of him and his work (John 1:45, John 5:39, Luke 24:27). Christ was our Passover Lamb sacrificed for us (I Corinthians 5:7, Luke 25:44, Exodus 12:46, Numbers 9:12). Jesus Christ is declared to be sacrificed for his people, by his "blood" being made a sin-offering for us (John 1:29, Hebrews 9:26, Hebrews 9:28, Hebrews 10:12, Hebrews 10:14, I Peter 1:19, Ephesians 5:2, 2 Corinthians 5:21). Jesus Christ is throughout the scriptures everywhere declared to accomplish for man who believes precisely what the ancient sacrifices did one time a year on the Day of Atonement (Galatians 3:13, Matthew 20:28, I John 2:2, I John 2:4, Romans 3:24-25, Ephesians 1:7, Ephesians 2:13). Jesus Christ suffered the penalty for us in order that we can have eternal life if we believe in him and what he accomplished for us.

Antinomianism

Antinomianism comes from the Greek words ant, meaning "against", and nomos meaning "law". Antinomianism means against the law. Theologically, antinomianism is the belief that it is not necessary for Christians to preach, teach, or obey any of the Old Testament commandments or the moral law. The teaching originates from the New Testament teaching that we are not required to observe the law of the Old Testament as a means to salvation. The basis for this teaching is from the reality that when Christ died on the cross he fulfilled the law (Romans 10:4, Galatians 3:23-25, Ephesians 2:15). It is taught that Christ is the end of the law and that righteousness cannot be obtained by works but by faith alone (Galatians 2:16-21, Romans 10:1-4). The teaching includes other relevant truth such as the fact that men are justified by faith without the deeds of the law (Romans 3:28).

There has been several versions of and justifications of Antinomianism down through the centuries. Some teach that once a person is justified by faith in Christ , they no longer have any obligation toward any moral law such as the Ten Commandments because God freed them from it. A variant of this position is that since Christ has raised believers up above the precepts of the law, they need to be obedient only to the guidance and work of the Holy Spirit which works through them after regeneration. Finally, others have opposed the preaching of the law to include the Ten Commandments on the ground that it is unnecessary and contrary to the gospel of Christ. People who may be considered Antinomian today are those that teach the we are saved by grace through faith alone and that a Christian has no obligations as a Christian to keep the commandments or to have a righteousness which comes from works because he cannot merit salvation. The teaching of laws and commandments to do moral things which place the Christian in bondage to follow a commandment or rules to obtain salvation or favor with God are seen as legalism by Antinomianism.

The most famous antinomianism controversies in Christian history occurred in the sixteenth century, and involved Martin Luther and Anne Hutchinson. In fact, it was Martin Luther who coined the word "antinomianism" in his theological struggle with his former student, Johann Agricola. In the early days of the Reformation, Luther had taught that, after New Testament times, the moral law and the commandments had only a negative value in preparing sinners for Grace by making them aware of their sins. Agricola denied even this function of the law, believing that repentance should be induced only through the preaching of the gospel of salvation by grace through faith in Christ. Agricola would not have agreed to a revivalist defining sin in a sermon based on God's law and encouraging the sinner to repent and turn to Christ. Moreover, many even today preach faith in Christ alone without defining sin.

The first major theological controversy in Protestant history lasted from 1537 to 1540. During this time Luther began to stress the role of the law in Christian life and to preach that it was needed to discipline Christians. He also wrote an important theological book to refute antinomianism once and for all: Against the Antinomians (1539). The Lutherans settled the matter by the formula of Concord in 1577, which recognized a threefold use of the law. The law was to reveal sin. The law was to establish what is right in society. The law was to provoke righteous living in those who had been regenerated by the Holy Spirit that had faith in Christ. Antinomianism misunderstood justification by faith alone apart from the works of the law as sanctification. The Holy Spirit performs the work of sanctification in the heart of the believers as a completely separate work in addition to justification.

The threefold use of the law

The law serves the purpose of bringing men under a conviction of sin, and makes him aware of his inability the meet the requirements and demands of the law and standard of righteousness. The law school them to bring them to Christ. Man becomes aware of himself as a transgressor because of the law and he sees himself as a sinner with the inability to save himself. Men can then come to Christ and turn to him for salvation when they realize the law and see their inability to keep it and their helpless condition to rescue themselves from self (Galatians 3:24-25). Sin is the transgression of the law (I John 3:4).

The law restrains sin and promotes godliness on the earth. The law is for the world at large and is necessary because of the reality of sin and its devastating effect upon the people that break it and others. In this aspect it is not a means of grace but designed to reveal to men what the standard of righteousness is. The law is good if we use it lawfully. The law was not made for a righteous man but for the lawless and the disobedient, for the ungodly and for sinners, for unholy and profane, for murderers of fathers and murderers of mothers, for manslayers, whoremongers, them that defile themselves with mankind, for people that steal men, for liars, perjured persons, and if there be any other thing contrary to sound doctrine (I Timothy 1:8-10). Keeping the law doesn't save us. The law defines sin for us. We then turn to Christ and trust him to save us, forgive us, strengthen us, heal us, forgive us, and make us whole. We pray and depend upon Christ to enable us by his grace to stand.

The law is finally a rule of life for believers and is utilized to remind them of their duties in terms with their relationships of love with other people and with God. In this aspect it leads them in the way they ought to conduct themselves and how they are to live life on the earth to please God and to love others. We love God because he first loved us (I John 4:19). We keep his commandments because we love him (John 14:15 & I John 2:4). This use of the law is denied by the Antinomians. However, the law provides the awareness of sin and the definition of transgression (Romans 4:10, I Timothy 1:8-10). The law also provides a standard of righteousness in connection with the doctrine of sanctification. The grace of God has appeared to all men, teaching them to deny ungodliness and worldly lusts, and to live soberly, righteously, and godly in this present world (Titus 2:11-12).

Antinomianism would deny the use of law to define ungodliness and for the use of a moral code or standard for Christians based on the law. Certain men have crept into churches undetected to turn the grace of God into lasciviousness and denying the only Lord God, and our Lord Jesus Christ (Jude 4). People can fall and be overtaken by faults or weaknesses and vulnerabilities but they will still need restoration in the spirit of meekness and will need to know the standard of righteousness (Galatians 6:1-3). Timothy was exhorted, "In meekness instructing those that oppose themselves; if peradventure God will give them repentance to the acknowledging of the truth; and that they may recover themselves out of the snare of the devil, who are taken captive by him at his will" (II Timothy 2:26). The Apostle James denoted, "Let him know that he which converts the sinner from the error of his way shall save a soul from death, and shall hide a multitude of sins (James 5:20). Sinners must be instructed as to what the definition of sin is and why it is wrong to practice sin as a confessing believer. These letters or verses were written to Christian believers or Pastors. If we say that we have no sin, we deceive ourselves, and the truth is not in us. If we confess our sins, he is faithful and just to forgive us our sins, and to cleanse us from all unrighteousness (I John 1:8-9).

Paul acknowledged that he had not yet attained perfection when he was near the end of his life. However, he professed that he was pressing toward the mark (Philippians 3:12-14). In order to press toward a goal or an objective we must know what the target is. Men are hopelessly unable and utterly helpless to keep the law in their own strength or human ability due to the depraved nature of sin always at motion in the flesh as a law but they are empowered supernaturally from Christ by the Holy Spirit (Romans 7:14-25,Acts 1:8, John 15:4,Acts 2:38,Galatians 5:17-23). The depraved nature is called original sin and it is that which we inherited by the fall. We are born with the passion of sin working within us. The moral weaknesses or lack of moral strength in man with his vulnerabilities have been called the doctrine of inability. Paul said that he would not have known his own lust unless the law said, "Thou shall not covet" (Romans 7:7). Enough said. Temptation is when we are drawn away by our own lust and enticed (James 1:14). We all have indwelling lust that dwells beneath the surface as a principle and therefore are all still imperfectly sanctified from sin to one degree or another in the practical sense (Romans 7:4-23, I John 1:8).

Historical Theology and views of the Atonement

The Catholic, Reformed, and Lutheran view have always been that the satisfaction of Jesus Christ to God for his accomplished work was completed for us as a divine person. Therefore, it was not due to God for himself and was free to be credited to others including you and me. You could compare it to a requirement that you pass a pop quiz with a rule that someone else can take the test for you. The teacher knows that you will fail again and therefore has someone to test in your stead. From the time of Thomas Aquinas the Catholic Church has held that this was the value of the Atonement. Christ satisfies the conditions for us in our stead based on this view by his active obedience and his suffering and death.

The Reformed churches differ with the Romanists, Armenians, and some others in regards to the intention of the Atonement of Christ and the actual effect that it has based on its purpose. The Reformers held that the Atonement not only made the salvation of those for whom it was offered possible, but that the Atonement meritoriously secured its own application to them. The Reformers held that the Atonement ensured the certain and complete salvation for those whom Christ accomplished the work for.

The Roman Catholic Church has for the most part always believed that it is through the work of baptism that the merits of Christ cancel all sins before and after baptism. They also held that baptism translates the penalty of post-baptismal sins from eternal death to temporal pains. The Catholics also teach people guilty of sins after baptism must make up for those sins by good works of charity in this life, or by pain in purgatory in the next life.

The Armenians believed that the satisfaction of Jesus Christ makes the salvation of all men possible, and secures for them sufficient grace, but that the full benefits of what Christ did is temporarily suspended on the condition of the individuals freewill. This position makes the Atonement unable to produce any real salvation unless man cooperates with God's purpose and plan which is left up to him or her to do.

The Reformers that led the Protestant Reformation taught that the scriptures reveal the removal of our condemnation and guilt for sins of the past or future is due solely to the death of Christ in our stead. They teach that the suffering of believers today is temporary and disciplinary (Romans 8:1-34, Hebrews 7:5-11). They also taught that it was the blood of Christ that cleanses us from sin and that by one sacrifice he perfected us (Colossians 2:10, Hebrews 10:12-14, I John 1:7). They teach that salvation is conditioned upon trust in Christ's work to save us and we call that faith. The faith is actually given to us from God as a result of Christ's work (Ephesians 2:7-10). The Reformers teach that the satisfaction of Christ meritoriously secures actual and final salvation for us as beneficiary and not just a possibility of our salvation if we keep conditions. They also teach that if Christ saved us that good works or spiritual fruit are evidences of that salvation but do not merit that salvation. If the Reformed view is true for all of God's people then your final salvation is sure and you surely will be in heaven. You can't lose salvation if you have been saved. Christ will finish the work he started through you based on the scriptural data as stated in this paragraph alone.

All agree that the Atonement is sufficient to accomplish the salvation of any man or all men no matter how vast the number. People of various views also agree that the Atonement makes possible that every human sinner who ever existed could possibly be saved because of it. What can save one could save another. The Armenians agree with the

Calvinists that only those who believe will be saved. The Calvinist also agrees with the Armenians that anyone that dies in infancy is redeemed and saved. Both sides also agree that some universal benefits apply to everyone including the longsuffering of God with the entire human family that is lost. They also admit that Jesus did die in a sense for all men and that he removed the legal obstacles out of the way. They also acknowledge that the Atonement can be applied to one man as good as it could be applied to another.

The question before us all as Christians is what do we believe and why? Did the death of Jesus Christ make it possible for all to be saved but not render it certain that all will be saved? Does the Atonement simply make the salvation of the Elect possible or certain? Did the satisfaction of the Atonement secure salvation in its own application, and the means thereof, to all for whom it was specifically rendered? Did the satisfaction purchase and secure its own application with all the means, to all for whom it was rendered? Was the Atonement part of a divine purpose to accomplish the purpose of saving only God's Elect? How does a limited Atonement square with the love of God? Does God love everybody the same? Is it true that we are Eternally Secure? This book is designed to answer these questions and more and to encourage us in our understanding of the depth of God's love for us. It is also designed to help us to understand the basics of the gospel truth which have been misunderstood by some for centuries. It is also designed to help us grasp what Christ accomplished for us as believers with his work on the earth and in his role now in heaven. What must we do to get saved? Is it possible for us to be lost or eternally damned after trusting Christ to save us? What did Christ's work accomplish for us as believers? Can we know for sure that we will be in Heaven if we die tonight? Why? Some things are a done deal and other things remain a mystery.

Asking God for Mercy as a Sinner

The Pharisee and the Publican

A sinner can get to heaven because of God's mercy alone. Get up from there if you did fall and ask God for mercy. Jesus spoke a parable to those that trusted in themselves that they were righteous and despised others. These people compared themselves to others and thought they were much better and they looked down on others. (Luke 18:9-14). Jesus said the publican, the sinner, left the temple justified in God's sight instead of the righteous religious because the publican admitted he was a sinner and asked God for mercy (Luke 18:14). Admit you are a sinner and ask Jesus for mercy. John taught us, "If we say have no sin, we deceive ourselves, and the truth is not in us. If we confess our sins, he is faithful and just to forgive us our sins, and cleanse us from all unrighteousness" (I John 1:8-9). The Lord is merciful and gracious, slow to anger, and plenteous in mercy. He will not always chide: neither will he keep his anger forever. He has not dealt with us after our sins; nor rewarded us according to our iniquities (Psalm104:8-10). It is of the Lord's mercies that we are not consumed, because his compassions fail not. They are new every morning. Great is thy faithfulness (Lamentations 3:22-23). Mercy is why people get to Heaven. The Lord will have mercy on whoever he desires (Romans 9:18). We confess that we are sinners and ask for mercy and that is one way to receive it. Our effort to be good will not be good enough. A real disciple will ask God for forgiveness on a daily basis (Matthew 6:11-12). As it is written, There is none righteous, no, not one (Romans 3:10). All have sinned and come short of the glory of God (Romans 3:23).

Let us first explain who these people were. The Pharisees were the most prestigious and highly esteemed religious leaders during Jesus' day and they were Jews. The word "Pharisee" means "the separated or holy ones" and they was people who separated themselves from others They believed that their role in the world was to separate themselves from the sinners and they were strict observers of the law and their own interpretations of the law. They vowed to obey all of the rules regulations, commandments, laws, and ceremonial observances of the Jewish custom and religion. The Pharisees saw themselves as being more righteous than other people because of the things they did or didn't do. They despised others sometimes including Jesus and saw others as lawless heathens, including Jesus, who did not comply with their legal traditions which were based on their own interpretation of law.

The Publicans, on the other hand, was considered one of the most wicked and vile of sinners during Jesus' day. The publicans were the Jews that were appointed by the Roman emperor to collect the taxes from the Jews. The odd thing about being a publican during Jesus' day is that they could charge people as much tax as they wanted and they kept part of what was paid to them as their income. Consequently, they were often traitors, thieves, extortionists, and viewed as scoundrels by many people.

Jesus had picked out what was presumed to be the pillars of the religious community to compare them to the most despicable of the Jews that had the worst of reputations. The publicans were often defamed and primarily because how they were accused of collecting taxes. When you look at this profound story that Jesus told, keep in mind that many people in churches today in our Christian community may have one of these two attitudes about themselves and in regards to others.

Jesus spoke this parable to those that trusted in themselves that they were righteous and despised others, "And he spoke this parable unto certain which trusted in themselves that they were righteous, and despised others: Two men went into the temple to pray, the one a Pharisee, the other a publican. The Pharisee stood and prayed thus within himself, God, I thank thee, that I am not as other men are, extortionists, unjust, adulterers, or even as this publican. I fast twice a week; I give tithes of all I possess. And the publican, standing afar off, would not lift up so much as his eyes to heaven, but smote upon his breast saying, God be merciful to me a sinner. I tell you, this man went down to his house justified rather than the other: for every one that exalts himself shall be abased; and he that humbles himself shall be exalted" (Luke 18:9-14).

Jesus has just compared the people who thought they were the cream of the croup in terms of following his commands and the laws and compared them to those with the worst of reputations. Publicans were seen as the some of the worst of sinners and were often defamed. Who do you think that God would declare to be righteous more in your viewpoint? Most of us would think that the people who really did the most righteous works were the ones that God really admired or justified. However, God doesn't think the way we do nor does he evaluate people based on our assumptions.

The Pharisee certainly appeared to be righteous and holy and I am sure that he felt he was a good person. He saw himself as being more righteous than the publican and had what we could call a high standard of regulations for himself which he kept. The tax collector was by his own admission deep in sin and admitted that himself by his own confession. The tax collector felt ashamed before God and would not lift up his eyes to heaven but only said, "God have mercy on me for I am a sinner". God often sees people in general and sinners much different than people do.

The Pharisee was full of his own ego and was inflated with pride in his own works as a means to justify himself in the eyes of God. The publican realized that he was sinful and his attitude was that he could not justify himself in the eyes of God on the basis of his righteous works. The publican saw himself as someone who needed God's help and the Pharisee saw himself as someone that was being righteous before God because of the works that he had. The Pharisee likely saw himself as winning favor with God because of the many achievements or good deeds which he had done. He knew that others especially the publican did not measure up to him in terms of keeping God's laws or regulations.

God sees self-righteousness and religious pride as one of the worst type of sins. Why? God sees it this way because he knows that all men have sinned and he sees them as being unrighteous as far as good works are concerned. They simply don't and can't measure up to his expectations in regards to his laws. The Pharisees saw themselves as being holier than others and consequently they had a bad attitude which showed up in the context of relationships with people. They presumed that God saw them as morally superior to others because that is how they saw themselves. People that are like the Pharisees are not too warm and fuzzy with unrepentant sinners. They have the tendency to be fault-finders and professional critics. They will judge and condemn the sinner a lot and they will lack the kindness, love, compassion, and mercy in the context of their relationships with sinners or people in general. This makes it difficult to win souls or be an effective witness especially to the worst of the sinners who they would prefer to keep far from them.

The Publican went to his house more justified in the eyes of God more than the Pharisee. Why? God saves us when we see ourselves as helpless sinners that cannot justify ourselves in his eyes on the basis of our works. He gives us mercy when we realize that we need help and confess our sinfulness and admit it. God justifies the sinner by granting him mercy but he doesn't save those who think they are righteous enough because they are presuming that their goodness somehow measures up to his standard. This book is about how a loving God has chosen to save sinful men. The atonement is what God did to save us through the works of his Son, Jesus Christ.

When we look at the story of Pharisees that saw Jesus sitting down and eating with sinners you find that they were enraged and asked the disciples, "How can your teacher eat with the unclean publicans and sinners, Jesus answered and said, They that are whole need not a physician but they that are sick. But go ye and learn what that means, I will have mercy, and not sacrifice: for I am not come to call the righteous, but sinners to repentance" (Matthew 9:11-13). Let our hearts not forget about the mercy of God. The heart of evangelism is to meet sinners where they are at and to fellowship with them there. It takes mercy to listen to them and to hang out where they are at. Try to relate to them without criticism and condemnation. Keep in mind that mercy is what brings us to heaven.

Jesus made it clear that his role in the lives of sinners was to show mercy to them and not to offer sacrifices to God. (Matthew 9:13). Jesus was not preoccupied with offering a sacrifice to God of strict compliance with certain Jewish laws or traditions which could be used to justify separating himself from the sinner. He built a bridge for sinners to God. Saints are here to build a bridge for sinners to God. We can't do this if we don't love them as they are. Mercy tolerates our association or fellowship with the worst of sinners in order to build a loving relationship with them. God is love and he loves us unconditionally. Jesus related to people in mercy in order that they could be saved. Jesus came to seek and save them that are lost (Luke 19:10).

Jesus was defamed for eating and drinking with sinners and called a winebibber and a glutton. He responded by telling his critics that wisdom was justified in all of her children (Matthew 11:19). What men will think is wrong for one reason God will think is wise for another. Jesus knew that in order for people to be restored and made whole that mercy had to meet them in the sinful state or environment that they were in. The barrier had to be torn down. A true evangelist can't wait for them to come to church but will go to them. There is joy in the presence of the angels of God over one sinner that comes to a repentance (Luke 15:10).

God offers unchaste woman eternal life

Some people with what we presume to be a bad reputation can get to heaven before some of us who think that we have a good one. Never count someone out. Jesus was tired from his journey and went to Jacob's well to draw water. The disciples went to town to buy food and meat. Jesus met the Samaritan wman at Jacob's well and asked her to give him something to drink. She asked him as to how could he as a Jew ask her a Samaritan woman for water when he knew that the Jews had no dealings with the Samaritans (John 4:5-9). The Samaritans were the people that Jews had abandoned their faith to intermarry with in the Northern

Kingdom around 722 B.C. The law of God forbade the intermarriage of the Jews and the Gentiles who were not in a covenant relationship with God. The Jews knew they were under a curse and did not speak to them or have other dealings with them at all. Jesus as a Jew broke the custom and the traditions of the Jews by speaking to this woman and asking her for water.

The woman knew that the Jews did not talk to the Samaritans and had no dealings with them. The fact that Jesus initiated the conversation is undoubtedly a form of mercy and grace. Jesus set an example for evangelists in terms of initiating contact with the lost and meeting them at the places where you could ordinarily find them when they are there. Jews ordinarily would avoid coming to the well at a time when one would expect to find a Samaritan there. She reminded Jesus that Jews had no dealings with Samaritans at all (John 4:9). Jesus' approach was one that broke traditions and the customs of the religious people of his era.

Jesus then offered this woman the gift of God which was eternal life before mentioning anything in regards to her immoral lifestyle or her current situation. It confirms that the gift is without regards to our own works. Jesus was offering mercy when he spoke of living water and was referring to forgiveness, eternal life, justification, and new birth. He said that the only condition was that whoever wanted the water had to ask him for it (John 4:10). When people stand before God at his Great White Throne to be judged I want you to keep in mind that they go to heaven because they asked Jesus for the gift of eternal life. There is a list of sins that have been proven against everybody. The only way to enter into heaven is to have the gift of eternal life. The ones that go to Hell will only go because they did not ask Jesus for his gift of eternal life. All people have a list of sins. Salvation is the free gift of God for those that ask for it.

She did not understand him. The Samaritan woman told him plainly that he had nothing to draw water from Jacob's well with and that she wondered as to how he could give her living water. She mentioned Jacob who had built the well and asked was he greater than him (John 4:11-12). When we think about her response we can keep in mind that Jesus initiated this discussion with her. Most people don't come to church or a preacher and ask them how to get saved. Jesus went to where she would be found and stirred up the discussion to offer her mercy and eternal life.

Jesus then shifts the conversation from the earthly meaning of water to the spiritual meaning of the living water. He mentions that if one drinks of the water from Jacob's well that they would thirst again but that whoever would drink of the water that he would give them shall never thirst again. Jesus also said that his water would be a well springing up within them into everlasting life (John 4:14). Who could refuse having such a gift that would cause them to live forever and satisfy the deep thirst of our souls within? The way that the living water was described by Jesus surely revealed that it gave a deep satisfaction within and resulted in one living forever. The woman said to him, "Sir give me this water, that I thirst not, neither come here to draw again" (John 4:15). She had just asked Jesus for eternal life.

The evangelism now shifts. The mercy was offered. Grace or unmerited favor had been shown by virtue of the fact that he had interacted with her in the first place. She asked for the living water which we know is the equivalent of asking Jesus for eternal life. Jesus now turns to another component of evangelism. He shifts to her personal life and relationships and how she was living her life. Receiving mercy and eternal life had nothing to do with her works and it is gift of grace or unmerited favor. The Grace that grants a sinner eternal life also works with the sinner to teach them to deny ungodliness and worldly lusts and to live soberly in this present life (Titus 2:11-12). Jesus helped her and brought up her relationship which could, theoretically, enable her to see her sin and bring about a conviction. He did not avoid a discussion about how she was living her life although eternal life was a free gift without the condition of righteous works. The fact that Jesus brought up her husband reveals that he was on a mission to encourage her and souls to repent of sin when offering the free gift of eternal life. The eternal life is free and not conditioned on our works.

The Samaritan woman was not an angel and she had been with many different husbands. Jesus then tells her at the well in Samaria to go and get her husband and she told him that she did not have one. Jesus then told her that she had spoken truthfully and that she have had five different husbands and that the man she was with was not her husband. The woman was in an adulterous relationship with a man who she was not married to. She was apparently living with the man or sexually involved with him although she was not married to him (John 4: 16-18). When men had sex with a woman to lie down with her the law required him to marry her (Exodus 22:15). He was required to marry the woman he lied down with and not put her away for all the days of his life (Deuteronomy 22:29).

A lady that had sexual relationships with a man or several men while married to another was considered an adulteress. Why did Jesus tell her that she had already had five husbands? Jesus was letting her know that he was aware of each sexual encounter with each man that she had been with. He was also letting her know that he was cognizant of the fact that she was with yet another man now although she had already acted in some capacity of a wife with at least five different men before him. Here is a woman that may have lived her life as an adulterer with several men after marrying her first husband. She also may have been a woman that been rejected by men and divorced because of adultery more than once. In either case, she was in an adulterous relationship with a man she was not married to at the time of Jesus' encounter with her.

Jesus did not judge or condemn another woman that was caught in the very act of adultery but he did tell her, "go and sin no more" (John 8:11). It is plausible that Jesus brought up the husband of the Samaritan woman to encourage her to repent or to change her mind in regards to adultery. Jesus did not offer her eternal life on the condition of her leaving her adulterous relationship. He offered mercy and the living water of eternal life first. Jesus pointed out her sin to her but did not teach her to do anything to receive eternal life other than to ask. Jesus accepted her and loved her as she was when he met her. The living water was free to anyone who asked for it.

Jesus' request for her to bring her husband to him was his pointing out of her sin to her. When evangelists tell others that eternal life is offered as a gift from God it doesn't move the reality away that God will also confront us about sin. God desires that men and women turn to him in faith and trust in him to save them from their sins. When people receive salvation it is important for them know that God's intervention will give them eternal life and save them from their sins. They will be unable to break away from their own ways without his divine aid. We should view Jesus' statement to her to return to him with her husband as God's direct intervention in her life to restore her marriage and bring her out of an adulterous relationship. The gift of eternal life is free and there is nothing we can do to earn it nor do we have to work for it or cleanup for God to receive it but God will ask us to change our mind about sin. Some interpret Jesus' intervention as evidence that repentance of sin is required for eternal life to be received. The task of the evangelist is the encourage people to ask God for the free gift of eternal life while encouraging them to repent of sin. They turn to Jesus Christ to trust him for eternal life and their salvation from sin which they are unable to save themselves from.

The Samaritan women then said to Jesus that she perceived that he was a prophet. She then enquired as to where she should worship. This indicates that her heart was searching for how to do what God would desire for her to do in terms of worship. Jesus mentions that God is to be worshipped in spirit and in truth. The woman went into the city and told her story of how Jesus told her all that she ever did. Many people then believed on Jesus in Samaria because of the sayings of this Samaritan woman (John 4:19-39).

The Samaritan woman could have been called many derogatory names in our modern day use of terminology to described women that are immoral. She had not lived a moral life and had done nothing to do anything but to make her husband jealous and mad. She had not been a good wife and was a Samaritan woman with a bad reputation. Jesus offered to give her the gift of eternal life and something that would cause her to never thirst again (John 4:13-14). Jesus was talking about salvation which came from believing in him and trusting him for salvation. The one important lesson to be learned from this story is that Jesus is offering eternal life to immoral people who have done nothing righteous to earn it that did not deserve it. The people were very immoral in terms of their conduct and behavior. They could easily and justly be condemned to eternal damnation in the Lake of Fire and brimstone based on (Revelation 21:8). Why did he offer her eternal life? God loves and accepts the most immoral of people and offers them the wondrous gift of salvation and eternal life. It is because of the atonement. God gave his son that whoever believes in him would not perish but have everlasting life (John 3:16). Jesus was here to die for her sins on the cross too. He was the Lamb to take away the sins of the world (John 1:29).

The strange and bizarre thing about this story is what happens after he offered her the gift of eternal life. Jesus then tells the woman to go and call her husband and to come to him (John 4:16). The Samaritan lady told him that she did not have a husband and then Jesus told her that she had truthfully spoken because the man she was with was not her husband (John 4:17-18). Here is where common sense, exegetics, and a knowledge of the scriptures become important. Jesus told her to go and get her husband and Jesus knew that the man she was with was not her husband and so did she (John 4:17-18). Who was Jesus referring to then and why did he ask her to bring her husband to him? I believe that Jesus was simply trying to break the woman up with the man that she was in an adulterous relationship with. Jesus did not condemn another woman that was caught in the act of adultery but he told her to go and sin no more (John 8:11). We can conclude from this that Jesus wanted to avoid condemning and judging the Samaritan woman as the Lamb of God here to take away the sins of the world (John 1:29). He would die for her at the cross. Jesus also was in the business of pointing the adulterer away from sin.

Is there anybody Good enough for Heaven?

The first question in regards to our soul and eternity is whether or not we can be good enough to get to heaven. If you were to die tonight and had to stand before God would he let you into heaven? What would you say to God if you stood before him tonight as to why he should not throw you into Hell? Some may say to God that they have been a good person. Some others may say to God that they have done more good than bad. Still we could find another group of people that would likely say that they were not quite as bad as other people. God's verdict about mankind is final. God's verdict says, 'There is none righteous, no, not one" (Romans 3:10). The Bible teaches, "all have sinned against God and come short of the glory of God (Romans 3:23). We are all as an unclean thing and all of our righteousness are as filthy rags to God (Isaiah 64:6). Jesus said, "There is none good but one: that is God" (Matthew 19:17).

This book was written to remind us as to why folks will be going to heaven. Many of us have become much better people and have brought forth much fruit in terms of holiness and our conduct. However, it is the Atonement and Christ's continual intercession for us as our High Priest that ultimately secures our salvation and brings us home to him. God loves you. You will be going to Heaven because he loves you if you believe in him. You won't if you reject him and his Son, Jesus Christ, and the works he accomplished for you to save you from your sins. The Apostle Paul's words to the Galatian church was, "I marvel that you are so soon removed from him that called you into the grace of Christ unto another gospel: Which is not another, but there be some that trouble you, and would pervert the gospel of Christ. But though we, or an angel from heaven, preach any other gospel unto you than that which we have preached unto you, let him be accursed. As we said before, so say I no again, If any man preach another gospel unto you than that ye have received, let him be accursed" (Galatians 1:6-9). I do not frustrate the grace of God: for if righteousness came by the law, then Christ is dead in vain (Galatians 2:21).

Caught in the act of Adultery and Loved

This New Testament story reminds me so much of the entire book of Hosea. In the book of Hosea God encouraged the prophet Hosea to buy his wife back from her slave owners who used her in the sex industry as a prostitute. God didn't tell Hosea to throw her away but to buy her back from her owner. Gomer, the prophet's wife, was a prostitute and God told him to buy her back from her pimps for fifteen pieces of silver (Hosea 3:2). The relationship between Hosea and his wife Gomer symbolized God's unconditional love for his people. Although God could have divorced Israel he didn't throw her away because he loved her. The same is true with the church. Church folk are full of faults and inconsistencies. Have you ever met the perfect saint? I have not. Although God could throw many of us away when we mess up he continues his relationship with us because of the magnitude of his love. God commended his love toward us, in that, while we were yet sinners Christ died for the ungodly (Romans 5:8). Jesus purchased the church with his own blood (Acts 20:28). A challenge for Christian believers is to love sinners and even the fallen and the weak as Jesus did. We must love them in spite of their faults and inconsistencies in order to do this. Love covers a multitude of sin (I Peter 4:8). Love does not ignore or pretend. Love endures. Love corrects. Love is longsuffering. Love is kind. Love is faithful. Love thinks no evil. Parents who love their children don't quit them because of their faults, problems, lies, inconsistencies, and personal failures. God is our loving Father.

We learn a valuable lesson about the love and mercy of God from the story of the woman caught in the act of adultery. They caught her in the very act of adultery and brought her to Jesus and asked could they stone her. The law required that an adulterer and the adulteress be stoned to death. Jesus knew the hearts of the people that brought her to him. They wanted to trap him. If Jesus would have answered and said yes they would have reported him to the Roman governor because only the emperor of Rome could pronounce a death sentence. However, the Jewish law required stoning for an adulterer. If Jesus would have said no it meant that he was not be observing the law which required those caught in adultery to be stoned.

People have a tendency to be very judgmental and critical of sinners especially with what we classify as the real big sins such as murder, adultery, lesbianism, homosexuality, prostitution, sorcery and others. What about the mercy and love of God and where and when does it apply to sinners? How should we communicate the love and mercy of God to others in the context of our relationships? God did not come to the world to condemn the world but that through him the world might be saved (John 3:17). The word condemn means to judge someone as being guilty and worthy of punishment to include death or eternal death. Jesus did not condemn the adulterous woman and it is a good idea to figure out why.

First of all the scriptures teach that they brought her to Jesus to find a reason to accuse him of wrongdoing (John 8:6). They wanted to entrap him of pronouncing a death sentence to accuse him before the governor. Jesus stopped in the sand and wrote something in the sand Jesus then says, "He that is without sin among you let him cast the first stone at her" (John 8:7). Let this be a lesson to all people who that are quick to condemn others and to judge them as being guilty of sin and worthy of punishment. We are all sinners and have broken God's laws and deserve judgment ourselves which include the same punishment we think should be imposed upon others.

Whoever shall keep the entire law and offend it in one point is guilty of it all (James 2:19). The scriptures teach, "All have sinned and come short of the glory of God" (Romans 3:23). Jesus gives them permission to stone her but only if they have not sinned at all. Those that are quick to stone others are often living in a glass houses and are either guilty of the same sin or some other sin based on God's law. The Roman writer says, "Therefore, thou are inexcusable, O man, whosoever thou art that judgest: for wherein thou judgest another, thou condemn thyself: for thou that judge do the same things. But we are sure that the judgment of God is according to truth against them which commit such things. And do you think this, O man, that judge them which do such things, and do the same, that thou shalt escape the judgment of God? (Romans 2:1-3).

The story gets even more dramatic. Jesus stopped down and wrote on the ground again. They that heard were convicted in their own conscience and left one by one beginning with the oldest and then Jesus was left alone with the woman standing in the midst. The people had not realized their own sinfulness and why they were just as deserving of a condemnation and punishment themselves when they brought the adulterous woman to Jesus. They were quick to criticize, judge, and jump ready to stone this adulterous woman without considering that they deserved the same judgment.

People are more likely to be merciful when they recall their own condition and what they really deserve. Jesus had taught us, "Judge not that you be not judged. You will be judged with whatever judgment that you judge. Why behold the mote that is in a brother's eye, but do not consider the beam that is in your own eye? O hypocrite, first cast the beam out of your own eye first to see clearly how to cast a mote out of a brother's eye" (Matthew 7:2-4). Jesus was asking people to do an inventory of their own lives and to be sure to clean house before pointing out what others need to do in regards to cleanliness. He is not prohibiting us judging altogether but emphasized that the speck had to get out of our own eye first and before judging.

People are told to judge a righteous judgment (John 7:24). Ministers can do this by defining sin and pointing out to others what is right or wrong. They must interact with sinners with the same love, mercy, forgiveness, and compassion that Christ had and in terms how we want to be treated from others and with the mercy we want in eternity from God. Jesus said, "Judge not and you shall not be judged, condemn not and you shall not be condemned, forgive, and you shall be forgiven" (Luke 6:37). What we do will return to us and how we treat others will determine if God decides to judge us with the same law or others. Jesus taught that we must forgive others or our heavenly Father would not forgive us (Matthew 6:15).

Jesus is now standing here with an adulterous woman and all critics are gone. Jesus then looks at the woman and asks her as to where her accusers were and whether or not any man had condemned her (John 8:10). The adulterating woman says to Jesus that no man condemned her and Jesus then says to this adulterating woman, "Neither do I condemn you, go, and sin no more" (John 8:11). We learn from Jesus that he values his relationships with us. He loves us with an unconditional love. Jesus doesn't throw us away because people are critical, hateful, unmerciful, unforgiving and unloving. His love and mercy shows up in our lives first in his interaction with us in our relationship with him and with sinners in general. God hasn't thrown you away nor given up on you because of sin. Jesus told this woman to go and sin no more but he didn't address sin until he first defended her, made it publicly known that he did not condemn her although he was the lawgiver and Judge, and had showed her a depth of love and mercy as a lawgiver and judge. Her response to him in obedience would be because of her relationship with him which began in a divine unconditional love. We love him because he first loved us (I John 4:19).

Jesus would not penalize her because he came as the sacrificial Lamb of God to die in her stead to atone for her sins. She was saved! She was not saved because she had been righteous to say she had lived her life as a saint. She was saved on that day because Jesus interceded for her as a lawgiver and judge. Mercy saved her. Love saved her. She wasn't condemned but she could have been condemned. The lawgiver and the Judge who could have condemned her did not! Who is he that condemns when it is Christ that died, has risen, who is at the right hand of God making intercession for us (Romans 8:34).

God is so patient and longsuffering with people when they fail. The Romans writer says, "Do you despise the riches of his goodness and his forbearance and longsuffering; not knowing that the goodness of God leads us to repentance" (Romans 2:4). God is good and that is why people can get to Heaven if they believe Christ and trust him for their salvation. God is good and that is why people repent of sin. The love and kindness of God germinates within our souls and flows outward in our expression of love to him. God has atoned for sin through his son Jesus Christ. John the Baptist saw Jesus coming to him and said, "Behold the Lamb of God, which take away the sin of the world" (John 1:29). Sin was taken away by Jesus and he atoned for our sins as God's lamb. God's law required blood to be shed for sin to be removed and as far as God is concerned the shedding of blood is what purges sin and removes it (Hebrews 9:19-22). Jesus was her Lamb and ours and came to shed his own blood for sin. This is what our atonement is about but there is much more. Jesus said, "Verily, verily, I say unto you, He that hear my word, and believeth on him that sent me, hath eternal life, and shall not come into condemnation; but is passed from death until life" John 5:24). You won't be condemned if you believe in Jesus. He died for you.

A Thief enters Paradise with Jesus

A thief lived his life as a thief which led to his death by Roman crucifixion. Jesus told the thief as he and the thief died that he would be with him on that day in Paradise. The thief had done nothing in his life to deserve heaven but he went. He was condemned and rejected by people but he was accepted by God. Why did Jesus tell a convicted thief on his deathbed while he was hanging on cross that the thief would go

to Paradise? Why did Jesus say this? The thief had neither been baptized nor partook in the Lord's supper. He had done no works at all
but only believed in who Jesus was and that Jesus had a kingdom. The
story goes, "And one of the malefactors which were hanged railed on
him, saying, if thou be the Christ, save thyself and us. But the other
answering rebuked him, saying, dost not thou fear God, seeing thou
art in the same condemnation? And we indeed justly, for we receive
the due reward of our deeds: but this man hath done nothing amiss.
And he said unto Jesus, Lord; remember me when thou come into thy
kingdom. And Jesus said unto him, Verily, I say unto you, today shall
thou be with me in Paradise" (Luke 23:39-42).

Why did Jesus let the thief into Paradise after he apparently had lived
his entire life as a malefactor? The answer is simply that he admitted
that he was a sinner and he believed. He confessed he was guilty of sin
and believed that Jesus was a King with a kingdom. The rest is history.
He believed on Jesus and in Jesus and because of his faith he went to
Paradise with Jesus on the same day. Jesus had just been nailed to the
cross for him and for the sins of the world. Jesus had said in his ministry, "He that believes on him is not condemned, but he that believes
not is condemned already because he hath not believed in the name of
the only begotten Son of God" (John 3:18). The thief went to Paradise
because he believed and confessed his sinfulness it is as simple as that. It
was clear also that repentance was within his heart or inner man. There
was nothing that he had did right or righteous enough to argue that
he had been a good person as a convicted criminal nailed to the cross
to get his due reward and he admitted that himself. Many of us like to
think of ourselves as somehow having a righteousness good enough to
save ourselves but the prophet Isaiah said," But we are all as an unclean
thing, and all our righteousness are as filthy rags" (Isaiah 64:6).

Where is Paradise? Paradise at this particular time was a resting
place for the righteous dead and was located temporarily inside of the
earth but it was separated from Hell until after the resurrection of Jesus.

After the resurrection of Jesus from death Paradise was relocated in heaven itself in the abode of God with the Old Testament saints.

The lower part of the earth is called (Sheol) in the Hebrew and Hades in the (Greek) which are two different words which mean the same thing. The Bible teaches us that Hades is in the center of the earth (Matthew 12:40). Hades is the underworld and it was at this time of Jesus' saying divided into two parts. We see in Luke 16 that the righteous of those that believed went into Abraham's bosom which was one side of Hades and this was called Paradise. We find that the unrighteous or the lost went into the fires of Hell which was on the other side of Hades. A great gulf divided both sides of Hades (the underworld) so that none on either side could get to the other (Luke 16:26). Jesus was telling the thief on the cross that he was going to a place of comfort and rest in the Hades underworld with the Old Testament saints until his resurrection and then at that time he would be in heaven with the rest of the saints. Was this thief good on the earth? No. Jesus saved him from the Hell in Hades on the other side simply because he believed. Keep in mind that Jesus was hanging right there on the cross for him as the atonement for his sin. It was people like him and much more worse that Jesus had went to the cross for.

What did Jesus do after he died on the cross in Paradise or Hades to change the location of Paradise to God's abode in Heaven? Those that were waiting in faith in Paradise (Abraham's bosom) were led to heaven by Jesus after his resurrection and during his ascension into heaven. Jesus descended first into the lowest parts of the earth into Hades into the Paradise there (Matthew 12:40, Luke 23:43). When Jesus' body was put into the tomb his eternal spirit went into the different compartments of Hades. He went into the underworld into a place of comfort with the thief on the cross which he said was a Paradise of comfort separated from Hell by a great gulf (Luke 16:26, Luke 23:43). Jesus also went to preach on the other side of Hades which we call Hell where bad angels and human beings were being confined in and waiting for eternal punishment. Peter said, "Christ also have once suffered for sins, the just for the unjust, that he might bring us to God, being put to death, in the flesh, but quickened by the spirit: by which also he went and preached unto the spirits in prison: Which sometime were disobedient, when once the longsuffering of God waited in the days of Noah, while the ark was a preparing, wherein few, that is eight, souls were saved by water" (I Peter 3:18-20). Jesus gave the gospel to the souls that are in the prisons.

Peter and Jude also wrote in letters about the angels in prison (Abyss and Tartarus) that are confined and waiting for judgment (Jude 6, 2 Peter 2:4). Fallen angels are also locked up in the abyss until the great tribulation when they will be unleashed on the earth to unleash God's wrath (Revelation 9).

When Jesus went into Hades he had conquered death and, "When he ascended on high, he led captivity captive and gave gifts to men. He descended first into the lower parts of the earth. He who descended first is also the one who ascended far above the heavens that he might fill all things" (Ephesians 4:8-10). Jesus took everything that held his people hostage as a hostage to what he did on the cross which included Satan, death, sin, demons, Hades, sickness, disease, and more.

Paradise which was located in a place of comfort in the lower regions in the earth is now located in the abode and home of God in heaven. Paul had stated that he was caught up into the third heaven which he called Paradise and the abode of God (2 Corinthians 12:2). Those who believed God who were in Paradise had their sins removed by the blood atonement of Christ and were gathered together in another place. The Paradise is now heaven. The Paradise then was the abode of the righteous called "Sheol" in the Hebrew (Psalms 16:10). The remaining references to "Sheol" in the New Testament after the resurrection of Jesus refer to Heaven. Paradise has been removed from Hades to the third heaven and the host of captives who ascended with Christ was the Old Testament saints (Ephesians 4:8). Jesus moved Paradise from the place of comfort in a different compartment of Hades to the abode of God in Heaven. Therefore, Jesus promised the thief on the cross that he would be with him in the bliss of Heaven on the day his died for him on the cross.

Do you realize what the death of Christ and his atonement means for us if we believe? We are on the way to Heaven. Jesus encouraged us and promised, "Let not your heart be troubled: ye believe in God, believe also in me. In my father's house are many mansions: if it were not so, I would have told you, I go to prepare a place for you. And if I go and prepare a place for you, I will come again, and receive you to myself: that where I am, there ye may be also" (John 14:1-3). Believe Jesus and trust him for your salvation. What was needed to accomplish your salvation was finished at the cross. Jesus said, "It is finished" (John 19:30). How did the thief get to Heaven? People nailed him to the cross because of his sin. Christ saved him because the thief believed, admitted he was a sinner, and the truth that Jesus was nailed to the cross in his place. Eternal life in Heaven is a free gift. Can one lose a gift by demerit that they did not merit in the first place?

It Is Finished

These words may have been the most profound and loving words that Jesus Christ said regarding us and our salvation. He loves us and thus destroyed our enemy. The case against you which Satan had was thrown out of God's courtroom. The laws which could be used to prove your guilt before God as a sinner has been nullified and deemed unusable in God's courtroom as it relates to a Christian believer (Colossians 2:14). It is finished. The Devil would like to see us in Hell because of our guilt and sin but the entire record of our sin was nailed to the cross with the laws which were broken. Case dismissed.

Satan's had the legal right to hold mankind in bondage to him as a slave. Sin caused a barrier between God and man that could not be broken. The Devil earned this legal right to make Adam and his posterity his slaves when Adam fell into sin and consequently alienated and estranged himself and his posterity from God. This left Adam and his posterity alienated from God and only under the influence of a superior, organized host of more intelligent and wicked demons. Adam unknowingly gave Satan dominion over the earth in his place. Jesus reversed Satan's power over humanity to hold them as a hostage to him in bondage against their will. Jesus represented man to God to reconcile God to man by what he did at the cross. It is finished. Man is no longer denied access to God because of sin and the barrier is broken between God and man because of Christ's death on the cross in his place. Men no longer have to be held in bondage to a demon if they want to approach God to be set free in Jesus' name.

It is finished. The authority and the power which the Devil once had to use sin against men to keep them from approaching God has been ruined forever. The curse is broken because he was made a curse for us (Galatians 3:13). It is finished. The power of Satan over souls has been punished and spoiled. Jesus said, "All power in heaven and earth is given unto me", (Matthew 28:18). Jesus spoiled all principalities and powers, made an open show of them, triumphing over them in it (Colossians 2:15). It is finished. Mankind no longer has to be under the control of demons because they have no access to God to be set free. Men no longer have to be blinded by Satan and estranged from God because of the sin barrier between man and God has been destroyed. Jesus is the door (John 10:9). The men that enter the door shall be saved (John 10:9). God is reconciled back to man. It is finished. People no longer have to be sick because the Devil wants them sick. He was wounded for our transgressions, bruised for our iniquities, with his stripes we are healed (Isaiah 53:5). It is finished. Sin is finished. The Lord laid on him the iniquity of us all (Isaiah 53:6). It is finished. Sin is finished. It is finished. Death is done. Paul revealed, "O death, where is thy sting? O grave, where is thy victory? The sting of death is sin; and the strength of sin is the law. But thanks be to God, which give us the victory through our Lord Jesus Christ" (I Corinthians 15:55-57).

In the gospel of John, as Jesus was on the cross the Bible says, "Jesus knowing that all things were now accomplished, that the scripture might be fulfilled, saith, I thirst. Now there was set a vessel full of vinegar: and they filled a sponge with vinegar: and they filled a sponge with vinegar, and put it upon hyssop, and put it to his mouth. When Jesus therefore had received the vinegar, he said, "It is finished: and he bowed his head and gave up the ghost" (John 19:28-30).

When Jesus said "It is finished" as he hung on the cross he meant that he had finished the work that his Father had sent him to do. The Greek word for "It is finished" is "tetelestai" which means paid in full. The word was used as an accounting term which meant that a debt was paid in full. Jesus had paid everything to God that we owed him in order to purchase eternal life for us. He paid in full obedience to the law what was owed to God on our behalf. He paid the penalty for transgressing God's law for every sin. He finished the law and the curses which could come to us for transgression against the law. He finished all of the responsibilities of a High Priest as our intercessor and gave his body as our sacrifice to atone for our sins once and for everything. Sinners owed God obedience and their very lives and our just reward for sin is alienation from God, abandonment and estrangement from him, and physical and eternal death. Jesus paid our debt to God in full.

When Jesus said this he was proclaiming that the sin debt owed to his Father by his sheep was completely wiped out forever. Jesus eliminated sin by wiping out the debt. The Old Testament law was finished and the ordinances which proved we were sinners has been blotted out, taken away, and nailed to the cross (Colossians 2:14). What is paid in full? Your sin debts to God have been paid off. When a debt in canceled it doesn't exist. The thing that is owed at that time is gratitude. The curses which came to us for breaking the law were finished. Christ redeemed us from the curse of the law and was made a curse for us (Galatians 3:13). The Old Testament priesthood was finished and Jesus Christ became our Great High Priest that passed into the heavens as a sacrifice for us at the throne of Grace to intercede for us (Hebrews 4:14-16). The sacrificing of bulls and goats to atone for the sins of man was finished and Jesus by one offering of his body perfected forever the sanctified (Hebrews 10:14 & Hebrews 10:1-12). Sin was finished and nailed the cross, "for he made him to be sin for us, who knew no sin; that we may be made the righteousness of God in him" (II Corinthians 5:21). God sees us as being redeemed from sin because of Jesus' offering made for us to cancel our sin debt and strict legal requirements which were owed to God.

Jesus said, "For I came down from heaven, not to do my own will, but the will of him that sent me. And this is the Father's will: which hath sent me, that of all which he hath given me I should lose nothing, but should raise him up again at the last day. And this is the will of him that sent me, that every one which see the Son, and believe on him, may have everlasting life: and I will raise him up on the last day" (John 6:38-40). It is God's will that you believe on Jesus and trust him only for your salvation. It is God's will that Jesus lose none of the sheep which were given to him by his Father. Man cannot do anything to add to what Christ has already finished for him. We cannot do any greater work than what Christ has already accomplished at the cross. Man could not do anything to remedy or satisfy his debt which Jesus Christ has paid in full. It is finished. Believe Jesus. Trust him for your salvation.

Forgiving others as we have been forgiven

Sometimes it is good to remind yourself about how you have violated others and trespassed against both them and God. Then keep in mind that as both God and people have had to forgive you that you must and should do the same with others. When we don't forgive we will grow bitter in the heart and hold grudges. People stop loving others when they have not forgiven. They also will sometimes seek revenge to try to settle the score. Folks will say and do things out of malice when they hold grudges and that is when they can be the most vindictive and quarrelsome. Hatred can develop in the heart and sometimes murder comes as a result of the hatred in the heart. Gossip and backbiting are common trends when we think others have treated us bad or betrayed our trust. It can be hard to forgive but the thing that makes it easier to forgive is when we do a thorough inventory of our own ways, words, actions, deeds, and life and consider the gravity and magnitude of how our offenses have hurt and betrayed others. We want people to let our mistakes, sins, and blunders go and not to hold those sins against us and we want God to forgive us also. We should then forgive others and provide them the same mercy that we expect from them and from God also. Many of us could pretend that we haven't offended others but we all have. That offense is sin. Peter asked Jesus, How any times should I forgive a brother or sister that hurts me, Seven? Jesus said, Try seventy times seven. Jesus then spoke a parable to explain how that we should take our experience of being forgiven by Christ and communicate the same love and mercy to others in the world.

Jesus says in his parable, "The kingdom of God is like a king who decided to pay off the debts of his servants. One servant was brought to the king who had a great debt of about one-hundred thousand dollars. The servant could not pay the king what was owed. The King ordered the man with his wife and children to be auctioned off and sold as slaves. The poor man threw himself at the feet of the king and cried out for mercy and said, "Please give me a chance and I will pay you back. The king was moved with compassion and paid off the debt for the man himself and did not hold it against him.

The servant left the room and shortly after that he saw someone that owed him about ten or fifteen dollars. He grabbed the man by the throat and demanded that he pay him what was owed. The man begged him for mercy and time to pay the debt back but the servant would not do it. He had the man arrested and put in jail until the debt was paid. When the other servants saw what this man who had been forgiven himself of a debt had done they went back and told the king.

The King brought the man back into his courtroom and said, "You wicked servant! I forgave all of your debts which you owed me and I paid them off myself. I gave you mercy. You should have been com-pelled by the reality that your debts were cancelled and been merciful to your brothers and sisters who asked you for mercy. The King was upset and put the demanded that the man who had his debt cancelled to pay back the entire debt. That is exactly what the Father in heaven is going to do to each individual who had his debts erased that doesn't forgive unconditionally anyone that asks for his mercy" (Matthew 18:21-35).

Jesus spoke this parable to give us the perfect example of how that once we have been forgiven by God that God requires of us that we relate to people with love, mercy, and forgiveness. God has been merciful to us and have cancelled our debts and paid in full what was owed to God by us. We cannot pay God what is owed to him and inherit eternal life on our own. The wages of sin is death (eternal death and damnation), and the gift of God is eternal life through Christ Jesus (Romans 6:23). God desires for us to relate to sinners with love, kindness, forgiveness, goodness, and grace. As we read this parable it is consistent with what Christ said over in the book of Matthew, "For if you forgive men of their trespasses, your heavenly Father will also forgive you: But if you forgive not men their trespasses, neither will your heavenly Father forgive your trespasses" (Matthew 6:14-15). We have to forgive people although we don't approve of what they have done even when we have been betrayed, lied to, lied on, hurt, rejected, despised ridiculed, abandoned, forsaken, and more.

God desires for each soul to repent of the sin of un-forgiveness in order for the forgiveness of God to be applied to our lives. When we repent of sin we acknowledge to God that our attitude toward him and others have been wrong. We confess our sins to God and ask him for mercy. We are not like the servant in the parable above who wanted to see his fellow-servant arrested, thrown in jail and punished until he paid us back for what they did to us. When we forgive we can relate to others with the same love and mercy that Christ has shown to us.

Sometimes the heart can be full of cursing, bitterness, wrath, strife hatred, and even murder because of the sin not forgiving others. God can see our hearts and he knows if we are holding silent grudge against someone in the family, business, church, relationship, or family. The

Bible teaches in this chapter that the tormentors come to the one that doesn't forgive. Satan will use the sin of not forgiving others to harass our own mind in regards to what the person did or did not do which makes it close to impossible to have a loving relationship with them because of past events and hurts that we decide to hold on to. When God has forgiven people it means that we must relate to them in a loving and merciful manner also in our speech, hospitality, goodness, works, and the way of we interact with them in comparison to how we relate to others. Satan knows that if we don't let the offense go and forgive completely that the fruit of love and compassion cannot be reflected in our lives towards that person. The result is division, confusion, anger, wrath, revenge, and epic battles which come from hostilities due to bitterness deep within the heart from not forgiving.

Love and Acceptance from our God and Father

The story taught by Jesus called the parable of the Prodical Son is one of the most amazing gospel stories or parables in the Bible. The parable illustrates how that God continues to love his children when they have strayed away from the right way and he celebrates their return to him. God has a paternal love for us as a Father. In this story a man had two sons and the younger son wanted his inheritance early. The Father gave it to him and not many days after that the son left his father and took his journey into a far country. The young man wasted his substance on riotous living. He spent everything and blew it. A great famine came in the land and he was in a great need. He then went and joined himself to a citizen in that country and the citizen gave him a job feeding the swine. The young boy began to want to fill his belly with the husks that he saw the swine eating.

The son came to himself and thought that he should return to his Father's house because they had bread enough to spare to avoid dying of hunger. He said, 'I will rise and go to my Father's house and say, "I have sinned against Heaven, and before thee and I'm no more worthy to be called your son" (Luke 15:11-17). When he arose to go to his Father and while he was still a great way from home his Father saw him, had compassion, ran, fell on his neck, and kissed him. The son said to his Father, "I have sinned against heaven, and in thy sight, and I am no longer worthy to be called your son" (Luke 15:20-21). I want you to imagine with me that this was your son or someone that you loved dearly. How would you feel and what would you do? Would you reject them? Would you criticize them? Would you say a lot of mean and hurtful things about the mistakes they had made to make them feel bad about themselves? One important thing to remember about this story is that the Father never disowned him as his son.

The Father said to his servants to put the best robe on him. He told them to put a ring on his hand and shoes on his feet. He then says to them to bring the fatted calf, kill it, and let us eat, and be merry. He says this is my son who was dead and now is alive again. He was lost and now he is found and they began to be merry and to rejoice (Luke 15:20-24). The celebration was not a celebration of the mistakes that the son had made. It was a celebration that the son was now restored to his home and in fellowship again with his loving Father.

God doesn't throw away or abandon the children that he loves. He let the boy make his mistakes and fall into sin but he did not despise or reject him. He waited patiently for him to realize the blunders were wrong and ruining him. The Father still loved him and was there to receive him when he decided to return home. The Father knew the boy had wasted his inheritance. The Father knew the boy had been in the pigpen. He did not scrutinize him or ridicule and criticize him. The Father responded only in love and compassion. The boy symbolized the sinner and his fall and how a sinner often goes in self-will into a far country in the opposite direction as God would desire. People may waste some of their lives with where they go and with what they choose, who they hang out with, chosen friends, and in a pigpen in life. They can join themselves to the wrong people and to the wrong lifestyle. When they realize they are sinners and that sin is ruining them have made a barrier between them and God they can repent and change their mind about how they will live their lives. They can return to God the Father who loves them and wants them to have his best for them.

God comes to them to receive them in love and shows mercy even before they make it all the way back to him or home. This is what the Father did in the parable. God acts on their behalf and provides for them and this is what grace is all about. Grace is the unmerited favor of God and a gift that is undeserved. The Father gives the child his best to include a ring, coat, shoes, and a meal. The child did not earn any of these unmerited favors. The child wandered away from his Fathers' home but he changed his mind about his decision and believed that his Father knew best and had his best interests in mind. I believe that the fatted calf in this parable symbolizes the sacrifice that God has made for sinners for when they come from what they were doing to return to him. The Bible teaches, "This I recall to my mind, therefore have I hope, it is of the Lord's mercies that we are not consumed, because his compassions fail not. They are new every morning: great is thy faithfulness" (Lamentation 3:22-23). The Psalmist declared, "The Lord is merciful, gracious, slow to anger, and plenteous in mercy. He will not always chide: neither will he keep his anger forever. He hath not dealt with us after our sins; nor rewarded us according to our iniquities. For as the heaven is high above the earth, so great is his mercy toward those them that fear him" (Psalms 108:8-11).

God's Love Doesn't Condemn

The good news is that people can avoid Hell. Jesus lived a perfect life for us out of love and he died in our stead to secure forgiveness and salvation. Jesus suffered and died the penalty for our sins in order for us to have eternal life and to protect us from the wrath of God upon the sinners. God so loved the world that he sent his only begotten Son, that whoever believes in him should not perish but have everlasting life (John 3:16). Believe Jesus Christ and trust in him and what he has done for you only for your salvation. God sent not his Son into the world to condemn the world; but that the world through him might be saved (John 3:17). Jesus came to die for us so that we can live forever with him. He did not come to tell us that we are doomed to spend an eternity in Hell. Hell is for those that simply don't believe and that reject Jesus and his work as the only way for eternal life in Heaven. Jesus did speak of Hell more than he did about Heaven to warn those who he loved. Jesus said, "Verily I say unto you, "he that believeth on me hath everlasting life" (John 6:47). It is God's will that we believe Jesus for our salvation. Jesus said, "He that believes on him is not condemned, but he that believe not is condemned already, because he hath not believed in the name of the only begotten Son of God" (John 3:18).

God Accepts Us Because Of His Love

He that doesn't love doesn't know God. God is love (I John 4:8). Love when referring to God comes from the New Testament Greek word "agape" which means an unconditional and selfless action, attitude, and life to promote what is good and blessed in the best interest of another or the recipient thereof. God's love for us is his selfless interaction with us to promote us which is best exemplified through his Son, Jesus Christ by what he did for us to save us. God's approval of us and his love for us is not based on our personal righteousness or performance of good works. Our hearts fill with pride and self-righteousness when we think we are more righteous than others or can earn special favor with God because of our own performance. Our hearts also fill with fear of punishment and depression combined with a loss of joy and guilt when we see examine all of the biblical definitions of sin and see how terribly bad we are within our hearts and out.

Our performance doesn't measure up. Our desire to persuade ourselves and others that we have now arrived as good people will cause us to hide the truth about themselves. It becomes a cycle which can lead to despair if you fail and arrogance if you do excel. People feel proud about whatever they think makes them feel better than other people or about how they think they measure up to God's standards more in their comparison of themselves with others as his precious saints. Pride causes criticism, strife, division, and self-righteousness. People who need to hear the gospel can feel inferior, worthless, and rejected because of everyone's narcissistic or grandiose ideas of themselves. God accepts the sinner because of Jesus and not because of their performance, dress attire or his or her good deeds and personal holiness or sanctified life. The best saint is an ant as far as God's law is concerned. Whoever keeps the law and offends in one point is guilty of it all (James 2:10). God commended his love toward us that while we were yet sinners, Christ died for the ungodly (Romans 5:8).

The most ungodly of sinners can be saved from the wrath of God to come if they believe the gospel. Jesus died for us while knowing every ungodly and wicked thing we would do or imagine to do throughout our entire lives. Before God destroyed the earth with the flood during the days of Noah he saw that every imagination of the thoughts of the heart of man was continually evil (Genesis 6:5). Although people can fail there is nothing you and I can do to add or subtract to or from what Jesus has already did for us. God won't love us more or less because of us. The Devil enjoys using pride in our own goodness to puff our ego up when we compare our life story or goodness to others. He also enjoys using depression and guilt by making us feel unworthy of God because of our past or present struggles or failures. Jesus Christ doesn't hold charges against you because of what he did to dismiss those charges. Blessed are those whose sins are forgiven and whose iniquities are covered (Romans 4:7). Blessed is the man to whom the Lord will not charge of sin if he sinned (Romans 4:8).

Security in God is because Of Jesus

When we accept the reality that God saves us because of what Jesus did for us at the cross we will at that time end the repetition of feeling arrogant when we do well and depressed or sad if we fail God or come short of his glory. We should not feel insecure in our relationship with God but love him more when we realize who he is and what he did to save us. God can only approve of us because of what Jesus did. The gospel gives us assurance that God approved of us because of Christ's works, and not our own. As a result of our comprehension of the depth of God's love for us and that reality piercing our souls, we love God and keep his commandments. We love him, because he first loved us (I John 4:19). We can relate to others with kindness, love, forgiveness, mercy, and goodness because within our hearts we know our heavenly father has related to us in that manner. We are his children. We forgive because he forgave us. We want to share. We are secure in salvation but not because we think we are earning favor with God because of our own personal conduct. We feel secure because we know the price he paid and the fact that he purchased the church with his own blood (Acts 20:28).

Repenting and Believing the Gospel

When we turn to Jesus to trust him for our salvation and believe on him we repent. Repent means to change the mind and the purpose. The usage of the word conveys the idea of sorrow and contrition which are included in the definition. Jesus said, "No man can come to me, except the Father which hath sent him draw him: and I will raise him up in the last day" (John 6:44). To come to God in repentance and faith means that God has drawn us to him by his grace. Thank God that you and I don't have to rely upon ourselves to repent and to believe. God knows how to work sovereignly in our hearts to bring us to him. We do repent but he gets the credit. When people decide in the mind to change God helps them to turn away sin.

The Greek word for repentance is (metanoia) "to have another mind" but it cannot be defined to exclude a hatred for sin. The concept of repentance in the Bible involves more than a casual change of mind.

When a person repents they don't continue to willfully sin. Therefore, repentance is turning from sin and it involves a change in behavior (Luke 3:8). Godly sorrow works repentance and is a sorrow about one's sinfulness before a holy God

One cannot truly believe on Christ unless he repents and he cannot repent unless he believes. Teaching repentance does not add law to the gospel of grace nor does it add any requirements for the sinners to do his own works in order for him to be saved. It is not faith plus repentance that saves but a repentant faith. We come to Jesus with a heartfelt repentance, which includes a deep hatred for sin and a godly sorrow while we look to Christ believing, trusting Jesus and him alone to save us because of what he did for us at the cross.

Some people mistake in their belief that they must change their ways or clean themselves up in order to be accepted by Jesus or worthy of him before they make a decision to turn to Jesus in faith and ask Christ to save them. All of this is vain. We can only become what Jesus Christ intended us to be by believing him and trusting him to save us. Jesus has already accepted us. He already loves us. That is why he died for us. Repentance is when we realize that we are sinners and in our brokenness and sorrow for our sins against God within we turn to Jesus Christ in faith for the forgiveness of our sins and the salvation from our sinful condition. The fact that Jesus loves us unconditionally and has died for us to save us makes the decision easy.

God command all men everywhere to repent and to believe the gospel. Repentance means to turn away from all sin known after we change our mind about it. Faith and repentance are two sides of the same coin and one cannot exist without the other. To believe in Jesus and to believe on Jesus for your salvation means to recognize that you are a sinner in rebellion against God. Believing in Jesus doesn't mean that you simply add Jesus to your life as one of the hobbies you have without us consciously forsaking idols to follow him. Repentance and faith are not something that a sinner adds or contributes to his salvation on his own to save himself. The preacher preaches repentance and faith to the sinner and God works in the heart of the unregenerate sinner to enable him and grant him a repentant heart and to enable him to have God's gift of faith. God puts repentance and faith in the heart of the unregenerate or spiritually dead sinner by the preaching of the gospel message. Repentance and faith are supernatural results produced by God working new motives and affections deep within the soul. Repentance is not a work that the sinner somehow contributes with his faith to contribute to his salvation. Repentance and faith are the result of God's work of regeneration by the Holy Ghost. Faith and repentance are not something that we add or supply apart from the supernatural actions of the Holy Ghost affecting us to do it. This is grace at work. The unsaved, lost, spiritually dead, and blind are unable to generate a righteous thought, right affection, pure will, therefore God, in his grace, gives us freely, the faith and repentance needed that he expects in order for us to be born again and saved. It is the grace of God that works to save the sinner. The Bible teaches us that, "the heart is deceitful and desperately wicked above all things" (Jeremiah 17:9). God has to change the human heart and create in them a clean heart and renew a right spirit within them. God draws the sinner and they cannot come unless he does the drawing (John 6:37). The preacher must preach repentance and faith and that is where God works (Luke 24:47, Mark 16:15-16).

The Bible tells the preachers to, preach, "in meekness instructing those that oppose themselves, peradventure that God may grant them a repentance leading to the knowledge of the truth who are captives of Satan to recover them who are held hostage by him at his will (II Timothy 2:25). The Apostle viewed repentance as something that God worked sovereignly in the hearts of a sinner at the preaching of the gospel while men were being instructed to turn them away from sin and out of bondage to Satan. To instruct those that oppose themselves is to declare a Word from God power enough to persuade the sinner of how his sin is opposing him. God then grants the lost sinner repentance and brings him out of the snare of Satan.

Repentance and faith are thus things we do but activities that originates with God who works these gifts through us by his saving grace. A natural man does not accept the things of the spirit of God and cannot understand them (I Corinthians 2:14). A fleshly mind does not subject itself to God and his laws (Romans 8:7). God has to change the mind of the sinner in order for him to repent and turn to Christ to trust in him alone for salvation. He uses the preaching ministry and the operation of the Holy Spirit to do this.

The Holy Ghost turns our mind from godlessness to godliness and turns our skeptic and doubt to a faith that saves. The scriptures teach that He, God, who began a good work in us will perform it until the day of Jesus Christ (Philippians 1:16). Some have taught that repentance is us trying to add works to salvation which is solely by faith. However, repentance and faith are both on the opposite sides of the same coin of salvation. People repent in their own minds of sinfulness against God and because of godly sorrow for their own sinfulness they turn to Christ in faith and trust him and him alone for their salvation. They realize that their works do not save them but the death of Christ to atone for their sins at the cross because of the preaching of the gospel. Repentance, which originates from God in the heart of the sinner with saving faith, results in the hatred of sin and a change of behavior because of allegiance to Christ.

Some are led to believe that because they simply said that they accepted Jesus and professed that they believe him that they are saved even without the work of repentance within their hearts. The result of this style of ministry is a people who do not have a godly sorrow and a broken heart about their own sin and rebellion against God. It is possible to profess to believe God and to have a lifestyle inconsistent with one's profession of faith in Christ.

Repentance is a special gift that God gives to us from Jesus Christ. Repentance includes the hatefulness of sin. Repentance includes the enjoyment of the beauty of holiness and it comes with faith in Jesus which is also a special gift from God. It is an aspect of the Grace of God at work in our lives that turns us away from sin, "for the grace of God that brings salvation hath appeared to all men. Teaching us that denying ungodliness and worldly lusts, we should live soberly, righteously, and godly, in this present world" (Titus 2:11-12). The scriptures teach, "Him has God exalted with his right hand to be a prince and a Savior, to give repentance to Israel, and forgiveness of sin" (Acts 5:31).

When we see people overcome sin we know that it was the Grace of God that pulled them out of the condition that they were in. We can come boldly to the throne of grace to obtain mercy and grace to help in the time of need (Hebrews 4:16). How can people come out or break the cycle? Again, "For by grace are ye saved through faith, and that not of yourselves, it is the gift of God" (Ephesians 2:8). Again, scriptures teach, "Then God also to the Gentiles granted repentance unto life" (Acts 11:18). Paul taught, "In meekness instruct those that oppose themselves; if God peradventure will give them repentance to the acknowledgement of truth that they may recover themselves out of the snare of the devil, who are taken captive by him at his will" (II Timothy 2:25).

Paul says that we must instruct people who are contrary to their own selves. We must teach them why sin is bad or wrong. They are also in the snare of the devil and often unknowingly. We can ask God to give us his grace to repent which is an unmerited favor from God that enables us to repent of sin and then we can change our mind, motives, and purpose to sin. People cannot of their own ability stop a sin because someone told them that a particular lifestyle was sin. The Bible teaches, "If we say we have no sin, we deceive ourselves, and the truth is not in us. If we confess our sins, he is faithful and just to forgive us our sins, and to cleanse us from all unrighteousness" (I John 1:8-9). When we come to God to ask him to forgive us because of the sacrifice of Jesus for us, let us confess to God what our sins have been in our lives and ask him to pardon us and clean us from unrighteousness.

Repentance is a voluntary forsaking of sin as evil and hateful, with sincere sorrow, humiliation, and confession. It is a returning to God because we know we truly belong to him and because he loves us and is willing to forgive us if we repent. We repent with a determination to live, enabled by his grace, a life of obedience to him and his commandments. The evidence of repentance is the hatred and forsaking of secret as well as open sins, a choice to do what is righteous. The Bible teaches, "For godly sorrow works repentance to salvation not to be repented of, but the sorrow of the world works death" (II Corinthians 7:10).

Repentance is a constant denial of self and bearing of a cross without a looking or going back. Jesus said, "No man having put his hand to the plough, and looking back, is fit for the kingdom of God" (Luke 9:62). I want to encourage you now to believe that Jesus loves you. Trust Jesus Christ for your salvation. Ask Jesus to grant to you a godly sorrow for your sins and ask him to enable you to be forgiven and to repent without looking back or going back into your former lifestyle.

Moreover, ask him for his gift of the Holy Ghost which comes to give you power, conviction of sin, comfort, peace, and sanctification from sin (Acts 1:8, Matthew 3:11-12, John 14:26-27). Jesus taught that repentance and remission of sins should be preached in all nations, beginning at Jerusalem (Luke 24:47).

The Atonement: Nature, Necessity, Extent, and Perfection

How can a holy God save a sinful man?

The question is, "How can a sinful man be accepted by a holy God"? The Bible takes sin seriously. It sees sin as a barrier separating man from God (Isa. 59:2). Man was able to erect a barrier between him and God by his sin but he is unable to destroy that barrier. Consequently, God has a wrath against man because of his sin although his love and mercy wants to save him. The atonement is God's way of covering for the sin of man and reconciling himself back to man without destroying him. The message of the gospel in John 3:16 is that "God so loved the world that he gave his only begotten Son, that whosoever believes in him should not perish, but have eternal life". Jesus is a God that is good and loving and thus the very idea that any man would be lost and thrown into Hell, was and is abhorrent to him. Therefore, he offered himself as a victim in their stead, paid the penalty and having laid down his life as victim in their stead, and thus pacified an angry God. Christ is glorified by this as his Son; however, the cause of the atonement is the sovereign pleasure of God to save sinners by a substitutionary atonement with his Son laying down his life for them.

The Hebrew definition of atonement expresses the idea of atonement for sin by the covering of sin or of the sinner. The blood of the sacrifice is interposed or placed between God and the sinner, and in view of the blood of the sacrifice the wrath of God is turned away. The blood has the effect of warding off the wrath of God from the sinner. A dynamic example of this is when Moses put the blood of a Lamb on the doorpost of the Israelites and consequently the death angel passed over their firstborn child and only smote the firstborn of the Egyptians. Many passages of scripture in the New Testament speak of the wrath of God against the sinner and of God being angry at sinners (Romans 1:18, Galatians 3:10, Ephesians 2:3, Romans 5:9). Jesus Christ is the only way for a sinful man to be reconciled with a holy and just God. When men fall away from God, he as such owes God reparation. But he could atone for his sin only by suffering eternally the penalty affixed to transgression. This is what God would require in strict justice if he had not been actuated by love and compassion for the sinner. God appointed Jesus Christ to take man's place and he is the perfect expression of divine love for a lost sinner.

The meaning of the Atonement

The proper meaning of the Hebrew word for atonement means to make moral or legal repair for a fault or injury. Jesus did both for us. In the Old Testament theological usage, it expresses not the reconciliation effected by Jesus Christ but the legal satisfaction which causes the reconciliation with God. The Old Testament idea of the atonement is too limited to express what Christ did for us in the gospel. The atonement in the New Testament removes the guilt but also merits for us the reward of eternal life because of the active obedience of Jesus Christ. Moreover, Jesus Christ was the Second Adam and he satisfied the entire broken covenant of works, as left by the First Adam. Jesus Christ suffered the penalty of transgression which Adam and his posterity ought to have done. Jesus Christ also rendered the obedience to God when tested where the original Adam failed and this obedience was a condition to eternal life. We rejoice in God through our Lord Jesus Christ, by whom we have now received the atonement (Romans 5:11). It was by one man, Adam, that sin entered into the world and death because of sin, consequently, death passed onto all men because all men sinned (Romans 5:12). For by one man's disobedience many were made sinners, so by the obedience of one shall many be made righteous (Romans 5:19).

Substitution is the gracious act of a sovereign God in allowing one not bound to discharge a service, or to suffer a punishment in the stead of another. The discharge of the service and the suffering of the penalty by the Jesus Christ were and are vicarious. This means that is in the stead of as well as in the behalf of us. The term propitiation refers to the satisfaction by removing the divine displeasure of God with us because of Jesus' vicarious obedience and death on our behalf. The Hebrew writer says, "Wherefore in all things it behooved him to be made like unto his brethren, that he might be a merciful and faithful high priest in things pertaining to God, to make reconciliation for the sins of the people" (Hebrews 2:17). Jesus Christ is a faithful priest acting on our behalf to stop your past faults and failures from keeping you out of a relationship with God.

The atonement in the scriptures represents the expiation of guilt by means of the sacrifice of Jesus Christ in order to satisfy God. The use of the term Redemption is even more comprehensive. Redemption signifies deliverance from enslavement or ruin by the payment of a ransom by our substitute. Redemption is the act of Jesus Christ paying that ransom, when it is the exact equivalent to Atonement. Jesus redeemed us from the curse of the law by being made a curse for us (Galatians 3:13). Redemption is also our atonement as it means also a deliverance from some aspect of our lost condition, as death, demons, principalities, powers, and habitual sin (Colossians 1:13, Colossians 2:15, I John 3:8).

The Theology of Limited Atonement, Universalism, and Unlimited Atonement

Limited Atonement

Most Christians believe and agree that Jesus' sacrifice is limited to those that believe. The disagreement comes in terms of who is limiting the atonement. Has God limited the atonement and who it was for simply because he only willed for those whom he Elected and graced to be saved? Has the atonement been limited by man simply because of his refusal to be willing to believe the gospel and to trust Christ for his salvation? Did Christ die to make it possible for everyone to be saved if they believe? Did Christ simply die for those whom God Elected or those whom he knew would believe the gospel?

When an airplane or train comes to your town it is there for everyone who desires to travel to the next destination. However, everyone knows that it is there more specifically for those who will come to take a ride and not for the general population that won't. Jesus died for the entire world in order to save those that would believe in him and trust him for their salvation. His work doesn't just make salvation possible for all but it also saves those that believe on him.

The doctrine of limited atonement confirms that Jesus died for specific and chosen people to secure their salvation instead of just for the world in general to render salvation as a possibility for everyone, included those he knew would never believe the gospel. As we example these theological truths, keep in mind that God's love desires for all sinners to be saved while his divine foreknowledge of all future events is aware as to whom will believe and respond to the universal call. The invitation and call of the gospel is to all but God knew who would respond to it and who would not. The folks that God knew would respond to his call to repent and believe are called his Elect in the Bible. The Elect are also loved in a special way which was shall discuss later. It is biblical to say that when Jesus died that his sacrifice was sufficient to save all and that the gospel is for all. The gospel is for all and the atonement is for all in the sense that it is designed to reach all that will believe out of the multitudes of sinners.

Jesus came to earth with a specific purpose in mind to redeem people from every tribe, tongue, and nation (Revelation 5:9). Jesus died to save his people from their sins (Matthew 1:21). Jesus said that he as a shepherd laid down his life for his sheep (John 10:15). Jesus said that his sheep are those that hear his voice and he knows them and they follow him. Jesus said that he gives them eternal life and they shall never perish (John 10:27-28). Jesus also says that his sheep will not follow the voice of a stranger (John 10:5). They were chosen by God before the foundation of the world (Ephesians 1:14). Jesus said that these sheep of his were given to him by his Father and that he would lose nothing but that he would raise them up on the last day (John 6:37-40). Jesus said he had come to do his Father's will which we know included laying his life down for his sheep which were given to him by God before the worlds were formed (John 6:38). The Bible teaches that Jesus was wounded for our transgressions and bruised for our iniquities and that by his stripes we are healed (Isaiah 53:5). Jesus bore our sins to justify many (Isaiah 53:11). The Bible teaches that Jesus died not just to make our salvation possible but to justify us and to actually save us, not just to make us savable or the reality of our salvation possible and left up to us.

The doctrine of limited atonement also teaches that Jesus' death on the cross was a substitutionary or vicarious atonement for sins. The words mean to act on behalf of us and to represent us to God. This means that Jesus' life and death performed something for us which brings benefits and advantages to us. The vicarious suffering of Christ as our representative meant that we would receive salvation as a benefit from his death and as a result of what he did specifically for us. The scriptures teach, "God made him (Jesus Christ) to be sin for us, so that we might become the righteousness of God in Him" (2 Corinthians 5:21). The good news about the atonement is that since Jesus stood in our place and suffered for our sins on the cross and represented us in his life on the earth as well that we can never be punished in Hell for sin. In order for Jesus' atonement to be a real and a vicarious atonement for all of our sin once and for all then it must inevitably bring us a real salvation for everyone who Christ died for. Jesus didn't die to provide a theoretical salvation. He died and shed his blood to save. If Jesus was an actual and real substitute for those who he died for then all of those whom he died for will be saved.

When we say that Jesus Christ died a vicarious death in the place of all sinners but that not all sinners will be saved that is a contradiction. He died for the sinners that would believe on him. The sacrifice was for all in order to save those that would believe but not to save those who would always remain in a state of unbelief. The atonement removes sin altogether for believers and the sacrifice of Jesus was one offering in which he perfected forever them that are sanctified (Hebrews 10:14).

We see different elements involved in our atonement as explained in the testimony of the Bible. A complete understanding of these aspects enables us to understand what Jesus Christ actually accomplished in his life for us and by his suffering and death in our stead. A universal atonement would mean a universal salvation. What Jesus did was so powerful that if he had done it for everyone with no exceptions including those that would never believe it would mean that everyone "universally" would end up saved and nobody would go to Hell. Jesus offered his body as a sacrifice for the sins of people in their stead to remove the penalty altogether from the equation as a variable. His sacrifice secured their salvation and perfected the sanctified forever by that one sacrifice (Hebrews 2:14). If he had died for everyone including those whom he knew would not ever believe the gospel it would mean we would have a redemption for some without them being set free of guilt. It would mean that unbelievers could be condemned to Hell to pay for their sins although Jesus had already died for them to save them. This would also mean that if Jesus died for people who would never believe that gospel that he paid the price for their sins but did not save them. We would have a reconciliation that would leave some totally estranged from God without ever getting reconciled. We would have a propitiation (satisfaction to God) rendered for souls that kept some still under the wrath of God and doomed to eternal damnation. It would mean that there was a substitution or perfect offering rendered to a holy God that was not suitable enough to save some because of their unbelief and continuance sin.

The doctrine of a limited atonement teaches that the work of Jesus in the atonement was exclusively for the sheep that God knew at some point in the future would believe him and follow him. He died for everyone in general but only to save those that would believe. The sacrifice was sufficient to save all and is available to all thus the gospel goes to all. Jesus made it clear that he was laying his life down for his sheep and that they would not follow a stranger but would believe in him. Jesus also made it clear that the sheep knew him and that he knew the sheep and that they were given to him before he came and that he, Jesus Christ, would lose none of them (John 6:37-40 & John 10:27-28, John 10:5). The doctrine of a limited atonement is consistent with who Jesus said he was laying his life down for. We should leap for joy by knowing that Jesus loved us to the extent that he specifically had us in mind to accomplish a real salvation for us when he died in our stead. He did this not just to make salvation possible but to accomplish our salvation for us.

The Bible teaches that Jesus redeemed those that are set free and their debts are paid in full. The Word of God teaches that those who are reconciled to God have the wall of separation between them and God torn down altogether (Colossians 2:14). Christ's death on the cross for us fully satisfied the wrath of God. When Jesus died on the cross, he said, "It is finished" (John 19:30). The word finished is translated from the Greek word teleo, which was used to indicate that a debt had been paid in full. This is what Jesus accomplished on the cross for us. Jesus paid your entire sin debt completely which means that none of your sin can be held against you on judgment day which accomplishes a real, secure salvation. Jesus forgave all of your sin and cancelled his law, written rules, regulations, ordinances, codes, and commandments that you broke which was proven against you and me that opposed us; he took it away, nailing it to the cross (Colossians 2:13-14). When you arrived on earth you were already foreknown by God, predestinated, called, and then justified and sanctified to later be glorified (Romans 8:28-29). These awesome truths were foreknown by God. He knew who would believe the gospel and who would receive him and trust him for their salvation. Grace worked through us to enable these things to happen.

One thing that people think about the limited atonement view is that it somehow limits the value of the atonement of Jesus as being for the whole world. However, the limited atonement correctly recognizes that Jesus' obedience to God's divine laws on our behalf and his suffering and death in our stead accomplished salvation for us and lacks nothing. Jesus also loses nothing and none of his sheep that the Father gave him as he himself had already said he wouldn't (John 6:37-40). The death of Jesus Christ and his atonement has such a value for the world that Jesus has to do nothing else to save every human being that every lived on the face of the planet. However, God had as his purpose in mind when sending Jesus to the world to live in our stead and die as our sacrifice to God. Jesus came with no other purpose than to secure forever the salvation of those God had given to his son (Hebrews 7:25& John 6:37-40). Jesus came to do the will of his Father and to die for his sheep which were given to Christ before the foundations of the world God is omniscient. God knew beforehand the fall of mankind and had already planned for his Son to come as a savior for the world. God knew who would believe the gospel and who would repent. They are called the Elect and the chosen. These are they for whom Christ died although God doesn't desire nor is he willing that any should perish but that all would come to repentance (II Peter 3:9). The gospel is preached to all in order that men who could believe do believe.

Some people feel that the doctrine of limited atonement limits the love of God for humanity. However, the doctrine of limited atonement magnifies the love of God and it puts a pre-eminence on us having a relationship of love with a loving Father. The truth is that the atonement is sufficient and powerful enough to save all. The limited atonement leaves us with a God of love that died only for those whom he knew would believe the gospel. The doctrine doesn't diminish his love but reveals a depth of his love for his people to the extent that he saves them from their sins by his work in their stead.

The unlimited atonement view says that Christ simply died to atone for the sins of the entire world to make salvation a possibility for all but not necessarily to secure the salvation of anyone in particular but to leave salvation up to them. Would this magnify God's love or diminish it? Compare this view to the view that Jesus died in a loving manner for specific people that he loved to save them and that his suffering and vicarious atonement accomplished their salvation for them. In the view of the unlimited atonement God loves everyone in general but saves nobody in particular but gives them the option to be saved and leaves it up to them. The love of God is manifested even more if we see Jesus' work in his life in a vicarious atonement living and dying to save people he loved to hold them firmly in his hand to bring them to heaven with him. The question could arise as to why he wouldn't do this for everyone if he truly a loving God. The answer is simply that God does not love anyone less simply because they have chosen to reject him and the provisions to secure their salvation.

God told Noah to prepare the ark and then to warn people that the flood was coming to give them an opportunity to get on the boat. God knew the people would not respond but he did give them an opportunity to be saved. The ark and the message of a coming flood was for everyone in a general sense to us in our perspective but it was specifically for Noah and his family as far as God was concerned because he knew everyone would not believe Noah's message. God had Noah to build the boat for the people that would get on the boat but not for the people who would not believe his message. Likewise, Jesus came to save his people from their sins (Matthew 1:21).

One of the major objections to the doctrine of limited atonement is the many biblical passages that indicate that the gospel goes to whosoever that will come. However, God sends the gospel to all and it is universal and everyone that believes will be saved. God knew beforehand who would believe and who would repent as well as whom to call his own Elect and chosen. The Elect are chosen according to the divine foreknowledge of God (I Peter 1:2). This means that God knows all of the future and is able to see beforehand the end of the ages and the destination of all as well as whom would respond to the gospel call. They are called his Elect.

God sent Jesus here to die for the sheep that he gave to Christ. This does not mean that Christ's atonement is not sufficient to save all but that God's will was that his Son would be offered up as a sacrifice only for those that God knew would believe. Nevertheless, he did not sacrifice himself to atone for the sins of those who would never come to trust Jesus Christ for their salvation. That would mean that the people who would go to Hell for unbelief would be paying for sins that Christ had already died for. The Atonement was a permanent putting away of all of the sins of specific people forever to perfect and sanctify them by that one sacrifice and sin-offering (Hebrews 10:14). People will not pay for sins that Christ have already died for. The Good News is Good News because we know that Jesus Christ paid the penalty for our sins already and we don't have to worry about paying for them ourselves. It is double jeopardy to pay for sins twice.

The Roman writer says, "For whom he did foreknow, he also did predestinate to be conformed to the image of his son, that he might be the firstborn among many brethren. Moreover, whom he did predestinate them he also called, and whom he called, them he also justified: and whom he justified, them he also gloried" (Romans 8:29-30). God will finish the salvation that he started for his people and that is nothing but love. We must accept that the atonement is so far reaching and powerful that it accomplishes the purpose that God had in mind for it in the lives of each person that his precious blood was shed for. We are saved because we have faith in Jesus and have trusted him for our salvation because of what Jesus Christ did for us. Why did the thief on the cross get into Paradise? It was because he trusted that Jesus had a kingdom for him and he trusted Jesus to save him when he said, "Lord remember me when thou cometh into thy kingdom" (Luke 23:42). Jesus then says to him, "Verily I say unto you, today shall you be with me in Paradise" (Luke 23:43). Why? It surely was not because the thief had lived any kind of life good enough that could bring him in a just standing before God. If it is possible for anyone to be considered righteous because they have works sufficient enough in terms of keeping commandments and the law then Christ died in vain (Galatians 2:21).

Some passages of scripture points out that Christ's atonement is more general and have an unlimited scope. For example, John said that Jesus Christ is the propitiation for the sins of the whole world (I John 2:2). Jesus is also called the Savior of the world in John 4:42. Other passages indicate that Jesus' atonement was unlimited. For example, "For the love of Christ constrains us; because we thus judge, that if one died for all, then were all dead; And that he died for all, that they which live should not live unto themselves, but unto him which died for them, and rose again" (II Corinthians 5:4-15). Also, "To wit, that God was in Christ, reconciling the world unto himself, not imputing their trespasses unto them, and hath committed to us the word of reconciliation (II Corinthians 5:19). However, these passages of scripture can be reconciled with many verses where we see the words "world" and "all" used but not to mean every individual on the planet. For example, Caesar made a decree that the entire world should be registered but the scriptures then teach that they registered those in every city in the region but not the entire world (Luke 2:1). Pharisees also said "Look at how the whole world is going after Jesus"! We know that every person did not actually follow Jesus but that the word "world" was used by them to refer to the many out of the region that did follow him. Therefore, the word "world" and "all" does not refer necessarily to every individual. Keep in mind that the scriptures teach that Jesus came to give his life as a ransom for many (Matthew 10:28). The word "world" wasn't used in this passage and these words were proclaimed by Jesus when referring to himself. The world many doesn't necessarily mean all. Jesus said again, "For even the son of man came not to be ministered unto but to give his life as a ransom for many" (Mark 10:45).

The people who don't fully comprehend the doctrine of limited atonement also think that if Christ died for the Elect only that it discourages evangelism. Why evangelize if he died only for the Elect? We evangelize to all in order that the ones who will believe can hear the gospel and get saved. That is simple. The Elect or the chosen are those who will hear the gospel and believe. They trust in Christ alone and his blood and not their works for their salvation. God knew who they would be before the creation but we do not. Paul said that Evangelism is the power of salvation to those that believe (Romans 1:16). People evangelize because we don't know who will respond to the gospel call and who will refuse to believe. God knows and he knew before he made the world but we don't. We therefore preach the gospel in order that the purpose of God for the Elect will be fulfilled in their lives. Again, the Elect can be defined as those whom God knew beforehand. His foreknowledge extends to the knowledge that they would respond to the gospel call, repent, and believe the gospel (I Peter 1:2). The Apostle Paul taught that those whom God foreknew would also be glorified after being justified and sanctified (Romans 8:28-29).

Friends if the atonement of God was unlimited and if Jesus actually died for everyone including all of those that would not ever come to trust Jesus and believe him it means that every person would be saved regardless of their continued unbelief which leads to the doctrine of universalism. Nobody really has to go to Hell at all if Jesus died for all who ever existed or if he atoned for the sins of every man that set a foot on the face of the planet including those that would never believe in him or trust him for their salvation. The Atonement removes sin as a sin out of the record book of the offending party. God would not have Jesus to pay the penalty for their sins and then have them to pay for the penalty of their sins too. That would contradict the justice of God. Jesus Christ died for the sins of the world to save those that would believe and his death accomplished their salvation if they are his people. Jesus came to save his people from their sins (Matthew 1:21). People have a choice as to whether or not they will follow Jesus or reject him and his atonement which is sufficient to save all.

The doctrine of an unlimited atonement makes the redemption of souls a possible act but it doesn't make the particular salvation of anyone sure or real. Why? The unlimited atonement teaches that his death was not for anyone specific but everyone including those that would never repent and would never believe the gospel. This would mean that Christ's sacrifice doesn't actually accomplish anything for anyone until someone decided to have faith and only if they decide for sure that they will stay with Christ until the end. It also means if you hold the view of James Arminius, that you and others will not know for sure if you will be saved in the end until you have decided to stay with Jesus and obey him all the way up until the end of your life. If this is true, God has Christ dying for sins of people that God knew would not be saved in the end due to their sin. If the unlimited atonement was true it means that God had Jesus paying the penalty for sins of people who would have to turn right around and pay for the penalty of their own sins in Hell later. It could be misconstrued as the equivalent of making God unjust. In the doctrine of an unlimited atonement, God would punish people for sins that Jesus Christ atoned for with his body as a sacrifice for it and them. That would violate the Old Testament typology. The Lamb took away sins and after that sin could not be held against any whom the blood of the sacrificial Lamb was shed for. If this were true it would mean that Christ's atonement somehow was insufficient in that it did not atone for all of the sins or the people in which Jesus Christ himself had died and shed his precious blood for.

It is unreasonable and ridiculous to think that God would have Jesus Christ to atone for sins of people who would in fact be punished under the wrath of God. Jesus Christ would could not have atoned for sins of people who would spend eternity in Hell. The atonement erases sin out of God's record book and removes the penalty away for the transgressor and for everything forever. The unlimited atonement could not be a vicarious atonement if it were true. A vicarious atonement is when Christ suffers the penalty in the stead of another and having lived in obedience for another also to bring the benefit of salvation to the recipient of grace as an eternal gift. The atonement secures a real and certain salvation for specific sinners who put their trust in him. The sin covered in atonement by the blood of Christ can never be charged to the sinners account.

A universal atonement teaches that Christ died for the sins of every individual in the entire world and that as a result of his vicarious atonement for all that all men will definitely be saved and go to heaven. It means that nobody can be punished for their sins because of what Christ did for all. Although Jesus Christ died a death that is sufficient to atone for the sins of everyone in the world it is a true saying that he only died to secure salvation for those that would believe on him and subsequently be glorified in heaven. Jesus atoned for our sins once and for all by his one sacrifice for us to perfect us and sanctify us in God's sight (Hebrews 10:14). The Atonement removes all sin (past, present and future) to secure salvation and to perfect his people. Universalism is untrue in that it fails to recognize the many teachings that reveal that many professing believers that call Jesus Lord shall not enter into the kingdom of heaven (Mattthew 7:21-24). The Atonement would not have been for those who would never come to a saving faith in Jesus but it is for the believers that would repent and believe the gospel.

The unlimited atonement view teaches that it is possible for Christ as a Great High Priest to atone for the sins of people he gave his body as a sacrifice for without redeeming many of those people from the law, Satan, and the wrath of God to come. The truth is that the atonement accomplishes all of the purposes in which God designed the atonement for. We are saved by grace which is a gift from God and not by our own works lest any should boast (Ephesians 2:8-10). God enables his people to repent and believe the gospel by his grace and he delivers them from the law, Satan, and the wrath of God in Hell. Jesus accomplished salvation for us if you believe him. Jesus said, "Ye have not chosen me, but I have chosen you, and ordained you, that you should go and bring fruit, and that whatsoever ye ask of the Father in my name, he may give it to you" (John 15:16).

Why warn true believers if they cannot be lost?

How should we interpret scriptures which speak of the possibility of those perishing or being lost for whom Jesus Christ died? The passages are possibilities which are hypothetical but nothing that surely shall happen with the Elect and they reveal God's purpose to use gifts he has given to the church as a deterrent (Ephesians 4:11-12). It means that under the administration of his Spirit that God has factored in the paradox of freewill. We all must surely have a degree of freewill in order for us to have moral responsibility and to be justly held accountable to God as individuals on judgment day or to be rewarded. It is appointed to all men once to die and after that the judgment (Hebrews 9:27).

In the case of Paul's shipwreck, it was certain that none would perish and an angel told Paul that they all would be saved and that no loss of any mans' life among them would occur but that only the ship would be loss (Acts 27:22). The angel guaranteed they would survive the storm. However, Paul later saw that the sailors had let down anchors and were about to get out of the ship presumably to swim and he told them, 'Except you cut the ropes and remain on the boat you cannot be saved and will perish" (Acts 27:29-32).The promise that they had from the angel which guaranteed that all would be saved was a revelation which came from the angel that originated from God. It did not mean that they could do anything and still be saved. They had to follow the leader and not put themselves at risk. The message from the angel did not take away the reality that they could still be lost and perish if they got off the boat or refused to cut the ropes. That is why Paul had to warn them as to what to do and when to bring God's word from the angel to pass. God's promise that he had secured the salvation of his sheep because of Jesus' atonement doesn't take away the fact that the sheep still need to be taught, nurtured, warned, led, and instructed in terms of how to live life on earth in order to be saved in the end. The fact that God knows the end and has shared it with us doesn't mean that we will do nothing to bring it to pass. God has designed ministry to perfect the saints that they won't be lost in the end which could, theoretically, happen if they sin willfully or depart from the faith (Ephesians 4:11, Hebrews 10:26-31, II Peter 2:1-22, Jude, Revelation 3:15-22).

These passages and others can be interpreted as probable events that are preventable because of the provisions which Christ himself have made for us to bring us safely home to heaven with him. Eternal Security or the perseverance of the saints does not suggest that one can live any way and still make it to heaven. It does teach that God knows his sheep and they hear his voice and follow him. He gives them eternal life and they shall never perish (John 10:27-29). Jesus also promises that his sheep shall not follow the voice of a stranger but will run from him (John 10:5). God has made provisions with Jesus' role as our High Priest, his sacrifice, Christ interceding for us, atonement, the Holy Ghost, ministers, angels, and other means to bring his people to heaven with him. Some things are possible but not necessarily probable and on the same principles must be explained such passages which warn the saints not to fall away from the faith but to stay in Christ and bear fruit. Yes people can be lost in the end. It is possible. It could happen No they won't. We should view these things as paradoxes which cannot be reconciled with our logic. Pastors and ministers must also do the work they have been gifted to do to bring all to the unity of the faith unto a perfect man (Ephesians 4:11). Jesus Christ died to atone for our sins and that is the good news. He provided for us a salvation that was sure and he is our surety.

The Day of Atonement and the shadows prefiguring Christ

The Day of the Atonement in the scriptures is when the priest took the blood from the perfect sacrifice and carried it within the veil and sprinkled the blood in the mercy seat (Leviticus 4:5). This signified the application of the perfect sacrifice to the covering of sin, and its acceptance by God. God removed the guilt and the penalty from the offending sinner because of the blood offered on behalf of the sinner. The effect of the sacrifice of the blood on the Day of Atonement was always forgiveness, "And it shall be forgiven him was the constant promise (Leviticus 4:20-31, Leviticus 6:30). The atonement was the covering of sin by removing the offense of sin from the offended, God, because of the sacrifice offered. The atonement removed sin judicially and sins which were past could not be charged against the offender anymore.

The Old Testament sacrifices by the priests were called "shadows" of which Christ is the "body" and they were called "patterns' of things to come (Hebrews 9:13-24, Hebrews 10:1, 13, Hebrews 10:12). The Hebrew writer declared, "By the which will we are also sanctified through the offering of the body of Jesus Christ once for all" (Hebrews 10:10). Again, "Wherefore, when he come into the world, he saith, sacrifice and offering thou wouldest not, but a body thou hast prepared me" (Hebrews 10:5). The law having a shadow of good things to come, and not the very image of the things, can never with those sacrifices which they offered year by year continually make the comers thereunto perfect (Hebrews 10:1). Finally, "by one offering he hath perfected forever them that are sanctified" (Hebrews 10:14). Jesus Christ himself gave his body as our perfect sacrifice one time for all sins to save us from the wrath of God to come.

The Hebrew writer goes on to say, "This is the covenant that I will make with them after those days, saith the Lord, I will put my laws into their hearts, and in their minds will I write them. And their sins and iniquities I will remember no more. Now where remission of these is, there is no more offering for sin. Having therefore, brethren, boldness to enter into the holiest by the blood of Jesus, by a new and living way, which he hath consecrated for us, through the veil, that is to say, his flesh, And having a high priest over the house of God; Let us draw near with a true heart in full assurance of faith, having our hearts sprinkled from an evil conscience, and our bodies washed in pure water. Let us hold fast our profession of our faith without wavering for he is faithful that promised" (Hebrews 10:16:23).

The gospel message is that Jesus Christ saves us from our sins through what he specifically did himself as our High Priest with his own body as a perfect sacrifice for our sins.

Jesus Christ affirmed that the law as well as the prophets spoke about him and his work (John 1:45, Luke 24:27). Jesus is declared to be sacrificed for his people, by his "blood" being made a sin-offering, (John 1:29, Hebrews 9:26, I Peter 1:19). John the Baptist saw Jesus coming and said, "Behold the Lamb of God, which take away the sin of the world (John 1:29). How did Jesus take away the sin of the world as the Lamb of God? Jesus accomplished this as a sacrifice for the sins of his people to remove guilt and the penalty of sin as our substitute based on God's laws which prefigured him and his work on the cross which was God's sovereign will. Jesus is everywhere in the scriptures declared to accomplish for the man that believes in him exactly what the ancient sacrifices did in the Old Testament. The Romans writer says, "For all have sinned and come short of the glory of God; Being justified freely by his grace through the redemption that is in Christ Jesus: Whom God hath set forth to be a propitiation (satisfaction to God) through faith in his blood, to declare his righteousness for the remission of sins that are past, through the forbearance of God; To declare, I say, at this time his righteousness: that he might be just, and the justifier of him which believeth in Jesus" (Romans 3:23-24).

Redemption in the Covenant of Redemption

Jesus Christ is our Surety, a word that is used in Hebrews 7:22. A surety is one who engages in legal activities and becomes responsible for ensuring that the legal obligations of another will be met. In redemption Jesus Christ became our surety by the undertaking of the responsibility to meet the conditions of God's covenant with man in obedience to the law and by bearing the necessary punishment to meet the demands of the law for us.

God required his Son, who appeared in the covenant as the Surety and Head, and as the Last Adam, to make amends for the sin of Adam which ruined him and his posterity. Jesus was sent to do what Adam had failed to do by keeping God's law and commandments to secure eternal life for God's Elect people. In order for Jesus to do this he had to assume human nature and be born of a woman, and assume the nature of Adam with his vulnerabilities, yet without sin, (Galatians 4:4,5, Hebrews 2:10,11,14,15, Hebrews 4:15. Although Jesus as a Divine being was superior to the law he was placed under the law in order to pay the penalty for sin and to merit everlasting life for his elect people, Psalms 40:8, Galatians 4:4,5, Philippians 2:6-8, John 8:28-29). Jesus would under this covenant after having earned forgiveness because of his sacrifice and obedience as the Lamb of God agreed to renew their lives through the power of the Holy Ghost which made it certain that true believers would dedicate their lives to God (Hebrews 2:10-13, John 0:16, John 16:14-15). God promised to his Son everything he needed to secure the redemption of his elect people. God prepared him a body that was uncontaminated with sin and free of corruption as the First Adam had before the fall (Luke 1:35, Hebrews 10:5). God gave him the Holy Spirit without measure which was an unlimited supernatural endowment of power to accomplish the task (Isaiah, 42:1, 2, John 3:31, Isaiah 61:1). God promised to deliver him from the power of death and enable him to destroy to dominion of Satan over men which was gained after the fall and to establish the Kingdom of God on the earth (Acts 2:25-28, Isaiah 42:1-7, Psalms 16:8-11). God promised to enabled him to send the Holy Ghost to form his spiritual body on earth to instruct, guide, and protect the church (John 15:26, John 14:26, Acts 2:33). God promised to give to his Son a seed which no man could number so that his kingdom would embrace all nations and many languages (Psalms 72:17). God promised to give to Jesus all power in heaven and in earth to govern the world and the church, (Matthew 28:18, Ephesians 1:20-22, Philippians 2:9-11). God promised to reward him as a mediator with the glory which he had as Son with the Father before the world was (John 17:5).

The gospel message is that Jesus Christ has redeemed us from the curse of sin and death and the consequences of the fall of the First Adam. Jesus Christ has earned eternal life for us because of his obedience and his death in our stead as our sacrifice. Jesus Christ has set us free from the governmental control and dominion of Satan. Satan had the legal right to enslave man and to have dominion over him as a result of Adam's fall and man's alienation and estrangement from God because of sin. Adam's sin resulted in the entanglement of his posterity with demons as a consequence of being alienated and estranged from God. The broken relationship with God resulted in an entrapment with a superior intelligence of devils. Jesus redeemed us by setting us free from the bondage to demons by the ransom of his own blood which atoned for our sins to God. The Redemption of Jesus Christ involves setting us free from the powers of darkness and the translation of us into the kingdom of his Son (Colossians 1:13). People are delivered and set free if they believe and they want to be free.

The role of the Priest in our Atonement

The priest was a man taken from among men to represent them in things pertaining to God and particularly his anger and wrath against man because of sin (Hebrews 5:1). He wore the names of all of the tribes on his breastplate. He placed his hands upon the scape-goat and confessed the sins of the people (Leviticus 4:3). All of the people had access to God only through the priest, especially the High Priest (Numbers 16:5). The priest offered sacrifices for the people and for their sins and he interceded for them to turn away the wrath of God (Hebrews 5:1-3, Numbers 6:22-27). Jesus Christ is declared to be our Priest both in the Old Testament and in the New (Psalms 110:4, Zechariah 6:13, Hebrews 5:6). The instant that Jesus finished his work on the cross the veil of the temple was rent in twain, and the whole sacrificial system was discharged because of his office as priest and that he made the perfect sacrifice once and for all sin (Matthew 27:50,51).

Jesus as our High Priest then offered his body to God as a perfect sacrifice for us and in currently interceding on our behalf. The work of Jesus Christ as our High Priest in respect to us as sinners is called redemption, that is, deliverance by ransom (I Corinthians 7:23, Revelation 5:9, I Timothy 2:6). Jesus Christ is the sacrifice which is the ransom. We are redeemed because of his bearing of the curse of the law in our stead, and he redeems us by offering his bleeding sacrifice to God. The scriptures teach, "We have not a high priest that cannot be touched with the feelings of our infirmities; but was in all points tempted like as we re, yet without sin. Let us come boldly to the throne of Grace that we may obtain mercy, and find grace to help in time of need" (Hebrews 4:16). Jesus Christ grants us grace to help which is a divine enablement to do that which we cannot do without his help and special aid.

We are set free from the stronghold of demons originating within human beings after the fall because Jesus' role as the Second Adam restores us in a relationship with God that we lost after the fall and because of the First Adam. We also can bear spiritual fruit but only with Christ's aid. He is the vine and we are the branches and without him we can do nothing (John 15:1-5). God was in Christ, reconciling the world unto himself, not imputing (counting) their trespasses unto them, and hath committed unto us the word of reconciliation. Now then we are ambassadors for Christ, as though God did beseech you by us we pray you in Christ's stead, be ye reconciled to God. For he hath made him to be sin for us, who knew no sin; that we might be made the righteousness of God in him" (II Corinthians 5:18-21). Jesus Christ is our High Priest and he is also our sin-offering to God in order that our own sin will not and cannot be credited to our account or to us as a record charged against us. God simply wants us to repent and believe the gospel in order to be saved.

A Vicarious Atonement

A personal atonement would have been provided by the offending party which is us. However, a vicarious atonement is provided by the offended party which is God. In either case, the penalty of the sin must satisfy in a manner consistent with the justice of God. A personal atonement provided by us would have excluded the element of mercy from God because we would suffer eternally damnation in Hell if we tried to supply our own atonement. We cannot build our own bridge to God or to Heaven. A personal atonement could not have resulted in redemption. A vicarious atonement leads to reconciliation with God and everlasting life through Jesus Christ. Some ask as to how a just God could transfer his wrath against moral offenders to an innocent party and treat the innocent Jesus as if he were guilty. The answer is that it can be legal if it is expressly authorized by the lawgiver. God is the Judge and the lawgiver. The Judge need not but can permit this. The method is just and righteous since guilty person is aware that the substitute is and has suffered for him. The method is also righteous and just since the person enduring the penalty is not indebted to justice for himself and does not owe his services to the government for his own wrongdoing

God therefore was righteous and just to permit in his own government Jesus Christ to suffer the penalty of our sins for our atonement to reconcile God back to us. Jesus Christ took the place of sinners. He took the place of sinners, and their guilt was imputed to him, and their punishment was transferred, to him. The vicarious sufferings of Jesus Christ were both the sympathetic sufferings of a friend in order for us to have mercy and the substitutionary suffering of the Lamb of God for the sin of the world. There are several passages of scripture which speak of our sins as being laid upon Jesus Christ, and of his bearing of our sin or iniquity, (I Peter 2:24, Hebrews 9:28, John 1.29, II Corinthians 5:21, Isaiah 53:6, 12). The gospel message is that God laid your sin on Jesus Christ out of love for you to repair your relationship with God and to grant you the gift of eternal life in heaven.

The Moral Influence Theory, Penal Substitution, & Governmental Theory

The Moral Influence Theory

Throughout history there have been different theories of the atonement and most of them have an important aspect of truth in them as revealed from the Bible. The moral influence theory of the atonement is widely held today and emphasized the importance of the effect of Christ's cross on the sinner. The view originated with Abelard, who emphasized the love of God, and it is sometimes called exemplarism. The theory holds that when we look at the cross we see the greatness of divine love. We then respond to love with love and we no longer live in selfishness and sin. The theology teaches that the sight of the selfless Christ dying for us sinners moves us to repentance and faith. We then teach that if God will do all of that for us then we ought not to continue in sin. We repent and turn from sin because of what Jesus did for us and we are then saved by becoming better people.

There is truth in this theory. However, taken by itself alone it is inadequate. We can only reject this teaching if it stops with God's love and represents to the world that this is all there is to the atonement. If we teach that Jesus Christ was simply displaying God's love without teaching what he was doing for us it represents the cross as simply a public display of love or showmanship. If someone was in a river drowning and someone jumped in to save him and lost his life in the process, he or she that was rescued would recognize the love and sacrifice involved. They would also know what they were saved from and where they are now in comparison to then. They would also respond in gratitude and recognize how they were saved. But if he or she thinks they are sitting safely on the land and was told that someone jumped into a river and lost their life to save them out of love, he would see no point in it and think it was a senseless act. Unless the death of Christ does something to save a sinner it is seen as nothing but a senseless act and is not understood as a demonstration of love. People need to know that Jesus died in order to rescue them for Hell, Satan's stronghold in the soul, and the bondage of the will to sins that men must be rescued or set free from. The Bible teaches, "We love him because he first loved us" (I John 4:19). Love is a seed that is planted when presenting the gospel message and it produces the fruit of obedience and a loving response to God. God's love alone does not save us and we must believe in him and in as to why he died for us. What does he save us from? The theory is true when combined with all of the other doctrinal truths in regards to the atonement.

The Atonement as Victory

The theory is that because of sin people rightly belong to Satan God offered his son as a ransom, a bargain that Satan readily accepted When, however, Satan got Christ down into hell he could not hold him down. On the third day Christ rose triumphant and left Satan without his prisoners and the ransom he had accepted in their stead. This was called the devil ransom theory, the classical theory, and sometimes the fishhook theory of the atonement. In the end Christ's atoning work means victory. The Devil and all his demons are defeated. Sin is conquered because of what Jesus did for us. It is to be noticed that this view is accurate in that Christ's Atonement is what secured the victory over Satan. However, Jesus' vicarious obedience and death was the price God's divine justice and wisdom deemed necessary to be paid by a divine person suffering as a Lamb in our stead. The price was not owed to Satan but was the sacrifice needed to reconcile God back to man by breaking to barrier that sin caused which resulted in our spiritual bondage to Satan. The Devil was the only spiritual being interacting with men due to the barrier. The barrier must be broken to make a way for us to come to God to be set us free from the curse and demonic strongholds resulting from the fall of the First Adam. The Bible teaches, He that continues to commiteth sin is of the devil; for the devil sinneth from the beginning, For this purpose the Son of God was manifested, that he might destroy the works of the Devil (I John 3:8). The Colossian writer also declared in regards to Jesus, "Who hath delivered us from the power of darkness, and hath translated us into the kingdom of his dear son: In whom we have redemption through his blood, even the forgiveness of sins" (Colossians 1:13-14).

The Bible also teaches, "And having spoiled principalities and powers, he made a she of them openly, triumphing over them in it" Colossians 2:15). The children of God are delivered from the power of and the kingdom of Satan and translated into the kingdom of Jesus Christ. They are no longer slaves to demons because of the work of Christ on the cross. They have been set free and are no longer captives. Jesus came to preach deliverance to captives (Luke 4:18). How can Satan have us bound if Jesus has set us free? The Atonement is seen as a ransom paid by Jesus with his own blood to set spiritual slaves free from demonic bondage. Satan and his demons lose the legal right to enslave us which was transferred to them by Adam and by us due to in according to this view. Be advised that this view of the atonement is also true. Jesus Christ is the only one that can set a sinner free from enslavement to principalities and powers of Satan. The blood of Jesus has the effect of spoiling (ruining) principalities and powers of the Devil which control the life of a sinner and the effect of translating a believer from the control of the Devil's and kingdom and into the control and jurisdiction of the kingdom of God. Believers now have victory over Satan and have been given the authority to cast out devils (Mark 16:17). The scriptures teach that we once were as others who disobeyed God because they were controlled by Satan, "Wherein in time past you walked according to the course of this world, according to the prince of the power of the air (Satan), the spirit that now works in the children of disobedience: Among whom also we all had our conversation in times past in the lusts of our flesh, fulfilling the desires of the flesh and of the mind: and were by nature the children of wrath, even as others" (Ephesians 2:2-3).

Penal Substitution

The Reformers held that the moral law is not to be taken lightly. The wages of sin is death and that is the problem for sinful man (Romans 6:23). The Reformers taught that Christ took our punishment and that he appeased the wrath of God in our place. The substitution theory holds that God punished your sins by the suffering and death of Jesus Christ. The Penal Substitution view maintains that Christ suffered the full penalty of the law and was punished for sin.

Some say that Christ did not suffer the penalty of the law because it included remorse and eternal death. However, the penalty is simply divine displeasure involving the withdrawal of the communion with the Holy Spirit. This is the case with all people. Jesus Christ suffered this displeasure and abandonment (Matthew 27:46), however, spiritual death was not possible as a divine person. He suffered the kind and degree of pain which divine wisdom, interpreting divine justice required a divine person suffering in our stead to suffer as the penalty for sin. Therefore, the temporal suffering of one divine person is a full legal equivalent for the punishment of those whom he died for. It was not possible for an eternal and divine person to experience eternal death. The punishment of Christ was not a substitute for the execution of the penalty of the law but the penalty of the law executed on him as our substitute and in our place.

Governmental Theory

Hugo Grotius taught that God as the governor of the universe relaxed his rule by transferring punishment of sin to Christ because he did not want sinners to die. The Governmental theory, which presupposes all of the truth in the "Moral Influence Theory," maintains that justice in God is not vindicatory, but is to be referred to a general Governmental rectitude, based on a benevolent regard for all beings under the moral governments. It teaches that the law is a product of God's divine will and therefore is relaxable. God's sovereign prerogative includes the right of pardon. But the governmental rectitude explained above, in view of an indiscriminate pardon would encourage the violation of law which God won't do, determines God to condition the pardon of human sinners upon an imposing example of suffering in a victim related to mankind and to himself, to demonstrate that sin should not be engaged in with impunity. Therefore, Christ's suffering, according to this view, were not punishment but an example of a determination to punish hereafter. They were not designed to satisfy divine justice, but to impress in the mind of the universe a deterring motive. This theory is truthful in that God can relax law if he desired. However, law required sacrifice for sin and the guilt of the offending party was transferred to the spotless sacrifice as a matter of divine law in the Old Testament. Therefore, Jesus Christ fulfilled the law as the Lamb of God with his sacrifice for the sins of humanity. Moreover, only a real bona fide punishment could be an example of a punishment, or a proof of God's determination to punish sin. The law required a sacrifice by the

Priest on the Day of Atonement to remove sin. Jesus was our priest and our perfect sacrifice to remove our sin and take it away.

The Gospel is that Jesus was our Priest to represent us to God

Jesus was and is our priest and that is the good news. A prophet is God's representative to man. A priest, on the other hand, is man's representative to God and both are appointed by God (Hebrews 5:4). The priest has a special privilege to approach God and to speak and act on behalf of the people. A prophet emphasized the moral and spiritual duties of man to God whereas a priest stressed the rituals and proper observances needed to approach God. A priest is taken away from among men to be their representative. His work is to offer gifts to God and sacrifices for their sins. The priest, Jesus, also makes intercession for the people (Hebrews 7:25). This means that Jesus died for us and rose again as our sacrifice to God and for the purpose of acting on our behalf in terms of speaking to God and representing us before God. That is good news because of the reality of Hell and the certainty of the wrath of God to come.

The remarkable thing about the priestly work of Jesus Christ for us is that contrary to how the Old Testament priest functioned, Christ is both the priest and the sacrifice to God on behalf of the people. The priestly work of Christ on our behalf is represented in the letter to the Hebrew Christians. Jesus Christ is described as our real, eternal, and perfect High Priest. He takes our place as a sacrifice to God for our sins which take away our guilt and he acquires a real and perfect redemption for us (Hebrews 7:1-28). In the Old Testament God removed a curse from the people when they looked up upon the symbol of the brazen serpent. The brazen serpent was not poisonous, but represented the embodiment of sin, Christ, sinless, was made sin for us. As the lifting up of the serpent signified the removal of the plague from the people the lifting up of Jesus Christ for us on the cross effected the removal of sin. The looking up of the brazen serpent in the Old Testament brought healing to the people who were bit by poisonous snakes, likewise faith in Jesus Christ brings healing and salvation to souls that are sick. Jesus said these things himself in regards to his suffering and death for us and what it accomplished in comparison to the brazen serpent that was lifted up in the Old Testament (Mark 10:45). The gospel message is that Jesus Christ is our priest and he is representing us before God and if we look at what he did for us on the cross and believe we can be healed, cured, saved, delivered, and freed from the bondage disease (physical and spiritual).

In the Old Testament there are numerous indications that the Mosaic sacrifices were typical of the more excellent sacrifice of Jesus Christ for us and our sins. There are statements which indicate that the Old Testament sacrifices where a type of and prefigured Christ and his work for us at the cross (Col 2:17). The Bible teaches that Jesus accomplished for sinners in a higher aspect what the Old Testament sacrifices were said to have done for those who brought them, and that Jesus accomplished this for us in a similar way (Galatians 3:13, II Corinthians 5:21). Jesus is called "the Lamb of God", in John 1:29, which is said because of the prophesy about him in Isaiah 53. He is also called "our Passover that was slain for us" (I Corinthians 5:7). The Old Testament sacrifices were not the real sacrifice that could atone for our moral guilt and remove corruption and pollution, but only shadows and types of the coming reality of what Jesus Christ himself would get accomplished for us. The tabernacle of the Old Testament was called, "a figure for that time present; according to which he offered both gifts and sacrifices that cannot, as touching the conscience, make the worshipper perfect", Hebrews 9:9. The next chapter in the book of Hebrews says that those sacrifices could not make the offerers perfect (Hebrews 10:1), and could not take away sins, (Hebrews 10:4). The Old Testament sacrifices offered by the priests in those days symbolized the suffering and death of Jesus Christ for us, and how that we would obtain forgiveness and acceptance with God only when they were offered with our sincere repentance, and with our genuine faith in God and his method chosen for our salvation. The sacrifices in the Old Testament had significance but only in the aspect that they taught us God's plan for redeeming us by the sacrifice of Jesus Christ for us.

The gospel message is that Jesus Christ is a chosen Lamb and his sacrifice on the cross for our sin actually takes our sin away as far as God's plan is concerned. He wants us to trust in what Jesus did for us and to believe that Jesus finished everything at the cross. The Hebrew writer sums up the gospel message by saying, "Seeing then that we have a great high priest, that is passed into the heavens, Jesus the Son of God, let us hold fast our profession. For we have not a high priest that cannot be touched with the feeling of our infirmities: but was in all points tempted like as we are, yet without sin. Let us therefore come boldly unto the throne of grace, that we may obtain mercy, and find grace to help in the time of need" (Hebrews 4:14-6). Jesus is currently in heaven and he knows about your weaknesses. He is ready and willing to speak an act on your behalf and give more mercy and grace to help you to overcome when you need it.

The work of Jesus Christ on the earth as our priest and our sacrifice finds its completion by his intercessory work for us. Jesus actually works for us now in the sanctuary of God in heaven based on the revelation provided for us with the role of priests in the Old Testament tabernacle. The Old Testament tabernacle only symbolized the true sanctuary of God in heaven.

The Hope from the Gospel

It is the good pleasure of God to saves us by his sovereign choice of a vicarious atonement. Jesus Christ is the fruit of the choice of God. The angels sang at the birth of Jesus, "Glory to God in the highest, and on earth peace among men in whom he is well pleased", Luke 2:14. Jesus came to reconcile a sinful world back into a relationship with himself which could not be done because of sin (Colossians 19:20).

It please God that in him should all fullness dwell, and, having made peace through the blood of his cross, by him to reconcile all things unto himself; by him, I say, whether they be things on earth or things in heaven. And you, that were sometime alienated and enemies in your mind by wicked works, yet now hath he reconciled in the body of his flesh through death, to present you holy and unblameable and unreproveable in his sight: If ye continue in the faith grounded and settled, and be not moved away from the hope of the gospel, which ye have heard, and which was preached to every creature which is under heaven; whereof I Paul am made a minster (Colossians 19:20-23). Your hope is in the gospel. Believe that you are at peace with God because of what Jesus did for you at the cross. We can only be without blame and reproof in his sight and before him because of the gospel message and the magnitude of what Jesus accomplished for us.

The Bible teaches us that God cannot overlook sin because of his holiness and the fact that his justice demands that sin is punished. We are told throughout the scriptures that God will not let the guilty be cleared (Exodus 34:7 and Numbers 14:18). God hates sin and his entire being moves against sin. The wrath of God is revealed from heaven against all ungodliness, and unrighteousness of men, who hold the truth in unrighteousness (Romans 1:18). The Apostle Paul argued that it was necessary that Jesus Christ should be offered up for us as an atoning sacrifice for our sin, in order that God might be just and remain just while justifying the sinner. The justice of God had to be maintained by punishing sin but the love of God would also be revealed in his plan to save the sinner from his deserved end. The atonement was necessary because of the nature of God.

Sin is not merely a moral weakness that comes from a morally depraved nature. Sin is more heinous. Sin is lawlessness. Lawlessness comes from a transgression of God's law. Guilt makes us a debtor to the law and requires either a personal atonement or an atonement made by someone else on our behalf. God would not have sent Jesus here unnecessarily. If it were possible that we could save ourselves and been made righteous by keeping the law of God then Jesus Christ died in vain (Galatians 2:21). The Bible teaches that the suffering and death of Christ was necessary to remove our sin. The Hebrew writer says, "And almost all things are by the la purged with blood; and without shedding of blood is no remission. It was therefore necessary that the patterns of things in the heavens should be purified with these; but the heavenly things themselves are better sacrifices than these. For Christ is not entered into the holy places made with hands, which are the figures of the true, but into heaven itself, now to appear in the presence of God for us" (Hebrews 9:22-24). The gospel message is that Jesus Christ shed his blood for you and entered in to heaven itself into the presence of God for us. Jesus appeared to put away sin by the sacrifice of himself (Hebrews 9:26). Jesus offered gifts and sacrifices to God for us which will be needed on the great Day of Judgment. It is appointed to men once to die and after that the judgment (Hebrews 9:27).

The atonement is made to render satisfaction to the person offended and wronged and not by the offending party but by the offended. The atonement propitiates God and reconciles him to the sinner. The reconciled God justifies the sinner who accepts the reconciliation and the method. The sinner is reconciled to God because Jesus Christ atones for his sin. The idea of the atonement is simply Jesus covering the sin of the sinner by the blood of the sacrifice offered for him in heaven. The wrath of God is turned aside because of the blood. To atone means to appease. Many scriptures speak of the wrath of God toward the sinner and the fact that God is angry with sinners (Romans 1:18 & Ephesians 2:3). It is the atonement of Jesus Christ made possible by his blood that reconciles us back to God if we believe. The Bible says, "But God commended his love towards us, in that, while we were yet sinners, Christ died for us. Much more then, being now justified by his blood, we shall be saved from wrath through him. For if, when we were enemies, we were reconciled to God by the death of his Son, much more, being reconciled, we shall be saved by his life. And not only so, but we also jo in God through our Lord Jesus Christ, by whom we have now received the atonement" (Romans 5:8-11).

The Gospel and extent of the Atonement in the Eternal Covenant

The Bible teaches that Christ purchased our salvation and that his work is and was not simply to make salvation possible but to actually save, to reconcile God to man and not just to render him reconcilable, "But God commended his love toward us that while we were yet sinners, and Christ died for us. Much more then, being now justified by his blood, we shall be saved from wrath through him. For if, when we were enemies we were reconciled to God by the death of his Son, much more, being reconciled, we shall be saved by his life. And not only so, but we also joy in God through our Lord Jesus Christ, by whom we have now received the atonement" (Romans 5:9-11). The work of Jesus Christ extends to his enemies and those that are ungodly. Jesus can save and reconcile or make amends for the ungodly and any and the whole question becomes for who and why.

The Bible refers to an Eternal Covenant between the Father and the Son in regards to the atonement for our sins. Jesus Christ spoke of this covenant that pertained directly to us while he was executing it on the earth. He looked at Peter and said, "I appoint to you a kingdom, as my Father have appointed unto me. That you may eat and drink at my table in my kingdom, and sit on thrones judging the twelve tribes of Israel" (Luke 22:29). You are truly blessed if Jesus has appointed you to sit in his kingdom with him to Judge the nations. Jesus also spoke of those that were previously given to him by the Father. He says in regards to his own sheep, "My Father which gave theme, is greater than all and no man is able to pluck them out of my Fathers hand" (John 10:29). Jesus died for his sheep which the Father gave to him. He says, "I am the good shepherd; the good shepherd gives his life for the sheep" (John 10:11).

Jesus said to the unbelieving Jews, "I told you, and ye believed not: the works that I do in my Father's name, they bear witness of me. But you believe me not, because ye are not my sheep, as I said unto you. My sheep hear my voice, and I know them, and they follow me: And I give to them eternal life: and they shall never perish, neither shall any man pluck them out of my hand" (John 10:25-29). Jesus says, "As the Father knoweth me, even so know I the Father: and I lay down my life for the sheep" (John 10:15). The church is purchased with his own blood (Acts 20:28). Jesus said in regards to his purpose in earth as it relates to you and his covenant, "All that the Father giveth to me shall come to me; and him that comes to me I will in no wise cast out. For I am came down from heaven, not to do mine own will, but the will of him that sent me. And this is the Father's will which hath sent me, that of all which he hath given me I should lose nothing, but should raise it up again at the last day. And this is the will of him that sent me, that every one which see the son, and believe on him, may have everlasting life: and I will raise him up at the last day" (John 6:37:40).

Jesus came to earth to do the will of his Father. The Father gave him sheep which were assigned to him providentially. Those that have been assigned to Jesus will believe and they will come to him and Jesus specifically says that he laid his life down for them because they are the ones that are his sheep. Jesus says that of all that was given to him that he would lose nothing as a shepherd. The Gospel message is news so great that it is hard to fathom. I can't argue with Jesus that it is his sheep that he laid his life down for. He will bring his sheep to his kingdom and he will keep them. The Ephesian writer said, "According as he hath chosen us in him before the foundation of the world, that we should be holy and without blame before him in love: Having predestined us unto the adoption of children by Jesus Christ to himself, according to the good pleasure of his will" (Ephesians 1:4-5). As to whether Jesus Christ died to atone for the sins of everywhere or simply for his sheep has been the subject of theological debates for centuries.

When debates are over we follow God's great commission and preach the gospel to every creature (Mark 16:15). Jesus knows who his sheep are and they will hear him and follow him and he gives them eternal life (John 10:27-28). The call to receive reconciliation with God because of the atonement is a universal call to all. The Elect are the sheep that God foreknew would respond to that universal call and believe on him and continue with him until the very end to glorification in heaven (Romans 8:29-30). Jesus says, "For many are called, but few are chosen" (Matthew 22:4). Christ came to do the will of the Father and to redeem his people as a result of a specific plan for you as one chosen before the foundation of the world (Ephesians 1:4-5).

The Extent of the Atonement

Catholic, Lutheran, and Reformed churches have always maintained that Jesus was a Divine being and therefore the satisfaction of the atonement in his active or passive obedience was not due to himself or from himself, and free to be credited to others. Second, the satisfaction of Christ for us was of an infinite value because it satisfies the claims of the law and of justice. As to the intention of the atonement and the effect of it we find different viewpoints. The Reformed Churches all agree in opposition to the Romans, Armenians, and supporters of an indefinite atonement, that the satisfaction of Christ is perfect in the aspect of the atonement not only making the salvation of those for whom it was offered possible, but of meritoriously securing and earning its application to them and consequently their certain and complete salvation in the end such as on the day of judgment.

The Romans hold that through baptism the merits of Christ cancel the guilt of all sins original and actual preceding that baptism and that post-baptism sins result in temporal pains instead of eternal damnation. They also believe that the post-baptismal sins must be absolved by good works of charity in this world or in the next by pain in purgatory.

The Armenians are those followers of the doctrine of James Arminius in the 1600's that maintain that the satisfaction of Christ makes the salvation of all men possible, and secures for them enough grace but that its full effect is suspended on the condition of the free choice of the people. Therefore, when you are forgiven it doesn't necessarily mean that your salvation in the end is secure on the Day of Judgment based on this view. Your salvation in the end will depend upon what you decide to do with your freewill after your conversion. This view is the result of many other views held by Professor James Arminius as with other groups.

The truth of the Atonement is proven in the scriptures. The Bible refers to the removal of condemnation based solely on the death of Christ, and the scriptures represent that all of the suffering of believers in this life are for disciplinary purposes (Romans 8:1-34, Hebrews 12:5-11. The scriptures teach that the blood of Christ cleanses from all sin, and that we are complete in him and that by his one sacrifice that he perfected us (Hebrews 10:12-14, I John 1:7, Colossians 2:10). The Hebrew writer says, "For by one offering he has perfected forever them that are sanctified" (Hebrews 10:14). Salvation is not conditioned upon what we do or fail to do to merit salvation but only on trust in Christ's work, and this faith is given to us as a result of Christ merit and him gifting us by his grace. The Ephesians book says, "That in the ages to come he might show the exceeding riches of his grace in his kindness toward us through Jesus Christ. For by grace are you saved through faith; and that not of yourselves: it is the gift of God; Not of works lest any should boast (Ephesians 2:8). The satisfaction of Christ meritoriously secures actual and complete salvation for its beneficiaries, and not simply to possibility of salvation upon conditions. The Lord Jesus fulfilled the conditions of the law or covenant by perfect obedience and a satisfaction to divine justice in his life and death at the cross. Whoever exercises faith in Jesus Christ shall be saved by him because of the nature and the extent of the atonement. The blood of Jesus secures the final salvation of those that are his sheep that were given to him by the

Father. Jesus is the shepherd that laid down his life for the sheep (John 10:11,15). The sheep hear his voice, follow him, and are given eternal life and shall never perish (John 10:28). The sheep will not follow the voice of a stranger (John 10:5). Consequently, the sheep obey Jesus and bring forth the fruit that he had chosen them and ordained them to bring forth which should remain (John 15:16).

There are many passages of scripture in the New Testament which warn Christians as to what could happen hypothetically to them if they did not continue in the faith. The scriptures reveal God's action against the tendency of people and as a means that God employs in his administration to fulfill his purposes. God deals with cities like Jonah to warn them in order to avoid what could hypothetically be a certain doom. In the case of Paul's shipwreck, it was certain that none would perish according to the angel, and yet at the same time it was made clear to them all that they would perish except that they abode in the ship (Acts 27:24-31). God had secured their salvation and paradoxically they still needed to be warned not to leave the boat. The warnings were a means to fulfill God's purposes. Although it was not probable that any of them would be lost or perish it was possible if they didn't stay where they were told to. The same concept should be applied in principle to passages which explain what will or can happen to saints if they willfully sin or do other things contrary to the Word of God continually Hebrews 10:26-30).

The Atonement secures our salvation completely and Grace teaches us to deny worldly lusts and to live soberly, righteously, and godly in his present world (Titus 2:12). The spiritual gifts given to the body of Christ are to perfect the saints in regards to conduct and living godly for Christ while on the earth (Ephesians 4:11-12). We shall know the tree by the fruit that it bears (Matthew 7:16). Those that profess they know him and do not keep his commandments are called liars and the truth is not in them (I John 2:4). We know that keeping rules do not save us and that Christ secured our salvation by the Atonement but our conduct and lifestyle is the fruit which provides the evidence as to whether or not Christ planted us in the kingdom and reveal whether or not we are one of his sheep. We also bear in mind in regards to this matter that regeneration is birth into the kingdom and sanctification is growth which occurs in stages of spiritual development throughout our lifetime. This is finalized after death when mortal puts on immortality and corruptible puts on incorruption.

Sanctification

I speak of sanctification to make it clear that the scriptural doctrine of the limited atonement secures our salvation but it does in no way provide for us a license to sin. He that has begun a good work in us will perform it until the day of Jesus Christ (Philippians 1:6). The work that Christ does within our hearts through operation of the Holy Ghost will sanctify us within. The work of God within us will reflect in outward expressions in our works. The radical change in life and what we call righteous works are not the basis for our just standing before God but Christ alone. The tree is known by the fruit that it bears (Matthew 7:20)

After the Reformation John Wesley spoke of entire sanctification as second gift of grace distinct from justification. He spoke of sanctification as a creative work of God on the inward man and as a process John looked at it as a process held the belief that a believer should look forward to full sanctification in this life as an act of God accomplishing in their lives what he saved them for.

Some viewed sanctification different and not as a supernatural work of the Holy Ghost in the renewal of sinners but as a mere moral improvement that was brought by man simply decided to do better Throughout the years you and I both have seen many teachers encouraging us to be holy and to live a godly life. All of these things should be viewed as a work of God by the Holy Spirit through men that God gifted in the church to bring sanctification to the life of the believer. It is God work. The letter of Titus says, "Not by works of righteousness which w have done, but according to his mercy he saved us, by the washing of regeneration, and the renewing of the Holy Ghost" (Titus 3:5).

Sanctification is a supernatural work of God. The scriptures describe sanctification as the work of God, the fruit brought from the union of Christ with a believer which comes when we abide in him and stay attached to the vine as a branch ((John 15:4). It is a work of God in man and thus cannot be a work of man (Ephesians 3:16). The manifestation of Christian virtues are spoken of as a work of the Holy Spirit and as fruits of the spirit (Galatians 5:22). We cannot make spiritual progress alone. We will only bear fruit in time as God does the work through us using the instrumentalities of gifts which he distributing in the local church (Ephesians 4:11).

Sanctification takes place in the inner life of a man in his heart. When the inner nature is changed and renewed we must undoubtedly conclude that the person has been born again (John 3:3). Jesus said that unless we are born again that we cannot see the kingdom of God (John 3:1-5). When the inner nature is changed there is bound to be a change in the outward expression of the man in terms of his speech, behavior, dress attire, people associated with, habits, and his overall motives behind what he says or does. Sanctification affects what is done with the body and the soul.

When it is said that a man takes part in sanctification as stressed by many it does not mean that he is an independent agent of the work so as to make sanctification partly the work of man and partly the work of God. God does the work and man is the instrument that he uses to include the person that is being sanctified. The man that has been born again has a new inner nature but he is subsequently free to co-operate with the work that the Holy Ghost is doing through him or her or to stubbornly strive against the work of the Holy Spirit. Regeneration happens as the new birth once and sanctification is something that follows as the saved man or woman yields to the work of the Holy Spirit in his life. It is possible to grieve the Holy Spirit. Paul exhorted, "Grieve not the holy spirit of God, whereby ye are sealed unto the day of redemption (Ephesians 4:30).

The Bible teaches that you do have sin and that the saints that have departed are now entirely sanctified. The Hebrew writer speaks of the spirits of just men made perfect (Hebrews 2:23). He was speaking of the men who had departed that were now already in heaven. These saints are the ones that are without blemish (Revelation 14:5). God is the one that is able to keep us from falling and to present us faultless before the presence of his glory with joy (Jude 24). The process will not be completed in its entirety in this life. Thus even Paul, acknowledged when he was at the end of his life and ministry that he had not yet attained perfection but that he was still pressing toward the mark (Philippians 3:12-14).

It is important in our time and hereafter when thinking of the church anthropologically and teaching the call to service and obedience that we emphasize that God and not men is the author of sanctification. The spiritual development of a man is not a human achievement but a work of divine grace. Man deserves no credit for whatever God uses him for to contribute to his own sanctification instrumentally. Man is responsible to yielding to God's movement but doesn't get any glory for achieving what he cannot do in his own strength.

Sanctification in this life is not imperfect in the parts but only in the development of the parts. When a human baby is born the parts are perfect except in a few scenarios. The development of the parts of a baby is incomplete and the baby has to be fed and it takes time for the baby and his parts to reach maturity in development. The parts of a baby are perfect in their design but not in the intended development of what each part were made for. The Christian is perfect as far as his new inner nature is concerned. However, he is imperfect in the development of that nature and in the application of the Word of God to his spiritual life on earth in an ungodly world.

Perfectionists throughout history deemed it necessary to lower the standard of the law and to externalize the idea of sin in order to maintain the theory that sinless perfection could be attained in this life. However, sin is not just doing something such as adultery or murder. Sin is the very wants that dwell deep within the nature of man which is still corrupted from the fall of Adam. Paul thus stated, "I would not have known lust except the law said no to covet" (Romans 7:7). Moreover, John says, "If we say we have no sin we deceive ourselves and the truth is not in us. If we confess our sins he is faithful and just to forgive us and to cleanse us from all unrighteousness" (I John 1: 8-9).

Sanctification results in good works and in a lifestyle radically different from our prior life. The good works will not in a meritorious way somehow earn for us heaven. God will reward us for them in heaven. The fruit of good works also reveal to us and the world whether or not we have been converted and born again. The born again will not habitually sin as a deliberate and willful lifestyle (I John 3:8-10). Whoever is born of God sins not and he keeps himself and the wicked one touches him not (I John 5:18-19). When one is born again it is true that there are some external things that they won't do. Nonetheless, they do not attain perfection to a degree that they are without blemish. He cannot say he is without sin at all on earth or he deceives himself (I John 1:8). Who can say I have made my heart clean, I am pure from my sin? (Proverbs 20:9) A Christian must pray daily for his own forgiveness and forgive others on a daily basis too (Matthew 6:12). The Lord would not ask his disciples and the world to use vain repetitions in prayer as the heathens (Matthew 6:7). Hence, men would be prohibited to pray for forgiveness on a daily basis for sins which are already forgiven. Paul admitted that he had not yet attained perfection in this life but that he was pressing toward the mark (Philippians 3:12-14). He also described his struggle with a fleshly nature which brought into bondage his will which delighted in the law of God (Romans 7:14-25). The Atonement is the perfect sacrifice of Jesus Christ once and for all sins to perfect us forever because of his vicarious suffering and death. He perfected us by that one offering forever to sanctify us based on his work to save us (Hebrews 10:14).

A Comparison of Theological Systems, Election, Predestination, and Security

We shall discus two historical systems of theology and their origins and their doctrines. I have not adopted any system as my personal belief, creed, or doctrine but the Bible. As we compare one set of beliefs with the other please keep in mind that both system of beliefs have their origin in the Bible. Most Christians must believe all of God's revealed truth in the Bible although some truth may be paradoxical and we may not be able to be reconcile them altogether with other truths in the Bible nor with our finite minds.

James Arminius lived from 1560 to 1609. He was born at Oudewater, the Netherlands. He was educated at the universities of Marburg (1575) and Leiden (1576-1581), at the academy at Geneva (1582, 1584-1586, and at Basel (1582-1583). He was a Pastor of an Amsterdam congregation from 1588-1603), and a professor at the University of Leiden from 1603 until his death.

The theological stance of James Arminius was similar to that of the pre-Augustinian church fathers and as did later John Wesley. In many ways his theological stance differs from the Augustine-Luther-John Calvin tradition. This type of Protestant theology rose in the Netherlands after the Reformation. It teaches justification by grace alone and that there is nothing meritorious in our faith in Christ itself since it is only through grace that fallen humanity can exercise faith.

One of the distinctions of Arminianism is the teaching on predestination. Predestination is the biblical doctrine as to what God decided about our final destination before he created the world. James Arminius saw predestination in God's plan as a pre-decision on God's part to save the ones that repent and believe. Thus it is called conditional predestination; since God's predetermination of the destiny of people is based on his foreknowledge of the way they would freely reject Christ or freely accept him.

or believe. Consequently, the view maintains that salvation is not pre-determined by God in the sense that he makes it certain that anyone in particular such as the Elect will surely get to Heaven because of the direct influence and actions of his grace. The theory holds that the Elect are chosen because God knows they will come, repent, and believe and thereafter they may or may not persevere until the end. God knows.

John Calvin lived from 1509 until 1564. He is considered the Father of the Reformed and Presbyterian doctrine and theology. John was born in Noyon, Picardie. His father was a notary who served the bishop of Noyon, and as a result, Calvin, while a child, received a canary in the cathedral which would pay for his education. He started his training for the priesthood at the University of Paris, his Father, because of a controversy with the Bishop and the clergy decided that he should be a lawyer. He later became a Protestant. Calvin was trained in grammatical exegetic in his legal studies and became a biblical theologian.

The theological view of John Calvin which we call Calvinism can be defined in the upcoming paragraphs or sentences.

In regards to theology, he taught that God is an absolute sovereign, infinitely wise, righteous, benevolent, and powerful, determining from eternity past what the future would be regarding every event according to the counsel of his own will. He taught that God has a vindicatory justice that was part of his divine nature and consequently it demanded the full punishment of all sin. He taught that God would not relax his vindicatory justice to punish sin because of his will.

As to Christology, he taught that Jesus was a mediator and one person that had two natures. He taught that the human and divine nature was unmixed, and kept all of the attributes distinct. He said that the personality of both were eternal and immutable. He said that in his actions each nature was united as one person.

In regards to Anthropology, he taught that man was originally cre-ated in a condition that as physical, intellectual, and moral faultless-ness. He taught that the guilt of Adam's sin is a judicial act of God immediately charged to the account of each of his descendants from the moment they begin to exist and before anything they do on their own. He taught that as a consequence of this that all people including babies come into existence in a condition of condemnation and without any influences of the Holy Ghost on them in their moral and spiritual lives. Consequently, men are born to some degree under the control of Satan and deprived of the original righteousness which had been in Adam prior to his fall. They have the prevailing tendency in their own nature to sin that is the nature of sin and worthy of the full wrath and punishment of God (Ephesians 2:1-3).

The nature of man after the fall is corrupt but his will if free. However, he is spiritually dead, and totally unable to do spiritual good and to do what is his duty to God to do. It is important to understand that these things are true. Paul described a law that was at war within the members of his body that brought into bondage his will although he delighted in his mind doing those things he knew was right (Romans 7:14-23).

As to Soteriology, Calvin taught that the salvation of man was absolutely of grace. He taught that God was free to save none, few, many, or all according to his sovereign and good pleasure. Calvin made salvation an act of God and not of man. The view of James Arminius is that salvation is from God but that man has to cooperate with him and participate with grace.

He taught that in salvation Christ acted as a Mediator in pursuance of an eternal covenant formed between the Father and the son. Christ was put in the place of being subject to the law of God under the covenant on behalf of God's elect people as their substitute. Christ by his obedience and suffering discharged all of the obligations coming out of their relationship with the law by him suffering vicariously to discharge the requirement of the law, satisfying the justice of God, and securing the eternal salvation of those for whom he died. The Bible does teach that he is the mediator of a new testament, that by means of his death for the redemption of the transgressions that were under the first testament (law), they which are called might receive an eternal inheritance (Hebrews 9:15). Again, "But this man, after he had offered one sacrifice for sins forever, sat down on the right hand of God; from henceforth expecting until his enemies became his footstool, for by one offering he perfected forever them that are sanctified" (Hebrews 10:12-14).

Therefore, by his death he purchased the gracious influence of his Spirit for whom he died. The Holy Ghost infallibly applies the redemption purchased by Christ to all for whom he intended it, and in the manner and at the time for whom God had intended it for in his eternal covenant. This view teaches that repentance, faith, and the work of the Holy Ghost are gifts of grace in which the blood purchased to secure the salvation of his own Elect.

Justification is taught as a judicial act of God wherein God gives us credit for perfect righteousness because of Christ's active and passive obedience. God treats us graciously because he has pronounced that all the penalties of the law to be satisfied by Christ on our behalf and because we are entitled to the rewards conditioned in the original covenant with Adam which was met in the Second Adam, Christ. The blessings here on earth and in eternity come to us then because of what Christ did and not on our own merit. The scriptures do teach, "Being justified freely by his grace through the redemption that is in Christ Jesus: Whom God hath set forth to be a propitiation through faith in his blood, to declare his righteousness for the sins that are past, through the forbearance of God" (Romans 3:24-25).

The Bible also teaches, "Nevertheless death reigned from Adam to Moses, even over them that had not sinned after the magnitude of Adam's transgression, who is the figure of him that was to come. But not as the offence, so also is the free gift. For if through the offence of one many be dead, much more the grace of God, and the gift of grace, which is by one man, Jesus Christ hath abounded unto many. And not as it was by one that sinned, so is the gift: for the judgment was by one to condemnation, but the free gift is of many offenses unto justification. For if by one man's offense death reigned by one; much more they which receive abundance of grace and of the gift of righteousness shall reign in life by one, Jesus Christ. Therefore as by the offense of one judgment came upon all men to condemnation; even so by the righteousness of one the free gift came upon all men unto justification of life. For as by one man's disobedience many were made sinner, by the obedience of one shall many be made righteous. Moreover the law entered that the offense may abound. But where sin abounded, grace did much more abound" (Romans 5:14-20).

The theological position is that although absolute and total perfection is not attainable in this life it is necessary that each believer has complete assurance of his salvation now and while doing so strive after perfection in all things in the practical sense. Most believers will experience a fall if left to themselves without being kept by grace and many will fall temporarily, but God by him putting a keeping grace in our hearts, keeps believers from a final apostasy and from being lost in the end. Grace is the reason for the Election, repentance, faith, conversion, and perseverance of the saints all the way home to glorification. According to our Bibles, "For whom he did foreknow, he also did predestinate to be conformed to the image of his son, that he might be the firstborn among many brethren, moreover whom he did predestinate them he also called: and whom he called, them he also justified, and whom he justified, them he also glorified" (Romans 8:29-30). Jesus Christ summarized the truth in regards to his sheep and his role as a shepherd. He said, "My sheep hear my voice, and I know them, and they follow me. And I give unto them eternal life: and they shall never perish, neither shall any man pluck them out of my hand. My Father which gave them to me, is greater than all, and no man is able to pluck them out of my Father's hand" (John 10:27-29). Jesus declared, "As the Father knows me, even so know I the Father: and I lay down my life for the sheep" (John 10:15).

Foreknowledge, Predestination, Election, Eternal Security and Great News

God loves us and gives us eternal life as a free gift if we ask him for it. The eternal life is not contingent upon men and whether they would be faithful or not but on God's own determination to finish the work that he starts with them. The Bible teaches, "For we know that whom he did foreknow, he also did predestinate to be conformed to the image of his Son, that he might be the firstborn, among many brethren. Moreover, whom he did predestinate, them he also called: and home he called, them he also justified: and whom he justified, them he also glorified" (Romans 8: 29-30).

Predestination is God choosing our end at the beginning of time. Election is God's decision to pick us out to be saved and his choice of us as part of his family as his children. God's choice of us is based on his divine omniscience or foreknowledge and purpose of what our end will be. For example, The call, commission, life, anointing, conduct, and purpose of John the Baptist were determined by God before his birth. He was predestinated to an end which was determined by God in his eternal decree and accomplished in God's daily providence by the means of angels, the Holy Spirit, and even John's parents. The same is true in regards to the prophet Jeremiah. God revealed to Jeremiah that he knew him before he formed him in the belly and God had ordained him as a prophet to the nations in advance of his birth (Jeremiah 1:5). God is sovereign and has the right to determine what he does with his own creation and just who and what people will be.

John the Baptist

John the Baptist was a great example of the life of someone that God had elected prior to his birth to do a specific task and to live his life as one of exemplary obedience to God under the influence of the Holy Ghost. The Angel appeared to Zacharias, John's Dad, to announce to him that his prayers were answered and that his wife Elizabeth would bear a son and to call his name John. The angel then tell Zacharias that John would be great in the sight of the Lord and would neither drink wine or strong drink and would be filled with the Holy Ghost from his mother's womb. He mentioned that many of Israel would turn to the Lord their God because of John and that John would go in the spirit and power of the prophet Elijah to turn the hearts of the Father s to the children, and the disobedient to the wisdom of the just, to make ready a people prepared for the Lord. When Zacharias doubted what the angel said it was the angel Gabriel that stuck him with dumbness that he could not speak because of his doubt. Zacharias was not able to speak until the things the Angel spoke had come to pass (Luke 1:10: 25). John's life, character, anointing, and activities were heavily influenced, shaped and determined by the Holy Spirit even before his birth while he was yet in the womb of Elizabeth. Jesus said that among all that were born of woman that there is not a greater prophet than John the Baptist (Luke 7:28).

John the Baptist was one chosen from his mother's womb and in eternity past and set apart to be a specific person for the kingdom of God and his purpose. All have not been marked by God and set apart in such a manner as John the Baptist to the extent that they endure, live righteously, turn hearts to God, and endure with him until the very end of their lives. John was Elect, Predestinated, called, justified, and sanctified. These things were determined by God for the life of John the Baptist before he made any choices of his own. All people have not been set apart for use by God due to the influence of the Holy Ghost in the same manner. The Apostle Paul says these words to the church of Ephesus in regards to the church, "According as he hath chosen us in him before the foundation of the world, that we should be holy and without blame before him in love: Having predestinated us unto the adoption of children by Jesus Christ to himself, according to the good pleasure of his will" (Ephesians 1:4-5).

God's Foreknown and divine love

What does the Bible means when it says that God foreknew us? The Arminian maintains that Paul is referring to those that God knew would have faith in him and respond to his offer of grace to them. The foreknown are those that repent and believe according to the Arminian. The Bible verse in Romans 8:29-30 opens up the question as to the definition of foreknew. How did God foreknow them? What does this mean? Who are the foreknown and why? The Arminian maintains that the foreknown are those that God knew would believe and on the basis of this foreseen faith that he predestined them to salvation. On the other hand, Calvinists, do not accept this view because of their perspective of the meaning of the word from the original language of the New Testament and because of the system of doctrine taught about the word in the rest of the Bible. The Calvinist teaches that God set his heart on the foreknown or these certain individuals. This view of the foreknown is not simply that he knew they would do one thing or another but that God knew them in the sense that he decided to set his affection and love toward them in a special way relationally. The word foreknew in this manner is understood to mean fore-loved. The people who God foreknew are the ones marked for salvation because he loved them in a special way in advance of their creation.

The questions that are raised by these two interpretations are these: Did God Elect certain people for salvation because he foresaw that they would believe in him and repent and thus accept his gift of grace? Did God set the affections of his heart on certain people and chose them because of his love for them thus predestinated them that they should be called and given faith in Christ and saved because of the work of the Holy Ghost? Is faith that was foreseen the cause of God picking certain ones and predestinating them or Is faith the result of God giving it to them because he chose to pick them out due to his special love for them?

The truth about this is amazing and almost unfathomable. All men were not "foreknown" which is evident from the facts as stated in

Romans 8:29. The "foreknown" are also predestinated. Predestination is God deciding where someone would go in the end such as to heaven and making that determination before the creation. All are not predestinated, called, justified, and glorified, thus the "foreknown" in this verse referred only to specific individuals that God knew about.

When the Bible speaks of God knowing certain ones, it means that he had loved them and had a special regard for them that he did not have in regards to others. It is sort of like the illustration above. For example, in Amos 3:2, God says to Jeremiah, "Before I formed you in the womb, I knew you an ordained you a prophet to the nations" (Jeremiah 1:5). The meaning here is not that God simply knew about Jeremiah but that God chose to have a special relationship with him distinguishable from that of others because he held him in special regard as his prophet. Jesus also used the word "know" or "knew" in the sense of an intimate love relationship or the absence thereof in his ministry. He said, "On that day many will say unto him Lord, Lord, did not we prophesy in your name, cast out devils, and do many wonderful works in your name? And then will I say unto them, "I never knew you, depart from me you that work iniquity" (Matthew 7:22-23). Jesus knew these individuals but he knew that as being the workers of iniquity. He did not know them in the sense of having an intimate relationship with him predicated upon love. He knew their evil works and their character which was wicked. When Jesus says that he never knew them he meant that he never knew them in an intimate or personal relationship They were not individuals that he set his heart upon to love and to have affections for and consequently they will not be saved.

Paul also used the word know in the same way when he says, "But if one loves God, one is known by him" (I Corinthians 8:3). Also, "The Lord knows those that are his and let every man that names the name of Christ to depart from iniquity" (II Timothy 2:19). God knows all people in general but he knows the ones that he loves and that loves him in a special way because they are the ones that he foreknew. These persons are the ones that are called according to his purpose and we know that his purpose is to save them and to glorify them. The Lord knows those that are his because there is a loving relationship that he has established and maintained between he and them.

The word know goes far beyond a simple awareness of someone's existence when it is used in the Bible and referring to God and even to men. The word know is essentially a synonym with the word love. The word know means to have a peculiar interest in and to delight in or act with or on behalf of (Exodus 2:25, Psalm 1:6, Jeremiah 1:5, Hosea 13:5, I John 3:1, Matthew 7:21-24).

The faith that God foresees is in fact a faith that he creates within the believer (John 3:3-8, John 6:44, Ephesians 2:8, II Peter 1:2). Therefore, the eternal foresight of faith is based on God's knowledge of what he will do with those whom he chose. We know that this choice is based on his love for them before they were made. Jesus said, "My sheep hear my voice, and I know them, and they follow me" (John 10:27). We see here that the word "know" is used to refer to a special relationship in which that his sheep follows him and hear him. Jesus said, "As the Father know me, even so know I the Father: and I lay down my life for the sheep" (John 10:15). Please notice here that Jesus' knowledge of the Father is a knowledge based on a special relationship with his Father that he had with nobody else. Please notice that Jesus specifically says that he is laying his life down for his sheep. Jesus did this because he knew us and we were given to him. He said, "All that the Father give to me shall come to me: and him that cometh to me I will in no wise cast out" (John 6:37).

The Good News is that Jesus atoned for the sins of the people that he foreknew and loved before the foundation of the world. Paul mentioned to the church of Ephesus, "According as he hath chosen us in him before the foundation of the world, that we should be holy and without blame before him in love: having predestinated us unto the adoption of children by Jesus Christ to himself, according to the good pleasure of his will" (Ephesians 1:4-5). We have redemption through his blood, the forgiveness of sins, according to the riches of his grace (Ephesians 1:7).

Proof of the Perseverance of the Saints

The proof that the Bible provides that those that Christ loved before the creation will actually be brought to heaven without exception is enormous. As I present this proof please keep in mind that this proof does not alleviate the fact that each believer must continue to do what the Bible exhorts them to do in order for these beautiful promises to come to pass. Jesus said, "My sheep hear my voice, and I know them, and they follow me; and I give to them eternal life; and they shall never perish, and no one can snatch them out of my Father's hand" (John 10:27-29). Jesus promises that his sheep hear him and follow him. He also ensures that he gives them eternal life that they shall never perish. The type of death in this text would include the "second death" which is described as eternal punishment in the lake of fire (Revelation 21:8). Never means never. Another proof is found in the statement of Paul to the Romans church when he says, "For the gifts and the calling of God are not repented of" (Romans 11:29). This means that the grace of God revealed in his calling of Israel is never withdrawn as if he would change his mind and repent that he did it. The statement is in regards to his chosen nation. Although God is focusing on Israel in the text it is apparent that God doesn't change his mind when he has chosen someone for a purpose nor does he withdraw his grace by repenting. Paul also told the Philippian church, "Be confident of this very thing, that He who began a good work in you will perform it until the day of Jesus Christ" (Philippians 1:6). Jesus also said, "All that the Father give me shall come to me; and him that comes to me I will in no wise cast out. And this is the Father's will which hath sent me, that of all which he hath given me I should lose nothing, but should raise it again at the last day" (John 6:37-40). These verses reveal that chosen ones were given to Christ in advance and that it is not God's will that Christ would lose any of them. The direct revelation of Paul's words to the Roman church is that those that were foreknown were also predestinated, called, justified, sanctified, and that they shall be glorified (Romans 8:28-30).

The Truth about Perseverance and Election

The Election does not mean that some will be favored and privileged to get saved if they do their duty. The Election means that they are chosen to be saved in the end based on God's sovereign choice and not depending upon their works. It is an Election to a destiny of salvation. A question posed by Paul to the Roman church was, "Who shall lay anything to the charge of God's elect? It is God that justifieth. Who is he that condemns? It is Christ that died, rather, that is risen again, who is even at the right hand of God making intercession for us" (Romans 8:33-34). God justifies the Elect in his sight because of the Atonement. Christ makes intercession for them in prayer as their Great High Priest in heaven. The life and the vicarious suffering and death in their stead nullify any charge or basis for their condemnation. God leads his chosen to him both to believe and to continue with him until the last day. Jesus said, "No man can come to me, except the Father which hath sent me draw him: and I will raise him up at the last day" (John 8:44). Jesus also revealed that us coming to him was his choice and not our own doing, "You have not chosen me, but I have chosen you, and ordained that you should bring forth fruit, and that your fruit remain: that whatsoever you shall ask of the Father in my name, he may give you" (John 15:16). The fruit is godliness, holiness, and spiritual fruit which is produced by the Spirit and reflected in our lives (Galatians 5:22-25).

God chose Jacob instead of his brother Esau and before either child was born or had done good or evil, that the purpose of God according to election might stand, not of works, but of him that calls (Romans 9:11). God has mercy on whom he wills (Romans 9:18). Jacob was deceitful and tricky and yet God chose him before he was born and prior to him making any choices while knowing his works would not measure up. People this had to be a special kind of love which was unconditional and not based upon works and our responses in our lifetime to him.

The one thing about the Election I want you to remember is that not all of the called that came out of the world to join a local church are designated by God as his Elect. God knows who his Elect are. He knows those that are his (II Timothy 2:19). Many will come in response to the universal call but all that come are not God's chosen or Elect nor will they all be faithful to their profession of faith. The only way for us to know them is by their fruit (Matthew 7:20). Those that God has granted the gift of grace to remain in a steadfast relationship with him shall persevere in faithfulness until the end and glorification (Romans 8:29-30). They are the Elect or chosen. Some others who will have faith shall depart from the faith or deny the Lord that bought them and shall come to damnation (Timothy 4:1, II Peter 2:1-3). This group were called with all men but they are not the Elect. The called can fall away from faith and be lost in the end but not the Elect. God has granted a special grace to his Elect to persevere and to remain faithful until the end to be saved. Paul mentioned that the called shall be glorified (Romans 8:29-30), however, not all of the called are Elect as Jesus has taught us. The King will come to the supper to see the guests and he will find someone without the wedding garment on. He will ask as to how that particular servant came and ask that he is bound hand and foot, taken away, and cast into outer darkness with weeping and gnashing of the teeth. Jesus then says, "For many are called, but few are chosen" (Matthew 22:1-14). There is a vast difference between those whom God chose before the foundation of the world and everyone else that has received the universal call.

The Redemption and Perseverance

The covenant of redemption gave the sheep to his Son as a reward for the Son's vicarious suffering and his obedience to the will of the Father. Although the Bible provides many exhortations and warnings to the believers to remain steadfast and faithful it does not indicate that God will go back on his promise. It appears that those who are in

Christ and part of the reward given to him cannot be separated from the love of God or him (Romans 8:38-39). The reward was determined from eternity and before the creation and was not left contingent on unfaithful acts of men. He chose us in him before the foundation of the world that we should be holy and without blame before him in love. He predestined us to the adoption of children by Jesus Christ to himself, according to the good pleasure of his will (Ephesians 1:4-5).

The Purchase and merit of Christ's performance

The Atonement is what Jesus accomplished in our stead to purchase our pardon and acceptance by God. Christ paid the price. The righteousness of Jesus is the basis of us being declared just by God. Thus it becomes very improbable that one who is justified by the payment of a perfect obedience could fall under condemnation. Jesus' own statement proves that a true believer has eternal life and cannot be condemned whereas he said, "Verily, verily, I say unto you, he that hear my word, and believe on him that sent me, hath everlasting life, and shall not come into condemnation; but is passed from death unto life" (John 5:24). It is impossible for a true believer to be condemned on the Day of Judgment to the Lake of Fire. God is sovereign. That is what we must keep in mind. Condemnation including Hell and the Lake of fire has been reserved for the unbeliever.

Christ's intercession work for us in prayer

Jesus Christ is also making intercessory prayer for us now in order to bring us to him. Jesus prayed to God, "I pray not that you should take them out of the world, but that you should keep them from the evil. They are not of the world, even as I am not of the world. Sanctify them through thy truth, thy word is truth. As though hast sent me into the world, even so have I also sent them into the world. And for their sake I sanctify myself, that they also might be sanctified through the truth.

Neither pray I for these alone, but for them also which shall believe on my through their word" (John 17:1-19). Jesus prayed every believer prior to our arrival on earth.

He prayed for Peter also during his earthly ministry and said, "Simon, Simon, behold, Satan hath desired to have you, that he may sift you as wheat. But I have prayed for thee, that thy faith fail not, and when thou art converted, strengthen thy brethren" (Luke 22:31-32). The Hebrew writer put it like this, "Wherefore he is able to save them to the uttermost that come to God by him, seeing he ever lives to make intercession for them" (Hebrews 7:25). We know that Jesus will not have a prayer that goes unanswered and that he cannot offer a prayer up in vain. The intercessory work of Christ in prayer for us reveals his plan to finish the salvation of the believers that he called. Jesus is preparing a place in heaven for specific people and he will come to bring them to those many mansions with him. Jesus said, "Let not your heart be troubled; ye believe in God, believe also in me. In my Father's house are many mansions: if it were not so, I would have told you. I go to prepare a place for you and If I go to prepare a place for you, I will come again, and receive you unto myself; that where I am, there ye may be also" (John 14:1-3). As you read these verses about the mansions that Jesus has prepared for us in heaven I want you to remember Jesus' words, "if it were not so, I would have told you (John 14:2). Jesus said in his prayer for the believers these phenomenal words, "Father I will that they also, whom thou hast given me, be with me where I am; that they may behold my glory, which thou hast given me for you loved me before the foundation of the world" (John 17:24). These declarations by Jesus in prayer to his Father prove that it is his intent to bring those that believe in him to heaven with him!

The Truth about Perseverance and Freewill

I say to this that men will be free to the extent that they have a will to make one choice or another. The possibility that men can fall away and never return is real otherwise the warnings throughout the book of Jude, II Peter, Hebrews, and other passages would not be in the Bible. Whether or not some or many will fall away and be lost in the end or not is something that God knows. All Theologians would agree that if it does happen with any of the saved or the Elect that God was able to prevent it. The sovereignty of God includes his divine control over what the free choices of men will be in the future. God can also work through people in providence (his omnipresent daily governmental control of the universe) to motivate them to desire to do his will and to continue with him. Men with such encouragement from God can voluntarily do God's will as they are inspired by God. The Philippian writer says, "For it is God which works in you both to will and to do of his good pleasure" (Philippians 2:13). Solomon was inspired by God to write, "The kings heart is in the hand of the Lord, as the rivers of water: he turns it whithersoever he will" (Proverbs 21:1). Paul mentioned, "Being confident of this one thing that he which hath begun a good work in you will perform it until the day of Jesus Christ" (Philippians 1:6). God is omnipotent and thus is able to allow the will of men to remain free when keeping them in his hand. This is how we got the Bible which is the inspired Word of God. Jesus said that no man is able to pluck them out of his Fathers hand (John 10:29). Jude's declaration and benediction in his epistle says, "Now unto him that is able to keep you from falling, and to present you faultless before to presence of his glory with exceeding joy" (Jude 24). Men are able to fall away from God and God is also able to keep them from falling or to bring them back to him again and to present them before him faultless with joy in his presence. This is great news. God can straighten us up if we do mess up and he can keep us until the very end. The scriptures teach that God scourges and chastens his Sons when they disobey in order to bring the fruit of holiness in them (Hebrews 12:6-10).

The objection due to warnings in the scriptures

The warnings in the New Testament to Christian believers are designed by God to threaten believers in terms of what could possibly happen if they do willfully sin or fall away. The exhortations should be interpreted as having the intent to prevent the very things that they warn against or about. Those things that are possible can be avoided if the proper precautions are taken heed to. Jonah threatened that if the city did not repent that the entire city would be doomed. The prophecy of the destruction or doom of the city could have happened theoretically but did not. God knows all things that are possible as well as what exhortations, prophecies, warnings, and encouragements are needed in order to prevent them. The exhortations do not establish that any of the believers exhorted would not persevere, but only that God is using these exhortations and warnings as a means to prevent them from a final apostasy. Yes it is possible and that is why I encourage Pastors and Evangelists alike to do God's will and to warn everyone to repent including the churches. God has a plan to prevent those things that are possible from actually happening in order to accomplish his purposes.

A teaching that some had an actual apostasy in the New Testament scriptures

John says of them, "They went out from us, but they were not of us; for it they had been of us, they would have remained with us" (I John 2:19). Many scriptures indicate that people with faith had an apostasy (II Timothy 2:17-18, II Peter 2:1-2, Hebrews 6:4-6, I Timothy 1:19-20, I Timothy 4;10). It appears in Peters' epistle that the prophets who were heretics denied the Lord that bought them. Another perspective on this is that the Bible teaches that many who profess the faith that we perceive are in the faith are yet not in the true faith at all. They believe but they do not have a saving faith (I John 2:19, Revelation 3;1, Romans 9:6, I John 2:19). They are not all Israel which are of Israel (Romans 9:6). This verse means that all the descendants of Abraham are not truly Jews. For example, Isaac and Esau have two different mothers. Consequently, the descendants of Esau are not true Jews but hybrid. Likewise, some that are Christians are not. Jesus saw that some even in the church of Sardis had the name that they were alive and yet they were not alive but dead (Revelation 3:1). The clincher for this may very well be in the words of Jesus Christ himself regarding those that profess faith and call him Lord. Jesus declared, "Many will say unto me in that day, Lord, Lord, have we not prophesied in thy name? and in thy name have cast out devils? and in thy name done many wonderful works? And then I will profess unto them, I never knew you: depart from me, ye that work iniquity" (Matthew 7:22-23). Undoubtedly these believers appeared to be real and faithful believers and they thought for sure that they were but they never had a true relationship with Jesus Christ. The word "never" means that Jesus never knew them as one of his sheep nor in the same sense that he knew those whom he had a loving relationship with. The foreknown are also predestinated, called, justified, sanctified, and shall be glorified (Romans 8:29-30). The word "know" is used in scripture to refer to an intimate and loving relationship between two people to include the Father and the Son and the Son and his sheep.

God gave his chosen people to his son in the covenant of redemption as a reward on the condition that Jesus would obey as their representative and suffer and die for them to save them. Jesus plainly said, "for I came down from heaven, not to do mine own will but the will of him that sent me, that of all which he hath given me I should lose nothing, but should raise it up again at the last day. And this is the will of him that sent me, that every one which sees the Son, and believeth in him, may have everlasting life: and I will raise him up on the last day" (John 38-40).

One thing to keep in mind about those that the scriptures teach will or may depart is that God is sovereign. God is the Judge. He will decide on his own what the end of each soul shall be including his own. It is not of him that runs nor of him that wills but of God that shows the mercy (Romans 9:16). As much as we love to know that God will bring his Elect home to Heaven there remains no escaping the reality that some who were bought will be damned. False prophets shall creep in among the people and bring in damnable heresies denying the Lord that bought them (II Peter 5:1). According to Peter, the damnation of these prophets does not slumber (I Peter 2:3). Friends I don't know how one can deny the Lord that bought them unless they were once redeemed. As we appreciate the wondrous truth of Eternal Security we keep in mind that God is just. He allows the will of man to remain free to the extent that some, paradoxically, can depart from the faith although we presume that they were never saved or known in the same sense that his Elect were converted, sanctified, and known (Romans 8:29-30).

History of the Eternal Security doctrine

The doctrine was taught first by Augustine Hippo (354-430). He was perhaps antiquity's greatest theologian. Augustine was born in North Africa in Algeria. His writings greatly influenced Western Christianity and philosophy. He was the Bishop of Hippo and among his most important works were The City of God and Confessions. He held that the Elect could not fall away to the extent that they could be lost in the end, but at the same time he believed that it was possible for some others (non-elect) to be regenerated and born again or in a true faith and yet fall from grace completely and suffer eternal damnation in the end. This view distinguishes the Elect of God from the rest of those that are born again or in the faith. The view also reconciles the paradox of the reality that you have a New Testament that teaches both that the saved are Eternally Secure and that some shall depart from the faith or deny the Lord that bought them to await damnation (I Timothy 4:1-

Hebrews 6:4-9, II Peter 2:1-2). It teaches that the Elect are a specially selected group of born again believers that cannot fail and shall certainly get to Heaven as decreed by God (Romans 8:29-30, John 10:25-29, John 6:37-40). The other born again believers or "men of faith" may theoretically fall from grace and be lost in the end as evident that some shall (I Timothy 4:1-2). Much scriptural data seems to suggest that the scriptural basis of this Pre-Reformation view of St. Augustine is valid. God has wrapped some so tight in his hand that he has told us that they belonged to him prior to creation and that they will be in heaven in the end. God has also made it evident that some shall depart from the faith or deny the Lord that bought them to wait for damnation in the end. Who is who? Who is what? I think that is the mystery.

The Church of Rome taught that the continuance of the saints depended on their obedience to God which made the salvation of their souls in the end uncertain to them. The Lutheran church made it contingent on the continued state of faith but not necessarily obedience which made it possible to depart from faith. The Calvinistic churches maintained a form that provides the absolute assurance that each true believer will make it home to heaven in the end.

Many if not all of the Calvinists believe that God who is rich in mercy, according to his unchangeable purpose of election of his sheep, does not fully withdraw the Holy Spirit even though they fall. They believe that he does not allow them to proceed so far as to lose the grace of adoption and forfeit their state of justification which is based on Christ's work alone. They will not bring themselves to accept that eternal damnation is even possible for a true Christian.

The Armenians reject the above-stated view of the Calvinists and believe that the perseverance of the believers until the end is dependent on their desire to believe and good works. The Wesleyans adopted the views of the Armenians which left the Calvinists to stand alone. The Calvinists are virtually the only group of Christians that believe that a true Christian cannot completely fall from a state of grace to finally be lost.

Predestination

Many Christians won't discuss this doctrine in churches at all. Why? It is because it is difficult to comprehend the truth of it and reconcile it with other truth that we know. Some people interpret the doctrine to mean that God is more loving and partial to some in comparison to others if he predestined some for Heaven and chose to leave others to their own way. The doctrine also causes many people to feel that it is incompatible with freewill and the moral accountability of man to God if God is the one that ultimately determines a destiny in advance of creation. However, the truth was designed to be a source of inspiration and comfort to all of those that truly believe in Jesus that trust him for their salvation. Paul reminded the church of Ephesus about this wondrous truth, "According as he hath chosen us in him before the foundation of the world, that we should be holy and without blame before him in love: Having predestinated us unto the adoption of children by Jesus Christ to himself, according to the good pleasure of his own will" (Ephesians 1:5).

Now if we belong to God and are his Elect it means that he did choose us before he made the worlds because he loved us and he plans to bring us to our final destination. Heaven is our destination. Jesus said that many mansions were in his Father's house and that he was going to prepare a place for us. He also said that he was preparing this place in order that he could receive us back to himself that we would be where he was at and that if it were not so that he would have told us (John 14:1-3). The simple truth is that God is omnipotent, omniscient, eternal, and omnipresent. God determines the final destiny of a created being in advance of creation due to his omniscience of events that are yet future, the reality that he is already in the future as an eternal being, his sovereign control of all events in history, God's infinite wisdom, his eternal decrees, and a combination of all of the aforementioned. It is to be advised to all that God's sovereignty does not eliminate man's freewill or his moral accountability. God's infinite wisdom, judgment, and his ways are past finding out and none has known his mind to be his counsellor (Romans 11:33-34).

Conclusion about assurance of salvation and Perseverance

Jesus Christ paid the price to purchase the sinners' pardon and acceptance. The righteousness of Christ is the reason why the sinner is justified in God's sight. The justified shall not fall unto condemnation because of the perfect price that was paid for his redemption from past, present, and future sin. Christ also makes constant intercession for us who are given to him in prayer as our High Priest (Hebrews 7:25, John 11:42). The Election of the sheep does not indicate that they may be saved if they keep their part of the plan to save them but that because of the atonement they shall finally be saved. Each believing Christian should live with this assurance that they surely will be in heaven at their departure.

The main objections to these wonderful truths being comprehended and embraced have to do with possibilities and probabilities. Many believe that such doctrines lead to carelessness and a false sense of security in our present position and leave us with a confidence that God will secure our final salvation without any effort or continuance of our own. Some believe that the doctrine leads to immorality and an abuse of divine grace. People may argue that if we will always be saved then it really makes no difference as to how we live and what we do. Although salvation is sure as far as God is concerned in that we are elected, foreknown, called, predestined, and that we shall be saved because of the atonement; it still requires constant watchfulness, and diligence, and prayer to make that calling and election sure to us (II Peter 1:10). People that have been saved do certain things and other things they do not. Many are not in the faith although they profess him as Lord and they won't discover until the end that he never knew them as his children (Matthew 7:21-24).

Conclusion, The Decrees of God, Perseverance and The End Times

The enigma with the doctrine and freewill does exist and it can be comprehended to a degree. God is incomprehensible but knowable. God works in us both to will and to do his good pleasure (Philippians 2:13). Perseverance in holiness is the evidence of the genuine experience of our salvation. Men must continue and follow peace and holiness in order to see the Lord (Hebrews 2:14). Freedom of choice brings with it some paradoxes which are not easily reconciled with God's purpose and human comprehension. The things which are not God's purpose, plan, or will in terms of casting his own adopted sons away are always possible because of free moral agency. However, if a man does fall away and not make it to heaven after getting saved it can only happen if God decreed it. God has decreed to let free moral agents do certain things if they want to. God has also decreed not to allow some things to happen in history and with some people. God's decrees embrace all events to include what all of the free moral choices of men will be. He has decreed to allow men to do chose to do some things and has decreed not to let men do other things on other occasions. Therefore, man does not ultimately determine to thwart God's purpose in his life because of freewill. God's decree will determine what happens with each person's life. Let the study of God's decrees be a source of comfort to you in your life. There will be no need to fret or worry about any event in your life nor what the future may hold once you comprehend the divine decrees of God.

The decree of God is his eternal, unchangeable, holy, wise, and sovereign purpose. The decree is God's purpose and intent with a person's life, creation, good and bad angels, and all things to include every event in history. The decree is what determined what the future would be before the creation and it includes the history of angels, the fall of man, the Atonement, salvation, and all events and their causes, conditions, successions, and relations. The scriptural proof is vast and to keep it simple God said, "I am God, and there is none like me, declaring the end from the beginning, and from ancient times the things that are not yet done, saying, my counsel shall stand, and I will do all my pleasure" (Isaiah 46;10). The Lord of hosts hath sworn saying, Surely as I have thought, so shall it come to pass; and as I have purposed, so shall it stand" (Isaiah 14:24). Foreknowledge is God simply knowing the future. Foreordination is God deciding what the future will be and each event whatsoever the class. God knows the future because he has already determined the future. God's decree relates equally to all future events of every kind, to the free actions of moral agents, as well as to the action of angels, to the sinful as well as to morally right actions. God has decreed to do some things himself such as the creation. He has decreed to do other things through men, angels, Christ, creation, miraculous interventions, other events in his daily actions of providence. He decided the means, causes, effects, circumstances, and instruments and the events which would depend on them. God's decree determines only the future of an event, however, his decree does not directly cause the effect. As it relates to freewill God decreed that people are free. He decreed to design circumstances that divine foreknowledge did anticipate that free agents would act in and do in accordance with his plan. God foreseeing that if he made a certain free agent and put him in certain relations he would act freely in a certain way, and yet with that knowledge proceeded to make that individual and put him in precisely those positions, God would, in so doing, obviously predetermine the future of the free act foreseen. God in his work foreordained what he foreseen. God decreed to permit sin but not to cause sin. That is called the permissive decree. He has no responsibility for these acts whatsoever. God decreed to provide men with the choice to follow him or to rebel against him. God decreed to allow men to be the agents of good or the agents of evil. Men can worship God or Satan. God told Jeremiah that before he formed him in the belly that he already knew him and had in advance ordained him to be a prophet to the nations Jeremiah 1:5).

The decree of God embraces all events. God works all things after the counsel of his own will (Ephesians 1:11). The inhabitants of the earth are reputed as nothing and the Lord does according to his will among the armies of heaven and the inhabitants of the earth (Daniel 4:34-35). The people that crucified Jesus were gathered together to do whatsoever the hand of God and his counsel had determined beforehand to be done (Acts 4:27-28, Acts 13:29). The universality of God's decree s is seen from his providence. The providential government of God holds and decides the activity and future of all things in heaven and on earth as a whole, and every event in detail to include the free choices of men (Proverbs 16:33, Daniel 4:34-35, Matthew 10:29-30, Genesis 45:5, Philippians 2:13). The lot is cast into the lap but the whole disposal is of the Lord (Proverbs 16:33). God decides which way the lot turns. Those things which appear to be events happening by mere chance are actually controlled by God and decided by God. Joseph reminded us that his betrayal by his brethren to be sold into slavery was intended by his brother for evil but meant by God for the good (Genesis 50:20).

A decrees of God had their origin before what we know as time and are eternal (Acts 15:18, Ephesians 1:4, I Peter 1:20, 2 Thess 2:13, 2 Timothy 1:9, Ephesians 3:11).. The decrees of God are immutable and thus unchangeable according to the scriptures (Psalms 33:11, Psalm 102:27). God is immutable and thus unchangeable himself and therefore it is unlikely that he will change his purpose for saving one of his own. God has foretold the certain occurrence of many events, including the free actions of men, which have afterward surely come to pass. The basis for prophecy is foreknowledge of the future, the foundation of a event as being future, is God decree to declare the end and all event from the beginning (Isaiah 46:10). The immutability of the decree is the reason of the infallibility of the foreknowledge or of the prophec God knows the future and who will persevere until the end in advanc God has decreed all future events, he includes in the decree the cause conditions, and consequences. A man cannot simply wander away fror a sovereign God and not be saved if God has intended to save him or purposed to keep him in his hand.

A conditional decree to let man decide his own future or destiny would put God in a predicament to allow man to thwart God's purpose based on what man decides to do which was not already planned by God. This would subvert the sovereignty of God to make him, as to the administration of his whole government and the execution of his plans, dependent upon the uncontrollable actions of his own creatures. All events that are future are decreed by God including the free choices of men as we have seen. The decrees of God are sovereign which mean that they are based God's own plans and not mans (Daniel 4:32-35, Romans 9:15-18). Man's actions to include those which are contrary originate with God's decree first as the aforementioned passages prove. The decree of God is declared to depend upon his own good pleasure and the counsel of his own will (Matthew 6:25, 26, Romans 9:11, Ephesians 1:5). The decree of God is what determines what the free actions of men will be (Acts 4:27-28, Ephesians 2:10). God himself works in his people the faith and the obedience which are called the conditions of their salvation (Philippians 2:13, Ephesians 2:8, 2 Timothy 2:25).

The end is in God's control and has been determined by God in advance and that is important to remember. It is a specific decree called predestination but it does not eliminate the fact that men are free to choose. Men are not machines or robots but they are indeed under the rule of a sovereign God. Jesus' declaration that his sheep has been given eternal life and will never perish should not be taken lightly (John 10:28-29). God's decree determines all future events to include what the free actions of men will be and whether his sheep will be in heaven and if any of them will be lost. The decree encompasses the counsel of God in terms of who will be lost in the end and why. Shall God's own sheep be lost? Has not the Atonement of Jesus Christ accomplished the purposes of God? Conditions do exist and it is God that works through men by his power the conditions which are dependent upon men. God has also used Pastors, prophets, teachers, evangelists, and apostles to perfect the saints (Ephesians 4:11). They are roadblocks to keep men out of Hell. Freedom of the human will is why the exhortations and warnings abound throughout the New Testament to the church and run parallel to the promises that none of his sheep will be lost.

Hypotheticals and possible events

The angel promised Paul that none of the men on the ship would perish but only that the boat would be destroyed. After that, Paul told the men to cut the ropes and remain on the ship or else they would perish. All men were spared as the angel had said in advance but the promise did not remove the probability away that they could perish if they did not adhere to Paul's exhortation (Acts 27:31). Hypothetically, it is possible that those saved can be lost although we know it is not very probable. Promises never remove responsibility from any believer to do what he has the responsibility to do if he wants the promise to come to pass. Jesus Christ has gone to great length by his vicarious atonement to bring us to heaven with him. God works through us by the Holy Spirit to enable his plan to come to pass. There will always remain just enough paradox in freewill for it to be possible for something to go wrong to include a believer being lost in the end. However, a believer must live in the hope and confidence that he which began a good work in us will perform it until the day of Jesus Christ (Philippians 1:6). Cut the ropes and stay on the boat. The angel promised that they would be secure and not perish on Paul's ship but then they had to follow directions. The ship would have been wrecked and they would have drowned if they did not cut the ropes as Paul exhorted and if they would not have remained on the boat.

The major objection to what we could call "Eternal Security" is that the exhortations and warnings throughout the New Testament for believers including parables that Jesus spoke imply the contingency of the believer's salvation. The scriptures reveal contingencies. The believers have to keep the faith and do what his or her profession say to do, consequently each believer is liable to a final apostasy. As you examine all scriptures collectively, we find some who thought that they had been saved but they were altogether fooled. The words spoken by Jesus Christ to Many that called him Lord was that he never knew them (Matthew 7:21-24). As stated above, this means that they were not known in the sense that the sheep were known that followed him (John 10:27-29, Romans 8:29-30). God knew the Many that shall call him Lord on that day as having wicked ways but he did not know them in the same sense that he calls his sheep known.

It will always be true that if the believers apostatize that they will be lost in the end (Jude). The threats could be viewed as a deterrent for Christians to avoid the very thing that the threats were designed to prevent. We see the hypothetical destruction of a city that was doomed called Ninevah and yet Jonah the prophet being sent which resulted in a turnaround. For example, "And God saw their works, that they turned from their evil way: and God repented of the evil, that he had said that he would do unto them; and he did it not" (Jonah 3:10). The city was saved in the end although God was going to destroy them if they did not repent and turn from their wicked ways. When we see the Bible teaches us that God changed his mind it means that because men repented that God changed his purpose to destroy their city. God can change his mind. God could alter an original plan and make a second decree in advance of or subsequent to the first plan and change the purpose or original intent in the latter decree. I precaution all not teach that he will do this but only that he could if he so desires. A paradox does exist in the omnipotence of God. Jesus realized this he prayed to the Father in Gethsemane. Jesus knew that all things were possible for God and that it was even possible for him to remove from Jesus the cup of suffering purposed for his life which was an eternal decree (Matthew 26:39).

Many scriptural warnings abound which warn of the possibility of believing saints being lost in the end and the fact that some were once righteous and had now been forgotten and rejected by God (Ezekiel 18:24, Matthew 13:20-21, II Peter 2:20-21, Hebrews 6:4-6, Hebrews

10:26-29). They are likely hypothetical warnings of the consequence of apostasy with the design of preventing it. They are also designed to show the consequences of indifference and sin and the need for constant care and effort by Christians. We also know that these warnings show the consequences of abusing grace which is possible to do given that men can choose. These passages also reflect people that left from among us because they were not really one of us (I John 2:19). Again, it is possible although very improbable that someone who is saved can be lost. The warnings are given because of the possibilities of a final apostasy that do exist in the lives of believers who are free moral agents. God knows what the possibilities are as well as what will happen in the future. Jesus knew that if the mighty works which was done in Chorazin and Bethsaida had been done in Tyre and Sidon that the latter would have repented long ago (Luke 10:13). God knows what is needed and what could happen hypothetically under some circumstances along with the means needed to circumvent those events with those things that will finally come to pass.

Those who have believed in Jesus and have trusted in him for their salvation are said to be glorified in the end (Romans 8:28-30). They have assurance from Christ that he died for them and that they will not follow a stranger because they know him (John 10:5). Christ gives them eternal life and he knows them and they shall never perish (John 10:27-29). Never means never. The apostasy that is possible with true believers is capable of being prevented by God who is able to keep them from falling (Jude 24).

A Christian Pastor must exhort believers to continue in faith and to strive for godliness and perfection in his or her life and warn them of the consequences of apostasy (Hebrews 10:26). Nevertheless, we must never forget that Jesus was the Lamb of God that took away the sins of the world (John 1:29). We must believe that he will never leave us nor forsake us but will be with us always even until the end of the world (Matthew 28:20). We must maintain the confidence that the same God which began a good work in us will perform it until the day of Jesus

Christ (Philippians 1:6). Jude says as he concluded his book which had many warnings, "Now unto him that is able to keep us from falling, and to present you faultless before the presence of his glory with exceeding joy. To the only wise God our Savior, be glory and majesty, dominion and power, both now and ever, Amen" (Jude 24-25).

One of the biggest dilemmas in Christianity is that many were not what they thought they were or what they have had the name of being and have not been born again (Revelation 3:1). The church of Sardis had the name that they were alive but were dead. Churches must pray and seek God and make sure that they are in Christ and that they are the trees that he planted.

We must rejoice in knowing that God loved us before the foundation of the world. His love is exemplified in the vicarious atonement by his Son to secure our final salvation. We must continue to have confidence and hope that we will be in Heaven with Jesus because of what he specifically did for us to accomplish our salvation. We pray, fast, study, obey, give, keep his commandments and purify ourselves because we love him as he first loved us (I John 4:19 & I John 2:4). Can a Christian be eternally damned? The answer to that question remains yes that a professing Christian believer can be damned and lost in the end and Many that profess and call him Lord, Lord shall be (Matthew 7:21-24). Will one of God's own chosen, sheep or Elect be lost or eternally damned in the end? The answer to that questions will always remain no. The vicarious atonement of Christ for his sheep ensures their final salvation in the end. All of the visible believers are not all believers at all. The sheep also know him and follow him and shall not follow the voice of a stranger (John 10:5 & John 10:28). Who shall lay anything to the charge of God's elect? It is God that justifies. Who is he that condemns? It is Christ that died, yea rather, that is risen again, who is even at the right hand of God, who also makes intercession for us" (Romans 8:33-34). All that profess to be born again are not all God's Elect. All of those that have been graced to respond to the universal call to begin in faith have not been graced with the gift of perseverance. Many who

317

profess faith in Christ will not continue until the end. The Elect shall persevere until the end and be glorified. Jesus said, "For many are called, but few are chosen" (Matthew 22:16).

It is sure to God, that if we are Elected and called, we shall be saved in the end. However, the future is not known to us. We are not sure as to whether or not we shall continue until the end and thus we are exhorted and required to constantly watch, be diligent, pray, take heed to exhortations and warnings from the Pastor and scriptures, examine our lives, and make our calling and Election sure (2 Peter 1:10). That means to make sure yourself that you are in Christ by inventorying your life. John said, "If any say that they know him and do not keep his commandments that he is a liar and the truth is not in him" (I John 2:4)

St Augustine of Hippo

St. Augustine of Hippo was the first theologian to teach the Eterna Security of the Elect. Augustine taught that the Elect was eternall secure and yet at the same time he taught that some of the believer who had true faith and the new life were not elect and could fall fron grace to suffer eternal damnation in the end. This doctrine is consis tent with both scriptural themes that run parallel throughout the Nev Testament in regards to both Arminius and Calvinistic views of Eterna Security. A good example of this is that we are told that in the latter day some shall depart from the faith (I Timothy 4:1) and that false prophet shall bring in damnable heresies to deny the Lord that bought them t await damnation (II Peter 2:1-2). We are also taught that the prede tinated shall be glorified (Romans 8:29-30) and that Christ shall los none of his sheep (John 10:27-30, John 6:36-39). Hence, all the Elec are his sheep and shall persevere until the end and shall never peris nor have any eternal damnation (John 10:28-29).

The vicarious atonement secures salvation. The other men of fait are men of faith in their sight and in the sight of other men based o their profession and to a measure or degree their activities but they ma depart from the faith and be damned in the end (Matthew 7:21-24, I Timothy 4:1, II Peter 2:1-3, Revelation 3:1, Hebrews 10:26-31, Hebrews 6:4-6). Whether or not they were ever born again or a true Son of God is debatable and have had arguments constructed on both sides for centuries and both are persuasive. The Elect are known to God and were categorized as such before the foundation of the world but it is unsure to us as to who they are out of multitudes and thus we preach and evangelize to all and minister to all congregants alike. God knows those that are his and those that name his name are exhorted to depart from iniquity (II Timothy 2:19). This explanation provides a scriptural basis to reconcile the Calvinistic view of Eternal Security with the view of the Arminius doctrine. The men of faith that shall fall from grace are true men of faith in our sight but were never the Elect or the fore-known (Romans 8:29-30). Many are in faith in their own perspectives and they call him Lord but Jesus will say to many that he never knew them and to depart from him because they were the workers of iniquity (Matthew 7:21-24).

The heretics that denied the Lord that bought them were bought in their view and in the view of men but may not ever have been redeemed as far as the Lord was concerned. The Apostle Peter professed that their damnation is waiting because they denied the Lord that bought them by bringing in damnable heresies (II Peter 2:1). A literal interpretation of this verse would mean that they were at one point redeemed. The only way they could have later been damned if they were once redeemed or bought would be that the sovereign God decreed to permit them to fall away from their original state of redemption as free moral agents. The one thing for sure is that these apostate teachers are not one of his Elect and foreknown which he foreordained in advance to justify, sanctify, and glorify (Romans 8:29-30).

Atonement

As much as we may not fully grasp nor comprehend the reality of it the scriptures limit the Atonement. Those whom he suffered and died for are called "his sheep," John 10:11-12, "the elect," Romans 8:32-35, "his people," Matthew 1:21, and "his church," Ephesians 5:25-27, Acts 20:28. Jesus Christ suffered and died vicariously to accomplish the salvation of the church which is his people. All of our sins were removed once and for all by his sacrifice for us. God's love is for all and his vicarious atonement is sufficient to save all. The work of Christ was exclusively for those out of the multitudes that would believe and the benefits of his work is what achieved salvation for his people. We cannot add to Christ's work for us by anything that we do to make it more magnificent than what it already is. We cannot subtract from what he accomplished for us by anything that we do or fail to do to. We cannot make his work less satisfactorily to God to save us. The Christian will not be condemned on the day of Judgment if he has placed his trust in Christ to save him.

The sacrificial work of Christ goes hand to hand with his intercessory works which are both aspects of his atoning work. The range and scope of his vicarious atonement would not be broader than the range and scope of his intercessory prayer. Jesus Christ limited as to who his intercessory prayer was for when he prayed, "I pray not for the world, but for those whom thou have given me" (John 17:9). Does it really make a lot of sense for him to limit the range and scope of who his prayer was for when he was on the earth if he was in fact going to the cross to pay the price for everyone without exceptions? Jesus made it clear that he was not praying for the world but for those who were given to him by the Father. Jesus knew that everyone did not belong to him and would not belong to him. He also prayed for those who would believe who had not arrived to earth yet.

The belief that Christ died for the purpose of saving all people without exception including the unbeliever, leads to universalism, doctrine that all men will be saved in the end. It is impossible Ladies and Gentleman that those whom Jesus paid the price for in full would be lost and condemned due to their own guilt of sin. Moreover, if Christ had died to apply the benefits of his work to all it follows from that premise that he would save all without exceptions. Christ died to secure the final salvation of those whom had been given to him and they are the ones that would believe. The Atonement is sufficient to save all but is limited in its application to those who would repent, believe the gospel, and continue with him until the end. The gospel must be preached to all. God knows who will repent and believe. He also knows who will continue with him and be faithful and those that will depart from the faith.

It is paramount that we encourage believers to keep on believing that Jesus died for them and rose again in order to accomplish their salvation for them. This is the good news if they believe it. We must also continue to exhort Christians to repent of sin and to obey him. None should be careless or overconfident that he has security without responsibilities and duties which he shall not answer to the Lord for. The believers that have a spiritual union with Christ are branches that abide in him and bear fruit. The branches that are not connected to him are withered and thrown into the fire to be burned (John 15:5-6).

The purpose of threats and warnings to Christian believers

God knows all of those things that are possible or probable. The threats and warnings of a possible eternal damnation for true Christian believers are designed to prevent those things from happening. It was possible for that wicked city to be destroyed in Jonah's day but God sent Jonah to preach repentance which resulted in a turnaround. God spared them and his purpose for sending Jonah was achieved. The warnings and threats of doom served their purpose in his ministry and they were real events of destruction that could have come to pass. The New Testament warnings are designed as hypothetical warnings of the consequence of apostasy to prevent it, by showing the natural consequences that come as a result of indifference to sin, and the need for earnest care for our salvation. They also show the terrible and the dreadful consequences of abusing the gift of grace to the extent that a sovereign God of purpose can be provoked to change his mind. The abuse of divine grace to this degree can only occur under circumstances where they had an appearance of spiritual life to the fellow man but were dead in reality (Revelation 3:1, I John 2:19, Romans 2:28). It is possible for the saved to be lost although all provisions have been made to prevent such events from occurring. Sheep can wander astray and Christ has promised us that he would lose nothing when referring to his sheep or people (John 6:39). The question becomes as to whether or not the promise of Christ was a conditional promise or an unconditional promise. Does God leave it up to man to do his part or does God guaranty that he will bring it to pass because of the Atonement, Christ's intercessory work, and God working through the free moral agency of man by the Holy Spirit in his providence. I suggest that this entire book addresses the answer to this enigmatic question and especially the conclusion.

A scenario in which it is possible for one of God's own to be lost and damned in the end would be the case of a sovereign God withdrawing the restraining influence of his grace from the true believers life. The Grace of God is what enables us to stand (I Peter 5:12). As far as I know there is not a decree of God that he will allow any of his own people or sheep to be lost. However, the possibility exists due to the paradox with omnipotence. God can do anything. God is the only wise God that is able to keep us from falling and to present us faultless before the presence of his glory with exceeding joy (Jude 24). If men fail it means in order for that to happen that God would have decided for one reason or another to change his original purpose and intent to save someone who he had already saved and forgiven. The Atonement of Jesus Christ and his intercession for us is the reason why it is not very probable that this will happen with any of his sheep. God has promised that he has given us eternal life and that we shall never perish. He will bring those that he has loved to him. Nothing is able to separate us from the Love of God which is in Christ Jesus our Lord (Romans 8:39). Many things that God has not purposed to happen could happen if a free moral agent continues to do some things and if God then decides due to their own stubbornness to let them. God can change his mind, purpose, plan, and intent. God is God. The possible changes of God's are hypotheticals things that God could do if he so desires. God is sovereign and he has all power. We should fear God.

I, therefore, leave you with a few warnings, Jesus said, "And fear not them which kill the body, but are not able to kill the soul: but rather fear him which is able to destroy both soul and body in hell" (Matthew 10:28). He said this to his own disciples who were his chosen sheep. Likewise, The Hebrew writer said, "If we sin willfully after that we have received the knowledge of the truth, there remains no more sacrifice for sins, but a certain fearful looking for of judgment and fiery indignation, which shall devour the adversaries" (Hebrews 10:26-27). This exhortation is to admonish the Hebrew Christians that it is possible for believers to fall into the same judgment that the unsaved or God's enemies shall fall into. It is a judgment for the lost sinner who are knowingly or unknowingly the enemies of God to be cast away to Hell.

Moreover, be it known unto you assuredly that it is possible for anyone to backslide and not be able to return to having a relationship with Christ. When they fall they are utterly helpless and unable to restore themselves. Recovery and restoration is man's responsibility but is not within his ability. God must work within the spiritually dead to restore them to the place of spiritual renewal. Falling down and not ever being able to get back up can happen to those who profess and believe to have been endowed with spiritual power from on high. The Galatian writer said, "Brethren, if a man be overtaken in a fault, ye which are spiritual, restore such a one in a spirit of meekness, considering yourself, lest ye also be tempted" (Galatians 6:1). The key for fallen saints is that the spiritual reach out to them in humility and intercede for them to restore them spiritually. This may take exhortation, rebuke, prayer, casting out devils, confession, the laying on of hands to impart spiritual power, and words of encouragement and comfort. If they are not restored it is possible that they will be lost as the scriptures testify, "For it is impossible for those who were once enlightened, and have tasted of the heavenly gift, and were made partakers of the Holy Ghost, and have tasted the good word of God, and the powers of the world to come if they shall fall away, to renew them again to repentance; seeing they crucify to themselves the Son of God afresh, and put him to an open shame" (Hebrews 6:4-6).

Many exegetical interpretations abound as to why the above-stated passage of scripture is in the Bible. I am quoting this verse with no preference to anyone's theological opinion on the subject matter. Some say these people could have never had the Holy Ghost and that they could not have ever been born again. Others say that the verse refers to those who reject the gospel after being exposed to it and consequently they blaspheme against the Holy Ghost which is the unpardonable sin. Still there are those that simply teach that this verse proves that the born again and those that have received the gift of the Holy Ghost can fall away and never be able to repent again after continuing to willfully sin. Consequently, they can be damned in the end. Who are these people? This becomes the question. The word "if" is the key word in the verse above. John taught us that that the born of God does not continue to commit or practice sin because he is the born of God (I John 3:9). One must trust Jesus for their final salvation and feel confident and secure that he or she will be in heaven if they were truly born again. The born again will not willfully practice sin according to the testimony of the scriptures.

Repent and return to a relationship with Jesus Christ before it is too late! It is still possible for you to be damned to Hell in the end if you don't repent now. Repent of lies. Repent of adultery. Repent of stealing. Repent of fornication. Repent of homosexuality and lesbianism. Repent of whore-mongering. Repent of hatred, bitterness and not forgiving others. Repent of witchcraft and sorcery. Repent of extortion. John the Revelator said, "Blessed are they that do his commandments, that they may have right to the tree of life, and may enter into the gates into the city. For without are dogs, and sorcerers, and whoremongers, and murderers, and idolaters, and whosoever loveth and maketh a lie. I Jesus have sent mine angel to testify unto you these things in the churches. I am the root and offspring of David, and the bright and morning star" (Revelation 22:14-16). John the Revelator also said, "He that overcometh shall inherit all things; and I will be his God, and he shall be my son. But the fearful, and unbelieving, and the abominable, and murderers, and whoremongers, and sorcerers, and idolaters, and all liars, shall have their part in the lake which burneth with fire and brimstone which is the second death" (Revelation 21:8).

The conclusion of the matter is that Christ died for us and rose again to accomplish our salvation once and for all. Yes it is possible to be lost in the end but very improbable at all if you are born again. Hence, we can find some truth on both sides of the debate that has lasted for centuries among theologians. God is sovereign and he will Judge all men and he has not left that up to us. The Most High will do as he pleases among the heavens and with the inhabitants of the earth (Daniel 4:32-36). God shall have mercy and compassion on whoever he wills to have mercy and compassion on (Romans 9:15). So then it is not out of him that wills nor out of him that runs but of God that shows mercy (Romans 9:16).

The Roman writer summarized God's wisdom and judgment in the following manner, "O the depths of the riches of both the knowledge and wisdom of God! How unsearchable are his judgments, and his ways past finding out! For who hath known the mind of the Lord? or who hath been his counsellor? (Romans 11:33-34). God is unsearchable. We cannot put him in our own system of theology based on the Word of God and define him or his ways nor as to how he will judge specific cases.

God's purpose for your life

God is infinitely wise and omniscient and by far transcendent to our own logic, perceptions of reality or human comprehension. He simply cannot be found out, measured, predicted, and categorized in terms of his works, ways, and future Judgment consistent with how we would define, measure, predict, or label people. We can look at people and their history, speech, words, promises, patterns, motives, and so on and predict what they will do in the future with amazing accuracy. God has given us his Word and have left us with some mysteries.

We can and do know his Word is true but there comes a limit to what a finite mind can phantom. What we can know for sure that God will do in the future based on his Word? The decrees of God are his unchange-able purposes and plans before the creation that he has decided in his will to bring to pass in time. God, "declaring the end from the begin ning, and from ancient times things that are not yet done, saying, My counsel shall stand, and I will do all my pleasure: calling a ravenous bird from the east, the man that executes my counsel from a far country: yea I have spoken it, I will also bring it to pass, I have purposed it, I will also do it" (Isaiah 46:10). Now if God has said it we know that he shall do it The Lord of hosts have sworn, saying, Surely as I have thought, so shall it come to pass; and as I have purposed, so shall it stand (Isaiah 14:24) A sparrow cannot fall to the ground without God's purpose to allow i and we are more valuable to God than many sparrows (Matthew 10:29 31). God's power is able to keep the believer from falling and to presen him or her faultless before him in joy (Jude 24). It is up to God, no us, to present us before him faultless. Our destiny is the result of God': determination and power to keep us not us maintaining our salvatior by our own strength and good works.

Jesus said that no man is able to pluck us out of his hand or th Fathers' hand (John 10:28-29). We were sealed by the Holy Ghost unti the day of redemption (Ephesians 4:20). Apparently, the Holy Spiri has secured the believer until the day of redemption. This implies tha a true believer will be kept by the Holy Ghost up until the day of the Lord. Finally, the gift of eternal life implies that if it was taken away that it was never eternal in the first place but temporal. My hope is that every believer would celebrate Jesus and what he accomplished for us with the Atonement. Be cautious in your walk with Jesus also. He has a plan to accomplish his purpose for our lives and to bring us to Heaven with him. The exhortations from the prophets and Pastors have a specific purpose and we must take heed to them when they come to us from the Lord.

Men don't know it all

It is possible for us to ruin or sabotage God's purpose for our lives if the God who is able to keep us from falling allows us to fall away. A permissive decree of God would need to be the precursor to such an event happening. God would need to stop his omnipotent power from keeping us and change his original purpose he had in mind for saving us to let such a final apostasy happen. The Bible warns that such an apostasy could happen but gives no indication that it will occur with any of his sheep. This gives us enough reason to have a godly fear of God and it helps us keep in mind that we don't know everything especially the future. We don't have all the answers. We just must keep trusting that Christ will save us and finish the work he started within us. Men have a will of their own and that factor alone causes the paradox. Don't wreck the ship. In the case of the prophet Balaam, God put an angel and his donkey in the way to stop him but after Balaam didn't listen or adhere God then decided to let him go his own way which wasn't God's original intent or plan but Balaam's (Jude 24, II Peter 2:15-16). He was called a mad or insane prophet that loved the reward of unrighteousness (II Peter 2: 15-16). Notice that the Spirit inspired Jude to write about the prophet Balaam to a New Testament Church that was saved by the grace of God. A falling away and a final doom of some is surely possible and that is why we see the threats and warnings to the New

Testament church with Old Testament illustrations and examples provided. God wouldn't inspire his man to say it if it were not a possibility with some who were among the faithful believers in the church. We must warn professing believers and unbelievers alike about Hell and the Lake of Fire. We often don't really know their eternal end or where they are headed after they take their final breath as we presume we do. The decrees are magnificent theology but we don't know the end of any as do God.

The bad things that could theoretically happen with congregants and church folk ought not to take place. That is why they must be warned and encouraged to repent and believe the gospel again and to continue in the true faith until the end. Our perseverance is left in God's hand, nevertheless, God can let us leave his purpose for our lives and go our own contrary way as the angels and Lucifer did if we won't listen and take good advice from spiritual authority. Theology would call that a permissive decree. Jude warned us, "I will therefore put to your remembrance, though you once knew this, how that the Lord, having saved the people out of the land of Egypt, afterward destroyed them that believed not. And the angels which kept not their first estate, but left their own habitation, he hath reserved in everlasting chains under darkness unto the judgment of the great day" (Jude 5-6). Why would such exhortations and warnings exist for the New Testament church unless it was possible that some among the Christians could be damned in the end?

Jude also warned, "For there are certain men crept in unawares who were before of old ordained to this condemnation, ungodly men turning the grace of our God into lasciviousness, and denying the only Lord God, and our Lord Jesus Christ" (Jude 4). People are in churches but are living in an ungodly manner without any proof aside from their profession that they have a genuine relationship with Christ. Their damnation is possible if they don't repent. Some interpreted the grace of God as an alibi to be as lustful and lasciviousness in their deeds as they may desire. More restraint and precaution must be taken. The design of the Atonement was both to cause change in the redeemed through the Holy Spirit's power while they are alive on the earth and to accomplish salvation in the end for them because of Christ's work on the cross. Some have taken the cross of Christ and what he accomplished in the Atonement as an excuse to live ungodly. They presume that how we conduct ourselves and live our life on the earth really doesn't matter anymore. Christ came to save us from sin (Matthew 1:21).

Jude says, "Even as Sodom and Gomorrha, and the cities about them in like manner, giving themselves over to strange flesh, are set forth as an example, suffering the vengeance of eternal fire" (Jude 7). Who was Jude talking about and why did he bring up the Old Testament History? Friends he was using the destruction of Sodom and Gomorrha and what happened to the people that were burned with fire and brimstone when they were judged by God as an example to warn the New Testament church. A similar doom for a professing Christian is possible. The fire and brimstone mentioned in (Revelation 21:8) is the final end of the unrepentant soul and body of the wicked. There comes a time when we must have the ability to discern the difference between those who profess him as Lord that have not ever been converted from Satan or his demons at all from those who were once saved that have fallen away from the faith that are now spiritually dead. These people are to be identified separately from the Christians that are saved and still in the faith with Christ in the hand of the Father (John 10:28-29).

Jesus warned churches to repent

Jesus Christ himself said, "He that overcome, the same shall be clothed in white raiment, and I will not blot out his name out of the book of life, but I will confess his name before my Father, and before his angels" (Revelation 3:5). Jesus also said to the church of Ephesus, Nevertheless, I have somewhat against thee, because thou hast left thy first love. Remember, therefore from whence thou art fallen, and repent, and do the first works: or else I will come unto thee quickly and remove thy candlestick out of his place, except thou repent" (Revelation 2:5). Jesus said to the church of Laodiceans, "I know thy works, that thou art neither cold nor hot. So then because thou art lukewarm, and neither cold nor hot, I will spue thee out of my mouth. Because thou sayest I am rich and increased with goods, and have need of nothing: and know not that thou art wretched, and miserable, and poor, and blind and naked: I counsel thee to buy gold tried in the fire that thou mayest be rich; and white raiment, that thou mayest be clothed, and that the shame of thy nakedness do not appear; and anoint thine eyes with eye salve, that thou mayest see. As many as I love, I rebuke and chasten: be zealous therefore, and repent" (Revelation 3:15-19).

Listen carefully to what Jesus says to the church of Thyatira, "I know thy works, and charity, and service, and faith, and thy patience, and thy works, and the last to be more than the first. Notwithstanding I have a few things against thee, because, thou sufferest that woman Jezebel which calleth herself a prophetess, to teach and to seduce my servant to commit fornication, and to eat things sacrificed unto idols. And I gave her space to repent of her fornication; and she repented no Behold, I will cast her into a bed, and them that commit adultery with her into great tribulation, except they repent of their deeds. And I will kill her children with death; and all the churches shall know that I am he which searcheth the reign and hearts and I will give unto every one of you according to your works. But unto you I say, and unto the rest of Thyatira, as many as have not this doctrine, and which have not known the depths of Satan, as they speak; I will put upon you none other burden. But that which ye have already hold fast till I come. And he that overcometh, and keepeth my works unto the end, to him will I give power over the nations: And he shall rule them with a rod of iron: as the vessels of a potter shall they be broken to shivers: even as I received of my Father. And I will give him the morning star. He that hath an ear, let him hear what the Spirit saith unto the churches" (Revelation 2: 19-29 We see the encouragement to those that Christ loves and died for. The were encouraged to repent and to return to a lifestyle of spiritual pow and victory. We see a resurrected Savior encouraging the church to walk for him and to live on earth for him in such a manner that their lifestyle and works bring the praise, honor, and glory to him.

Jesus has promised that his sheep have eternal life and that they shall never perish (John 10:28-29). The plain truth is that we can know who has the eternal life that Jesus promised based upon their hearts, attitudes, actions, and by what they say and do. John stated, "We know that we have passed from death unto life, because we love the brethren, He that loveth not his brother abideth in death. Whosoever hateth his brother is a murderer: and ye know that no murderer hath eternal life abiding in him" (I John 3:14-15). John said the following in his Revelation from the Spirit on the isle of Patmos, "Blessed are they that do his commandments, that they may have the right to the tree of life, and may enter in through the gates into the city. For without are dogs, and sorcerers, and whoremongers, and murderers, and idolaters, and whosoever loveth and maketh a lie. I, Jesus have sent mine angel to testify unto you these things in the churches. I am the root and off-spring of David, and the bright and morning star" (Revelation 22:14-16). Christ removed all of these sins away for the believer and nailed them to the cross.

My advice for every professing Christian is to repent of sin and believe the gospel. Be sure that you are in the true faith and have believed the right gospel and that you are truly what you say you are and who and what you think you are. Many have been deceived. If you have believed Jesus and you trust him for your salvation you will not be condemned. You will also receive the promise of the Father which is the Holy Ghost (John 14). Your sins have been forgiven and Christ have accomplished your salvation for you if you have repented and believe. Christ will also manifest himself inwardly within your heart and outwardly in your lifestyle in such a manner that you will know that you have been born again. You will change. Jesus warned, "Ye shall know them by their fruits. Not every one that says Lord, Lord, shall enter into the kingdom of Heaven but he that does the will of my Father which is in heaven. Many will say unto me in that day, Lord, Lord, have we not prophesied in thy name? And in thy name have cast out devils? and in thy name done many wonderful works? And then will I profess unto them, I never knew you: depart from me, ye that work iniquity" (Matthew 7:21-24).

Be advised that Satan has come to send strong delusion in the church and to professing believers. This is the spirit of the Antichrist and it is now upon the earth to lie, deceive, steal, kill, destroy, and to lead souls to Hell. The Apostle Paul warned, "For the mystery of iniquity doth already work; only he who now let will let, until he be taken out of the way. And then shall that Wicked be revealed, whom the Lord shall consume with the spirit of his mouth, and shall destroy with the brightness of his coming: Even him, whose coming is after the working of Satan with all power and signs and lying wonders, And with all deceivableness of unrighteousness in them that perish; because they received not the love of the truth, that they might be saved. And for this cause shall God send them strong delusion, that they should believe a lie: That they all might be damned who believed not the truth, but had pleasure in unrighteousness" (II Thessalonians 2:7-2).

The believer shall not be condemned. God so loved the world that he gave his only begotten Son, that whoever believeth in him should not perish, but have everlasting life, For God sent not his Son into the world to condemn the world; but that the world through him might be saved (John 3:16-17). The word world in this text is referring to those whom God knew would believe in Christ and trust him for their salvation. He that believeth not is condemned already, because he hath not believed in the name of the only begotten Son of God (John 3:18). Believe in Jesus Christ and trust him for your salvation. The tree is known by the fruit that it bears (Matthew 7:20).

The mystery that will be revealed by Jesus to many on that final day of judgment when they stand before the Lord is that he never knew them as they professed and as they presumed. They will be told by Jesus Christ himself, "I never knew you, depart from me, you that work iniquity" (Matthew 7:23). They will say that they had prophesied. They will say that they had cast out devils and done other wonderful works. They will profess to him that he is their Lord but they will be told to depart from him because they were workers of iniquity (Matthew 7:21-24). I close by saying that this is the most shocking if not terrifying thing that the Lord wants you all to keep in mind as you travel through your Christian life. Jesus said that this would happen to many professing believers. People will stand before God on their day of judgment and discover that they were delusional and never saved.

This was not a warning but a solemn declaration of events that will happen when many stand before God to give an account of themselves to him about their life on the earth. The scriptures testify, "And it has been appointed to men once to die and after that the judgment" (Hebrews 9:27). They wondered what they must do to be saved when the early church started. The scriptures say, "Then Peter said unto them, Repent, and be baptized every one of you in the name of Jesus Christ for the remission of sins, and ye shall receive the gift of the Holy Ghost" (Acts 2:38).

God's answer to the Existential Crisis

God created man and placed him on the earth to have a relationship with him in and through his Son Jesus Christ. Man had freewill. He was deceived by Satan and rebelled against his creator. He has been alienated and estranged from his purpose on earth and in eternity. He does not know naturally the reason for his existence nor for his continuation past the grave. God's enemy is Satan the Devil. He was once a beautiful angel called Lucifer that had his abode in Heaven. But Lucifer rebelled with 1/3rd of the angels and became Satan the Devil and demons. Satan and his demons are now on the earth. They are the invisible enemies of God and man. Satan and his demons have deceived man regarding where he came from, why he is here, and where he is going to. Satan also deceived men as to how to solve his problems spiritually without God.

He has man thinking that he has the solutions in his own inventions or within himself and with the Devil and his cunningly devised strategies.

Man is rescued from his will that is in bondage to his morally depraved nature as a result of his relationship with Jesus Christ. Man was born a sinner and is in bondage to a depraved nature which he inherited from Adam as a result of the fall of man in the garden. Satan instigated the fall. Man is set free from the controlling domination of this depraved nature by his spiritual empowerment from God's gift of the Holy Ghost. The Holy Ghost is the power that raised Jesus Christ from the dead and Christ coming into man to help in spiritual power.

Man is set free from spiritual enslavement to the demons that dominate his mind as a result of his relationship with Jesus Christ who sets the captives free. Christ also gives the believer power to cast out devils and to heal the sick. Man receives eternal life and becomes part of an everlasting kingdom because he believes in Jesus Christ and accepts the work of the sacrifice of his Son on the cross for him. Man lives his life out on the earth as a Son of God that is born of the spirit once he repents of his sin and believes the good news of this gospel. He received God's spirit to live inside of him. He becomes part of an eternal kingdom that is within him and that is coming to the earth with Christ as King to reign forever. Man eliminates his guilt and his depression. He walks away from his anxiety and his fear as he puts his trust in the sovereign Christ alone. Man has all demonic forces casted out of his troubled mind. He escapes the wrath of God to come because of his faith in Jesus Christ and he lives forever in heaven in a mansion that was prepared specifically for him. Man lives his life out on the earth with the purpose of pleasing his Creator who is also his Savior. He strives to serve others with the Love of God whereas he has the God of love that is living inside of him forever. He loves God because he comprehends that God loved him first and that this wonderful love springs forth as love toward God and others.

Jesus Christ said these words, "For this is how God loved the world, He gave his one and only Son, so that everyone who believes in him will not perish but have eternal life. God sent his Son into the world not to judge the world, but to save the world through him. There is no judgment against anyone who believes in him. But anyone who does not believe in him has already been judged for not believing in God's one and only Son" (John 3:16-18).

Bibliography

Albright, W.F. Recent Discoveries in Bible Lands, New York: Funk and Wagnalls,1955.

Albright, W.F. "Old Testament and Archaeology of the Ancient East." In Old Testament and Modern Study: A Generation of Discovery and Research, ed, by H.H. Rowley. Oxford: Oxford University, 1956.

Arnold, Thomas. "The History of Rome as Three Volumes in One." London: Fellows, 1838.

Anderson, J.N.D. Christianity: The Witness of History. London: Tyndale Press, 1969. Reprint, Downers Grove, Ill: Intervarsity Press, 1970.

Blackman, E.C. "Jesus Christ Yesterday: The Historical Basis of the Christian Faith," Canadian Journal of Theology. Vol 7. April 1961.

Blaiklock, Edward Musgrave. Layman's Answer: An Examination of the New Theology: London: Hodder and Stoughton, 1968

Bruce, F.F. "Archaeological Confirmation of the New Testament." In Revelation and the Bible, ed. Carl Henry. Grand Rapids: Baker Book House, 1969.

Carson, E.J. An Introduction to Christian Apologetics, 3rd ed. Grand Rapids: Eerdmans, 1950.

Corduan, Winfried, No Doubt About it: The Case for Christianity: Nashville: Broadman & Holman Publishers, 1997

Craig, William Lane. Knowing the Truth About the Resurrection. Ann Arbor, Michigan.: Servant Books, 1988. Rev.ed of The Son Rises.

Folds, Eric. The Shroud of Turin and Historical Proof of the Resurrection of Jesus: Independently Published, 2020

Folds, Eric. God, The Gospel, and Atonement: Maitland, Florida: Xulon Press, 2014.

Folds, Eric. Science Discovers God: The Mystery of Quantum Physics and Light: Maitland, Florida: Xulon Press, 2013.

Greenleaf, Simon. The Testimony of the Evangelists, Examined by the Rules of Evidence Administered in Courts of Justice. Grand Rapids: Baker Book House, 1965 (reprinted from 1847 edition).

Josephus, Flavius. "Flavius Josephus Against Apion," Josephus Complete Works. Trans. By William Whiston. Grand Rapids: Kregel Publications, 1960

Kenyon, Frederick G. The Bible and Archaeology. New York: Harper & Row, 1940

Kevan, Ernest F: The Resurrection of Christ. London: The Campbell Morgan Memorial Bible Lectureship, Westminster Chapel Buckingham Gate, S.W.I., 14 June 1961.

Mcdowell, Josh and Bill Walton. He Walked Among Us: Evidence for the Historical Jesus. San Bernardino, Calif.: Here's Life Publishers 1988. Reprint, Nashville: Thomas Nelson Publishers, 1993.

Montgomery, John W., "Evangelicals and Archaeology." Christianity Today. August 16,1968.

Montgomery, John W., Faith Founded on Fact: Essays in Evidential Apologetics. Nashville: Thomas Nelson,1978.

Morrison, Frank, Who Moved the Stone? London: Faber and Faber,196?

Peters, F.E. The Harvest of Hellenism. New York: Simon and Schuster, 1971.

Ross, Hugh. "Astronomical Evidences for a Personal, Transcendent God. The Creation Hypothesis: Scientific Evidence for an Intelligen

Designer. Ed. by J.P. Mooreland. Downers Grove, Ill: Intervarsity Press, 1994.

Sanders, C. Introduction to Research in English Literary History: New York: Mcmillan Co., 1952.

Smith, Wilbur M. "The Indisputable Fact of the Empty Tomb." Moody Institute, May 1971.

Smith, Wilbur M. "Scientists and the Resurrection," Christianity Today. April 15,1957.

Sparrow-Simpson, W.J. "Resurrection and Christ," The Resurrection and The Christian Faith. Grand Rapids: Zondervan Publishing House, 1968. Reprinting from 1911 edition of Langsmans Green, and Co., published under the title, The Resurrection of Modern Thought.

Sproul, R.C., John Gerstner, and Arthur Lindsley. Classical Apologetics. Grand Rapids: Zondervan Publishing House,1984.

Tacticus. Annals. In Great Books of the Western World, by Robert Maynard Hutchins. Vol. 15, The Annals and the Histories by Cornelius Tacticus. Chicago: William Benton, 1952.

Yamauchi, Edwin. "Jesus Outside the New Testament: What is the Evidence?" Jesus Under Fire: Modern Scholarship Reinvents the Historical Jesus. Ed. By Michael J. Wilkins and J.P. Mooreland. Grand Rapids: Zondervan Publishing House, 1995.

About the Author

Eric Folds is the Pastor of The Christian Church of God, Inc and the Dean of Christian University and Theological Seminary. He has authored numerous books. He is a Consultant and a Nouthetic Counselor. He has studied Theology, Quantum Physics, Ancient History, Ministry, Archaeology, Apologetics, Behavioral Psychology, and Pastoral Counseling. He works with people that are traumatized. He 's an entrepreneur and a small business owner. He has seen the miraculous happen and lives radically transformed by the power of Jesus Christ as the risen savior. He is married to Kimberly Folds. Gabriel Folds and Joshua Folds are his two sons.

Lightning Source UK Ltd.
Milton Keynes UK
UKHW040631071122
411784UK00001B/17

9 781662 861